The Rise and Fall of Patriarchy

CHANGING OUR APPROACH TO JUSTICE, LEADERSHIP, AND POWER

MICHELLE PANAYI

Contents

CONTENTS

Author's Note

Dear Reader,

I ask only one thing of you: to have an open mind, as much as possible, when reading this book. Whilst I have written each chapter to weave into the next one with key themes progressing to the final chapter, there may be aspects that are confronting and may even provoke strong emotional opposition. In those cases, it may be useful to leave that section and return to it later or to leave it altogether and move on to other sections that you may find more helpful.

There are also descriptions of violence against women (including an alleged rape) and the views of men who buy sex with women that you may find difficult to read. When you read them, you may feel that it is a good idea to have a break from the book until the emotional charge has settled.

I do not think there would be much disagreement with the view that we all want to be happy, to be free from suffering, to reach our full potential, and to express and experience love (whether we are conscious of these desires or not is open to question). And so it is with this aim that I have written this book for us.

Best wishes
Michelle

About the Author

Michelle Panayi has worked as a consultant, human rights lawyer, and manager in the pro bono legal sector. She also worked for several years as a political advisor. This book is a result of her work, culminating with examining justice and power from a feminist—what some would call a radical feminist perspective, with additional insights from experts in a variety of fields.

Introduction

For two consecutive years, Elise suffered from chronic laryngitis. Both times, it left her unable to speak for nearly two months. Her doctor was so concerned the second time that she referred Elise to a throat specialist to find out if she had permanent damage to her vocal chords. The specialist was very gentle and kind as he examined her. He could see the impact that the laryngitis had on her throat but there were no signs of permanent damage, or an indication as to why she had the problem for so long. Then he questioned Elise further and she handed him a note.

The note contained details of when Elise was a victim of male violence and had been silenced afterwards by authorities. This was a light-bulb moment. The specialist said that he had seen a few cases like Elise's where such trauma later led to a physical manifestation with chronic laryngitis. It was many years after the event, many years after Elise thought she had fully recovered from the traumatic experience, but had intuited that it had a part to play with her illness and the specialist confirmed this. Fortunately and not surprisingly, she began recovering from laryngitis straight after consulting him.

Elise's experience is a powerful symbol of the abuses of patriarchy. So whilst I wish I could agree with Mary Beard in her book *Women and Power*, and say that western women have a lot to celebrate—to do so for me would be like saying we should be grateful for being permitted the right to vote and engage in any capacity in the workforce and education. I can't be in celebratory mode given the prevalence of male violence against women in all its forms, making it so difficult for many women to stay alive, let alone function in the public sphere and at home. Patriarchy has continued to cast a long shadow. Its distorted perspective on life and the world serves only to imprison women, children, and even men. It will continue to do so unless, in spite of our fear, we seek to live our truth the best we can and not allow the system to beat us.

Patriarchy has been in existence for thousands of years from the Neolithic era through to ancient Greece and Rome, where it became deeply embedded in society and still is throughout the world today. It is a system that places men predominantly in power and has a history of silencing women's voices. This is highlighted not only by Elise's case but by Mary Beard's examination of Homer's *Odyssey*. In this Greek classic, the young Telemachus tells his mother effectively to shut up when she requests that a bard sing a more joyful tune. So she dutifully does shut up and returns upstairs, reminded by her son that speech is for men only.[1]

Of course this is in the context of Greek democracy, established around the fifth century B.C., in which women were excluded from participation. Not only that, but women were viewed either as sex objects or the dutiful wife or dutiful daughter. Sound familiar? And the family unit mirrored the state: the man was the head of the household and if he wanted to use violence against his wife and children—that was his prerogative. He had to assert his power in his domain, and we are paying the price still today with a family violence crisis. Feminists were on the money when, decades ago, they pronounced that *the personal is political*.

Patriarchy's silencing of women takes many forms beyond threatening us to keep quiet, such as excluding women's voices in the telling of history and in the creation of our social, legal and economic structures. It also includes the lack of data on women's lives and perspectives. This has serious implications in areas as diverse as medical trials endangering women's lives and access to safe toilets—all in a world designed by men for men, as explained by Caroline Criado-Perez in her book *Invisible Women*.

But patriarchy not only silences and excludes women; saying we are the inferior sex rather than equal. It is much broader than that, playing out in our lives and our decision-making and that of our institutions, in some obvious ways, but also in more subtle ones. This means that if we are to break free from patriarchy's influence and control, we must examine it more closely.

Gender stereotyping is a key feature of the patriarchal thought system. Only certain qualities and roles are viewed as appropriate for each gender (such as housework for women and leadership roles for men). Patriarchy combines this gender stereotyping with valuing what are commonly referred to as 'masculine' qualities such as reason/intellect, strength, assertiveness, confidence, decisiveness, initiative, acting/doing, setting boundaries and saying no, and independence. These qualities can only have full and appropriate expression, though, when society and individuals also embrace what are commonly perceived as 'feminine' qualities.

The problem is patriarchy denigrates 'feminine' qualities and values. These include emotions such as empathy and compassion, intuition, listening, and relatedness. Interconnectedness, interdependence, and unity stem from the value of relatedness and are also linked to holism or a holistic approach (as later discussed). The stereotypical feminine realm also emphasizes humility, patience, and 'being' rather than 'doing', and the feminine is aligned with nature.

It's important to note that there is no basis to label certain qualities as masculine or feminine. This is merely part of patriarchy's simplistic view that the natures of men and women are inherently different when in fact many differences are due to socialisation. As psychologist and ethicist Carol Gilligan says, this gender binary has been so internalised in our psyche that instead of seeing it as culture we mistake it as natural.[2] And so these qualities and values should evolve to simply being known as positive attributes and values.

Patriarchy also treads the dangerous path of cultivating 'hyper-masculine' or toxic qualities. These develop when a person is not in touch with his or her 'feminine' side. They include aggression (I'm not talking here about self-defence or defence of others), seeking conflict, irrationality, narcissism, a sense of entitlement, and greed. A disrespect for and violation of other people's boundaries also thrive under patriarchy. The refusal to accept responsibility for one's mistakes and negative actions is cultivated as well, along with impulsiveness. But that's not all.

Patriarchy also fuels arrogance, as well as an 'us and them' mentality. Those who aren't part of one's group are viewed as the 'Other' without a common humanity. This gives rise to sexism— including the sexual objectification of women, homophobia, racism, and the mistreatment and abuse of employees or customers by managers or CEOs, for example.

The desire to dominate, control, and triumph over others is also valued by patriarchy, for it sees this as real power. This thought system thrives on creating fear and promotes acting in self-interest rather than shared interests. There is a conspicuous absence of working collaboratively towards a common higher goal or purpose. It's a case of 'my way or the highway.'

Controlling and dominating others also means that diversity—and the different perspectives and power-sharing that comes with it—is seen as a threat. As a result, conformism is at the heart of patriarchy: a sure killer of authenticity, creativity, innovation, voicing dissent, and promoting transparency. We see this play out in the workplace and with governments too often. Extreme examples include the terror of the Inquisitions by the Church, Hitler's Nazi Germany, and Islamic nations such as Iran and Saudi Arabia where women are imprisoned and tortured for advocating for women's rights. Importantly, the authorities in these examples equate terror and authoritarianism with justice.

But patriarchy also thrives on victims becoming oppressors too. How many times do you see people who are oppressed, mistreated or disempowered in some way, turn around and take it out on someone else or a particular group? It's the see-saw effect. Put someone else down to feel powerful and less insecure, less fearful, and less self-loathing. But behind that momentary sense of triumph and feeling of power, the fear, insecurity, anger, and 'not being good enough' remains. It's a vicious circle.

Other qualities that patriarchy values whilst devaluing the feminine include status, prestige, superficial charm, clever rhetoric, exclusiveness, fame, material wealth, and worldly achievement—all of which are associated with power. It also highly values physical perfection, though over the ages this emphasis has increasingly been placed on women. Indeed, ancient Athens was very materialistic and exemplified a culture resting in all these patriarchal values, so much so that Socrates (like present-day advocates for a more compassionate and just world) appealed to Athenians to instead value wisdom, truth, and kindness.[3]

Highly hierarchical organisational structures are a feature of patriarchy. This approach runs the risk of creating unnecessary layers of management, with executives out of touch with the work taking place on the ground as well as the resources needed at that lower but critical level.

The ancient Athenians strongly endorsed competitiveness, and this mentality continues today under patriarchy. Some argue that it is in itself problematic, whilst others say it is only a problem when triumphing is seen as the *only* worthwhile goal, or done at the expense of caring for others.

Patriarchy also prizes ambition. We can see harmful effects of this in the area of leadership where it can become all about getting ahead rather than seeking to give, climbing the career ladder and treading on others to keep climbing, and even taking credit for the work or ideas of others.

Patriarchy's refusal to value the feminine also leads to the misconception that honesty and sincerity are signs of weakness. Dishonesty in the pursuit of power is even seen as being clever, and a justifiable behaviour. I've known of corrupt people boasting of how smart they are and asserting that the victims of their scams were simply 'asking for it.' Whilst it has been said that power corrupts, I contend that patriarchy also corrupts.

And what happens to women when they are not permitted or encouraged to develop positive masculine qualities? This socialisation leads to them lacking the ability to say no without feeling guilty, as well as being unable to feel confident and assertive, be stern when needed, or take initiative. They become gullible and naïve, worry unnecessarily, and feel the need to please and accommodate others. They are also less adventurous, repress anger, and are more susceptible to feelings of despair.

This gender stereotyping has also led to patriarchy being very prescriptive about what men and women should wear and there is no equality when it comes to its modesty code. Women have to cover up more than men to be respected and viewed as religiously pious or dignified. And because patriarchy sees women through a lens of extremes, it also says on the flip side that we have to look 'sexy' to be attractive—and women have to be attractive to be valued. This usually means wearing very little at all and posing 'seductively' in an increasingly sexualised world. It doesn't make sense, just as mandating blue clothes for boys and pink clothes for girls doesn't make sense either.

It's curious that whilst we are finally acknowledging a link between gender stereotyping and violence against women, not many members of the legal profession, governments, and even a few women's advocacy groups use the word 'patriarchy,' or acknowledge how the patriarchal system is behind this stereotyping. This omission fails to take into consideration how letting go of these stereotypes, means also challenging the very foundations of our society. We really require radical change that is going to take a long time to fully implement, given patriarchy is so embedded in our psyche.

It is little wonder that we are grappling with high rates of depression and anxiety, suicide, child abuse, drug and alcohol addiction, pornography and sex addiction, and addiction to money/wealth and other forms of worldly power. Corruption is commonplace. So is bullying and sexual harassment. Violent crime and white-collar crime occur too frequently. Meanwhile, more and more children and adults are left feeling empty from repressing important parts of their humanity under patriarchy.

In order to be healthy whole people and reach our full potential regardless of our gender, we need to develop both the positive 'masculine' qualities and positive 'feminine' qualities within us. This will allow us to be truly kind and caring towards one another and ourselves, rather than privileging the ego and the never-ending pursuit of self-interest at the expense of others; of having to keep *taking* to fill a bottomless pit of scarcity.

Our society and the lives of women, children, and men have been devastated by patriarchy and its hold on our legal and political systems and the business and finance sectors. Its influence is also found in other areas that people may find difficult to confront due to their attachment to or strong identification with them. These range from religious and human rights institutions through to unions, the media, all political parties, political causes, and the science, health, and education sectors. Patriarchy's influence permeates everything, enforcing its interpretation of what constitutes power and leadership. This undermines attempts to create an equitable, peaceful, and compassionate society.

But many people have also been blind to the degradation of the environment and mistreatment and torture of animals stemming from patriarchy. It is patriarchy's emphasis on domination, control, and devaluing of the feminine that has made denigration of the environment and animals inevitable. Yet whilst I was growing up, it puzzled me whenever environmentalists, animal rights campaigners, and political parties linked to them, could not see this. And so they could not see the advancement of equality and respect for women (with the link to feminine values) as being critical to their success.

Capitalism's emphasis on the profit motive and patriarchy seem like a good fit with a liberal democracy which emphasises individualism. But patriarchy has also flourished in communist states run by brutal dictatorships.

Intriguingly, those countries which are the least patriarchal (compared to the rest of the world) are social democracies such as Iceland, Norway, Finland, Denmark, and Sweden. They focus on shared, collective interests whilst still respecting individual freedom, unlike communist nations. Whilst the Nordic countries are not a utopia and still have much more work to do in order to unravel the hold of patriarchy, they are leaders in this area in many respects. To varying degrees, they show us the benefits in letting go of patriarchy's distorted values. This creates healthier, more prosperous nations founded on egalitarianism, respect, and compassion. And they show hyper-capitalist nations that you can achieve prosperity without bowing down to the rule of the free market.

In the following chapters I explore how patriarchy has been embedded in the structures and decision-making of our society, the implications of this, and where patriarchy's influence is diminishing. I think we can agree that patriarchy is a harmful ideology. But in order for us to bring about its downfall we need to bear witness to its impact, what changes in the law have undermined it, and what more needs to be done. This discussion will hopefully help the reader identify the influences of patriarchy elsewhere and challenge it.

This book firstly examines patriarchy's influence on the teaching of law (law school being a cradle of worldly power). The damage it has caused here can also be found in other faculties as well and helps to explain why the law and various leaders have failed us in many respects. I highlight recent positive changes in the teaching of law and the profession in order to show that patriarchy is losing its hold in some aspects, but unfortunately it continues to have a strong grip in other areas.

The reader is then taken on a brief journey through our justice system to understand patriarchy's influence there and see where it is losing its power. The first stop is criminal law and the impact of a patriarchal 'might is right' approach focusing purely on punishment. This has led to an increase in prisoners re-offending and the imprisonment of many disadvantaged women who pose no risk to the community.

It is a method that can be likened to the martial approach in medicine of fighting and conquering every illness and disease instead of a holistic approach that includes working collaboratively with patients,[4] unless of course you are dealing with an emergency. The broad brush of a purely punitive approach in the criminal justice system contrasts with our increasing awareness of a more effective method to tackle crime: addressing the underlying causes. This includes working actively with offenders and those at risk of offending and empowering them to make good decisions.

Government investment in early therapeutic intervention and mentoring schemes is an important part of this holistic approach as is investing in disadvantaged communities and addressing family violence. It also includes addressing the harms of the multi-billion-dollar sex industry—harms that our society prefers not to confront even whilst claiming to be serious about violence against women. Innovations such as courts delivering justice in a therapeutic way and rehabilitation initiatives in prison are also explored.

You cannot have a discussion about the impact of patriarchy on the justice system without examining how sexism in the law has made it so much harder for victims of sexual abuse and family violence to access justice and be treated with dignity and respect. This is important since there are still judges, politicians, and lawyers who reject the idea that the law has ever been sexist. Improvements achieved through feminist advocacy are also discussed in Chapter Six, showing cracks in the patriarchal system. These activists' work gives us a better chance of having a society that doesn't engage in victim-blaming and is safer and more just than it currently is.

We often look to the police to help us be safe and expect them also to look out for each other. The last thing police officers need on top of dealing with traumatic incidents and violent crime in the community is having the anxiety of knowing their colleagues or supervisors haven't 'got their back' or worse are going to try to exploit or abuse them. Chapter Seven shines a light on the impact of patriarchy on law enforcement and how an independent review exposed a toxic culture of sexual harassment in Victoria Police. The review revealed not only the trauma for the police officers subjected to such abuse but also how patriarchy and the toxic masculinity it promotes prevents an organisation from being professional, respectful, and effective. Instead, barbaric cruelty thrives, and this is also borne out in police corruption and brutality.

Patriarchy has also hampered the justice system's ability to address sexual harassment. Calls for important law reforms were not heeded in the past, including in 2008 after an Australian Senate inquiry into sex discrimination. Given we live in a patriarchal society, it is not surprising that sexual harassment (like family violence and all forms of sexual abuse) is widespread and that radical reforms to address it have been rejected by successive governments.

It also says a lot about our celebrity-obsessed culture that the issue only gained the attention it warrants after high-profile celebrities in Hollywood spoke out about workplace sexual harassment including sexual assault in 2017, igniting the #MeToo movement. The Australian Sex Discrimination Commissioner then called for a national inquiry into the issue and in doing so came across her first hurdle. It was one that some of us already knew was coming: getting survivors to provide input when many had signed confidentiality agreements in order to receive compensation from their employers. In Chapter Eight, we explore the problem of confidentiality agreements and the way the law deals with sexual harassment. The chapter also outlines a holistic and radical approach to reforms for the reader to contemplate.

Patriarchy hasn't just had a negative impact on women being safe at home, in public spaces, and at work. It has also played a key role in racism. This is highlighted by the brutal treatment of Indigenous Australians and asylum seekers, as well as the racism migrants have experienced as far back as the gold rush era. Chapter Nine explores these matters, along with the various attempts that have been made to chip away at the patriarchal system of discrimination. To ensure a nuanced examination of race and cultural issues, this chapter delves into examples of when our law-makers have stood up to patriarchy by upholding the rights of women and children instead of abusive cultural practices and values.

Another important justice issue is the environment and the treatment of our fellow species. Chapter Ten provides an overview of the damage that patriarchy has unleashed. In seeking a new way forward, we need to change our perception about our connection to the environment, our connection to each other, and also the structure of our economic model. This can be achieved with guidance from scientists, environmentalists, mental health professionals, feminists, and other innovative thinkers, not just the business sector. We also need to be vigilant in not allowing our technological development to further alienate us from our natural environment, ourselves, and each other.

No discussion about patriarchy can be complete without examining its impact on leadership, and so Chapter Eleven paints a portrait of patriarchal leadership. Even when surrounded by an expensive, elaborate frame, it is an ugly sight to behold, composed with the aggressive dark strokes of a purely commanding style. I also explore whether it makes any difference putting a woman in the picture as leader.

So what makes a good leader? Much has been written about this topic dating back to ancient Greek and Roman times. I found it extremely helpful to draw together insights from several experts, including the world-class educator on leadership Daniel Goleman, and comparing them with what I have observed in the workplace. The portrait of a good leader is opposite to that of a patriarchal one. What stands out is a noble and gentle character, a passionate visionary who embodies positive 'masculine' and 'feminine' traits, including humility—an important quality that has increasingly fallen out of fashion in our age of self-promotion and the 'selfie'.

Finally this book explores what true power really means as opposed to patriarchal power, reflecting on the writings and perspectives of great philosophers, mental health professionals, and spiritual teachers, as well as from the life of a remarkable woman, Marie Byles, the first woman qualified to practice law in NSW.

Whilst some feminists argue the need for women to embrace rage and anger as a form of power and allow these emotions to lead the way in overthrowing patriarchy, other feminists such as Marie Byles remind us that there is a much deeper and stronger power for both women and men to access that brings peace to us all. It comes from outside the patriarchal system and guarantees its downfall beyond the radical changes needed in the law and our culture. It is through re-examining our notions of power and embracing the true power Marie Byles came to know that real hope lies.

This book is by no means an exhaustive examination of these themes, nor do I wish to take an academic or scholarly approach but merely contribute some points to the discussion on patriarchy that feminists began long ago. Whilst I focus on Australia, and in particular my state of Victoria, several of the issues raised correlate with the experiences of other states and countries.

-1-

There Must Be
A Better Way

I grew up in the 1970s and 1980s, consistently reminded by my patriarchal Greek heritage and Australian society that women and children (especially girls) did not matter as much as men, could not be intelligent, or were even objects to control and dominate. I was unable to relate to my Greek Cypriot culture nor my Australian one (though it afforded me slightly greater freedom), and so I stood outside both worlds.

I couldn't understand how we could live in a society with pornography and sexist advertising, which were pervasive. Prostitution, family violence, sexual abuse, and workplace sexual harassment were so embedded in the system that they were easily overlooked or just not talked about as being a serious problem linked to patriarchy. The list didn't end there. I was also confused by the gender pay gap, and that the modelling industry and high-end escort work (where a woman's worth and identity is reduced to her body's attractiveness as well as, in the latter case, sex acts) were the only areas where she could earn much more money than men. There were also too few women in power, and too many people who thought this was just how things were, including women.

Our situation reminded me of what the African American writer Richard Wright spoke of in his memoir *Black Boy*, of how smoothly black people acted out the roles that the white race had created for them in the early twentieth century. Wright said that most people of his race were not conscious of living a separate and stunted way of life. A part of them had shut off their minds and emotions from all that the white race had said was off limits. And even though they lived in a land that claimed there was equal opportunity, they knew what they were and were not to aspire to.[5] *The same can be said in relation to females and what the male race has mapped out for us*, I thought growing up. But if you tried to do something about it by challenging the system and its underlying causes, you were a feminist to be despised. The mainstream media had even succeeded in making feminism a dirty word.

But challenge it all I did and feminist I was, deeply admiring the women who had fought hard for so many rights such as the right to vote, access to education and the workforce, greater respect for women in sport and the arts, and continuing the fight against inequality in all its forms.

But I was also naïve. When I entered a well-regarded law school in the early 1990s, I thought I would encounter people from all different backgrounds who wanted to help improve society and serve humanity. Whilst we had for the first time a slightly higher percentage of female students than males, most students came from white, privileged backgrounds and from elite private schools where they were taught (as one male student put it) that they were essentially the pillars of society. Students in the faculty were judged by many according to what they wore (labels were important), law books were hidden in the library in the 'spirit of competitiveness', and some students tried to 'psych' other students out during exam time with misleading questions or misinformation for exam preparation. The law faculty had a serious, heavy atmosphere where both the intellect and appearances were prioritised above all else.

I also knew some students were struggling with depression and substance abuse, and a fellow student committed suicide in my first year. I was told by a friend that he was struggling with the competitive, alienating environment and didn't want to disappoint his family. Even the students who weren't struggling as severely were vomiting before entering exam rooms; they were so anxious and distressed.

So what was happening in the lectures of this highly regarded faculty? When I started law school, I assumed that our lecturers would be visionaries critiquing the legal system and explaining complex areas of law in an accessible manner through their enthusiasm and passion for teaching. I thought that they would bring the law to life in a caring environment. For the most part, I was wrong. Lecturers in the law faculty, as with other departments and universities (I am told), were there not necessarily because of their excellent teaching ability but more for their research and publishing acumen.

There was more than an air of prestige and status in the faculty, whilst law subjects were mostly taught with a dry, lifeless, intellectual style. Indeed cases were dissected with a scientific measure.

I remember some unfortunate highlights: firstly, my company law lecturer mainly addressed the ceiling as he spoke rather than speaking to the students in front of him. It was as if we weren't really there. We were fee-paying students (before our generation, university education was free) and we were paying to be ignored.

My criminal law lecturer, without prior warning, showed us a short film of an interview with paedophiles talking explicitly about what aroused them to offend; the purpose of showing the film none of us understood. When a couple of students privately complained to him that he should've warned us beforehand, given that they had been sexually abused as children, he revealed this to the whole class and was critical of the complaint. There was no sensitivity whatsoever, let alone kindness. There was also little if any discussion on addressing the gender bias that pervaded the criminal law, particularly for victims of sexual abuse and family violence. This was similarly the case in an elective subject on problems of the criminal justice system, where issues pertaining to family violence and sexual abuse, as well as prostitution, barely rated a mention.

I was beginning to see that the sexism in the law interpreted 'objectivity' to mean stripping away emotions such as empathy and so the very humanity of the legal system. This has allowed it to negate the experiences of women and children and be so unjust and cruel at times, as discussed in later chapters.

And so generally, the law faculty was indeed an alienating place. This was problematic given it was the breeding ground for future leaders and power holders in our society. A Federal Liberal government minister at the time visited our faculty and told us we were in the top ten per cent of the country—we were the future leaders who could make a significant contribution to Australia. I thought, 'God help us,' given the way we were being educated, leaving so many of us feeling empty inside.

Meanwhile, we continued grappling with our patriarchal learning environment. In my first year, my lecturer for legal process made it clear that feminists were wrong in arguing that law was taught in a patriarchal way and that it didn't matter whether textbooks used *he* most of the time instead of interspersing it with *she*. But there were those of us who could already feel the effects of never seeing the female pronoun in textbooks, and few female judges in cases cited and in the outside world.

Some of us felt our self-esteem plummeting despite our access to education, a phenomenon that Gloria Steinem wrote about in her book, *Revolution from Within*. She discussed a study by researchers from the University of Illinois of both male and female valedictorians who went on to college and universities. They found that the women experienced lower self-esteem than their male counterparts despite being high performers like the men. This was due to the impact of seeing fewer women in positions of authority, some women being treated with contempt, and a more competitive and adversarial style in classrooms.[6] I then discovered that feminist researchers examining law classroom dynamics concurred with such findings, saying there needed to be a more cooperative and less authoritarian style of teaching. They also emphasised the importance of a feminist perspective in teaching and content that brings the humanity of parties to the cases studied.[7]

Don't get me wrong. I was well suited for advocacy in the adversarial and competitive legal system. I was a high performer for the compulsory moot court (mock trial) subject and was singled out by the moot master for a special commendation for my oratory skills, which I appreciated. But it was also bittersweet: whilst my persuasive arguments won our defence side the case, I knew that on the facts of the matter and in the interest of upholding truth and justice, the prosecution side should have won. This plays out in our legal system where, unfortunately, there are times when the truth doesn't win because the art of persuasion does. We inherited this emphasis on clever rhetoric from ancient Athens, as it is greatly valued by patriarchy as an important form of power. Because of this focus on the art of persuasion, the ability to afford a highly skilled lawyer is critical in court. Given there are many people who can't afford a lawyer, greater government investment in and access to legal aid is essential to reduce the number of unrepresented litigants.

I received another rude awakening about the law when I undertook an elective subject called Elements of Forensic Medicine. A guest lecturer who was an expert on violent crimes spoke to us about a number of rapes and murders and the profile of the perpetrators and their criminal history. After the lecture, I asked him what rehabilitation was available for offenders in prison. He said 'none' quite matter-of-factly.

I walked away gobsmacked. How did our lawmakers think that simply locking people up and throwing away the key was going to stop them from reoffending? How could they think that simply punishing someone by putting them in prison was the answer? But then I realised that from a patriarchal, 'might is right' viewpoint, this would make sense. I don't mean to argue that punishment should not be involved in the criminal justice system, but in itself it will not stop re-offending, nor will the threat of punishment prevent offending without addressing the underlying causes of crime.

My saving grace in law school arrived mainly in the form of two elective subjects: Professional Practice and Law, Gender, and Feminism. Professional Practice was a clinical program where students undertook supervised legal work at a community legal centre. It was both enjoyable and rewarding since we were working on real cases with clients. I was also fortunate to have a wonderful lecturer who not only brought the law to life with passion but also truly cared about his students and clients, and had a great sense of humour.

Law, Gender, and Feminism finally gave me the feminist critique of the law I was yearning for and was also taught with much passion, vigour, and kindness. Taking it was one of the better choices I have made in my life despite other students warning me that if I did, no law firm would hire me. I decided to study it anyway, saying that I wouldn't want to work for anyone who had a problem with this subject. And as it turned out, it wasn't an impediment to obtaining employment.

Law, Gender, and Feminism challenged both the way law is taught and the claim that the law is impartial. Feminist legal scholars exposed its hidden gender bias and said that subjects should be taught addressing this bias wherever it arises rather than relying on a specialist elective subject alone to do this. Such an approach makes sense and should apply to the political system, as well. It would be better if all government portfolios took into consideration the feminist viewpoint rather than leaving it only to be considered under the women's portfolio. This cannot be emphasised enough, especially for the Justice/Attorney-General portfolio-holders. Such an approach elevates women's issues rather than keeping them marginalised. Shadow portfolio holders should also adopt this practice.

It is interesting to note here that feminists in the law used the term 'gender bias' rather than sexism. Perhaps the term 'sexism' was seen to be too emotive and radical by feminists to use. Maybe 'gender bias' is just a more polite way of saying sexism—but it is hard to imagine that these feminist legal scholars would seek to accommodate men and avoid offense. Or perhaps it was and still is from a desire to sound more intellectual about the issue— again playing into the hands of patriarchy and its values. I've heard people argue that if the bias is unconscious in a person or organisation, they are not sexist but have a hidden gender bias. According to these people the same goes with 'racial bias,' and such bias then leads to sexist or racist actions and laws respectively. I don't share this view, but we don't all have to agree.

Regardless of the above, back in 1994 the Australian Law Reform Commission (ALRC) recognised that many laws are gender biased and this is now accepted internationally and seen as a basic human rights issue. At the time, a United Nations World Conference on Human Rights stressed the importance of working to eliminate gender bias in the administration of justice. The ALRC also stressed the importance of recognising that stereotyped assumptions affect law making.[8]

Feminists also emphasised the importance of selecting cases to be studied in law school that included matters relating to women's experience, not just men's and included female judges where possible. The sexism in the law arose in areas as diverse as tort law (or the law of negligence), social security law, labour law, family law, superannuation law, sex discrimination law, the reproductive rights of women, family violence, sexual abuse, and pornography. We also learnt about the feminisation of poverty, particularly where women are solely responsible for the care of their children.[9]

By the time I finished law school, however, I was extremely disappointed overall with the way law had been taught and didn't bother to attend the graduation ceremony. As I said earlier, I was not alone in feeling empty; many other female students did too. Even a few male classmates were in touch with something being wrong with the curriculum and method of teaching.

We also knew we were leaving the faculty as 'half people', that our intellectual side had been developed at the expense of maturing emotionally. This was ironic given that commercial law firms would visit our faculty saying they wanted *well-rounded people* and *whole people* to work for them. And even if such people did exist, they wouldn't stay well-rounded or whole for long in these firms. The high workload and demanding and competitive environment consumed a person's life, and there would be little time for family and other interests: hence the known high divorce rate and depression in the legal profession at the time.

Even in the areas of social justice and human rights law, the environments were highly competitive and stressful, and there were many cases of bullying and sexual harassment—just like in the corporate sector. In 2005 I was talking to Josie, a rehabilitation officer for WorkCover in Victoria. She was extremely passionate about helping people recover from workplace injury. But what struck her was the irony that during the fifteen years of her work, the two worst organisations she had come across were legal organisations in the social justice/human rights area.

Since law school

Since the 1990s, the law has been changing and it has improved due to the persistence and hard work of feminists. But it has taken far too long and happened too late for many women and children, particularly in the area of family violence and sexual abuse. Some of the most critical reforms were only implemented in recent years as discussed in this book. There is still much needed reform in many areas to address sexism in the law and the patriarchal approach to solving societal problems that it has also contributed to.

There have also been some positive changes in the teaching of law and in the profession itself, but there are also more reforms needed. Let's take a look at these issues more closely.

A new way of teaching

There are now law faculties that have a specialized Law and Gender studies research section, which is progress, but we must ensure that all law students have access to a feminist perspective wherever relevant on all law subjects. To borrow the thinking of the African American civil rights leader Dr Carter G Woodson, the measure of progress is the content read, not just the numbers of people from a particular social group that read it, such as women or people from racial minority groups. He knew that when you control a person's thinking, you don't have to worry about them challenging the system as they quickly find their proper place and stick to it. Their education makes sure that this happens.[10]

Some lecturers are now teaching law in a supportive, collaborative way, rather than within purely adversarial and authority-driven environments. They bring the humanity of the parties in cases to life to help students develop their empathetic nature as well as intellectual skill, and this in turn engages the students. In this spirit, lecturers should also incorporate innovative approaches to the law that challenge the conventional approach and provide more tools for dealing with legal issues. This would increase students' interest in and passion for the law, as this approach encourages a creative way of thinking. These innovative approaches should be raised in the teaching of a core subject wherever relevant. In-depth examination as an elective subject, which some faculties provide, is also important.

Such innovations include therapeutic approaches to justice, discussed later in this book. In the family law context, they include a collaborative model for settling divorces in a respectful way outside the court process, focusing on the best interests of both parties. In a commercial context, they include the emergence of 'conscious contracts'. This might sound a bit New Agey, but it's actually a practical, common sense approach which makes contracts more meaningful and straight forward. The traditional convoluted contracts written within an adversarial context are replaced by agreements that are written in plain language that both parties can understand, include only relevant clauses, and which reflect the vision and values of contracting parties and assist with dispute resolution.[11]

These innovative approaches do not provide a perfect system that suits everyone but they do provide new ways of thinking and as I said more tools for the legal profession to work with.

More women in the profession

Seeing more women working in the legal profession, including in the role of judges, will boost female students' confidence. More female barristers are also being briefed due in part to federal government quotas under an equitable briefing policy for government agencies. But despite making up one third of the bar, women still had far fewer speaking roles in 2017 in the highest Victorian court compared to men. Jennifer Batrouney QC said there is still a long way to go before there is equitable briefing in relation to gender, especially in the civil courts.[12] And indeed, there is still sex discrimination including sexual harassment that women lawyers have to deal with including in law firms, as discussed in Chapter Eight.

Specific measures for student and lawyer wellbeing

There are some other simple measures to enhance student wellbeing. All faculties should actively encourage students to seek help when feeling anxiety or depression through onsite counselling services and classes on mindfulness and meditation. Such assistance can help students work through any mental health issues, become more self-aware, calm, and emotionally mature.

Faculties should also encourage students to participate in Mental Health week programs and provide feedback on the usefulness of such programs. All universities should be involved in law wellbeing conferences or forums to discuss what they can do to enhance wellbeing amongst students, lecturers, and those in the profession. Law faculties in Victoria are already doing this in collaboration with mental health experts, members of the judiciary and researchers.

It is critical that this happens globally since the depression amongst students and those in the profession continues. In 2017 the Dean of Law and Professor at the University of Capetown, Ms Penelope Andrews, investigated the issue after receiving an email from a student raising concerns that the hyper-competitive and alienating environment of the law school was putting the mental health of students at risk. As a result of this environment, using anti-depressants was the norm amongst students, along with alarmingly high consumption of alcohol.[13]

Ms Andrews found that some of the most up to date research in this area is in the United States. In 2014 a survey conducted at 15 law schools across the US found a quarter to one third of students suffering from mental health issues such as depression and the misuse of alcohol and drugs.[14]

In 2014, the American Psychological Association cited that lawyers were 3.6 times more likely than non-lawyers to suffer from depression, so a mandatory 'mental health' component was added in continuing legal education in several states as high profile lawyers across the US have been committing suicide. Some suffer depression from a highly stressful workload imposed on them but others are also workaholics, driven to win case after case for their self-esteem until they hit a wall.[15]

In Australia we also know that lawyers, especially those in the top tier firms, are still working excessively long hours in a culture of competitiveness, putting their health and safety at risk. This is due to senior partners believing that everything must be done to please the client, even if it involves the exploitation of staff. Like their counterparts in the United Kingdom and United

States they treat junior lawyers as if they are machines.[16] Nothing seems to have changed since my law school days, when it was apparent that if you worked for these firms you became enslaved to them. This can be likened to other sectors, such as the medical profession, where young doctors are being pushed to the brink working excessively long hours in a toxic culture, putting their health at risk as well as that of their patients. And we know that this certainly happens in factories and other industries as well.

This is a stark reminder that the values of patriarchy—prestige and status, worldly success, ambition and competitiveness, do not bring peace to oneself and others nor do they create happiness. We need to realise that we can have academically solid faculties that are also caring and friendly environments. The same ethos applies for workplaces. Focusing on the wellbeing of staff will naturally benefit the clients. This need for a different approach to work is non-negotiable: excessive work hours should never be the norm. No employer should be able to get away with saying to those who dare to protest—'this is how highly productive organisations work,' and behind that is the warning: *toughen up or else.*

But it's not just excessive work hours that we are talking about. It's the whole work life balance. Some people want a four day working week or to take some time off to simply be and recharge or spend time with family or go travelling, but they are afraid to because they may be perceived as less serious about their work and less committed to clients by their superiors. This isn't right. I remember when I was a backpacker in the United Kingdom watching a program on finance and the presenter showed the curriculum vitae of a high-profile CEO. In it was a gap year where he spent his whole time living in a mountain hut in Wales, re-connecting with nature. I thought that was simply brilliant.

–2–

Simply Locking Them Up Won't Work

Just as we take on our self-concept and at least some of our perceptions from our parents as we grow up, our society has inherited practices and ways of thinking from our ancient past that require re-evaluation. Historians tells us that not only were the Athenians competitive and materialistic, but they also valued a 'might is right' approach whilst viewing things as black and white, actions as good or bad,[17] without wishing to look deeper at underlying causes, asking the difficult questions, or conceding grey areas. Our criminal justice system has been founded on this way of thinking. It has assumed that just locking people up with lengthy sentences is the most effective way to tackle and reduce crime and create healthy, safe, communities. Given that we all want to feel safe and live in a vibrant, peaceful society let's investigate if this is true.

Back in 1987, Victoria was struggling with a crisis of overcrowding in our prison system that led to the emergency measure of using police cells as mini-jails.[18] This was a time when jail terms for serious crimes were increasing. Fast forward to 2018 and Victoria needed to expand prisons in a corrections system that already cost more than $1 billion to operate annually. The warning signs were flashing in the years leading up to this. Prisoner overcrowding was still happening, and police cells were again used as mini-jails whilst the then government claimed a tough-on-crime approach was the only answer. Not much had changed since 1987.

And so it is no surprise that research has shown that simply being tough on crime and building more prisons is not the answer to reducing and preventing crime. Recent statistics show that nearly half of prisoners in Victoria re-offend within two years.[19] According to the Australian Bureau of Crime Statistics, 58 per cent of prisoners have been in prison before.[20] The increasing prison population also makes it harder to deliver rehabilitation and education programs to all prisoners, which are essential to reduce re-offending and increase community safety.

This model of simply arresting and imprisoning people to tackle crime fails to take into consideration a number of factors critical to helping offenders get back on track and preventing crime in the first place. It doesn't include any examination of the underlying causes of offending and with that an examination of our patriarchal culture.

It is human nature, unfortunately, to avoid looking inwards at our faults and weaknesses; if something feels uncomfortable we want to place it in a vault in the dark recesses of our minds—which actually makes things much worse for us, preventing us from becoming better and happier people. We've been doing that with prisoners—not wanting to take a good look at who we are imprisoning and their backgrounds because it is too challenging, especially for those in power. And simply building more prisons as the answer to crime is far too costly and irresponsible.

It is not only extremely expensive in terms of construction to build prisons, but also in terms of cost per prisoner per year. So what does that mean on the ground? In 2013, the cost of housing a prisoner was $98,000 per year, yet the cost of supervising a person in the community and engaging them in programs under a community corrections order was $10,000 per year.[21] That's a huge difference. We can't keep asking taxpayers to keep paying for more prisons to be built whilst diverting much-needed resources from other areas, such as hospitals, schools, and housing.

And who are our prisoners? What are their backgrounds? Let's take a look.

Male prisoners

The vast majority of prisoners are men. Therefore, we need to tackle why more men commit offences. Here, we cannot overlook the part that patriarchy plays; gender stereotyping contributes to men developing hyper-masculine or toxic qualities such as aggression, narcissism, a sense of entitlement, lack of empathy, and greed. Associating dominating, controlling, exploiting or destroying others with being powerful is also a root cause. More specifically, violence against women is also due to sexism (including the sexual objectification of women) and gender stereotyping in general as well as the patriarchal notion of power. Where men are extremely shame-prone ie feeling deep-seated shame about being vulnerable in any way or helpless, they are also more likely to adhere to the patriarchal notion of power and lash out and attack others in order to feel 'powerful'.

We also know that overall, men are less likely to reach out for help through therapy by their own initiative, particularly if they are adhering to patriarchy's toxic view of masculinity and the false belief that men cannot experience or show vulnerability or be helpless in any way. This can also lead to substance abuse, with men self-medicating for anxiety or depression, and substance abuse is tragically common amongst the prison population.

I spoke further about this issue with a compassionate and astute medical practitioner and therapist. She said that it can be very difficult for therapy to work in some cases for men with addiction or anger management issues because they are not honest with their therapist. This wasn't a surprise to me as I had heard from other practitioners that resistance to recovery for addicts can be very strong, as it can be for the general population with negative attitudes and behaviours to overcome. We identify so much with our past and its grievances, and with our character flaws and harmful traits, that we wonder who we would be without them. There is a resistance to losing the very identity that is all a person knows, and a lack of faith in the happiness and freedom waiting for them on the other side. There can also, in some cases, be a resistance to accepting any responsibility for doing harm to others. Depending on the individual, this issue of responsibility can be quite painful to confront. Recovery requires a highly skilled and intuitive therapist, whilst the clients need to realise that they are wasting time and money unless they are prepared to be honest with their therapist and with themselves.

Prisoners and disadvantage

The vast majority of prisoners also come from disadvantaged backgrounds. Many have acquired brain injuries or psychiatric illnesses or disorders, lack secondary education, were homeless before entering prison, have backgrounds of family dysfunction and abuse, and close to half of prisoners were unemployed when imprisoned.[22]

Some sex offenders also claim they were sexually abused as children. But how true is this? Victoria's review into the management of serious sex offenders in 2015 (dubbed the 'Harper Review' because it was led by former Supreme Court Judge David Harper) said that some scepticism here is justified. It is difficult to trust the self-reporting of sexual abuse by sex offenders when they may be hoping to lessen the punishment for their own acts of abuse.[23] Such scepticism is supported by other specialists in the field, such as Dr Anne Salter, who has worked closely with sex offenders, saying that if it is in their interests to lie and they think they can get away with it, they will, even if it's to gain sympathy.[24]

Nevertheless, a 2012 Victorian study of children who were sexually abused between 1964 and 1995 found a link between being a victim of child sex abuse, especially for boys abused during adolescence, and later sex offending. According to the study, whilst the majority of child sex abuse victims do not go on to offend, victims of such abuse are more likely to commit violent and sexual offences than other members of the general community.

What this tells us is that early therapeutic intervention is not only beneficial for all victims of abuse. But more specifically for boys who are sexually abused, therapy will aid their development of healthy, respectful sexual attitudes and behaviours, as well as interpersonal and social skills. This is helpful not only for their sake but, as the 'Harper Review' says, for the sake of potential future victims.[25] They, along with all other young people, should also be taught what positive masculinity is and the importance of becoming a whole person within the context of true power discussed in the last chapter.

Indigenous Australians

The imprisonment rate of Indigenous Australians is alarming. In 2018 Change the Record reported they were 13 times more likely to be in prison than non-Indigenous Australians.[26] As we let that sink in, it's worth noting that this is true even within the context of the wide-reaching recommendations made back in 1991 by the Royal Commission into Aboriginal Deaths in Custody. Its recommendations included ceasing the incarceration of Indigenous Australians for minor offences that should have had no custodial sentence, such as public drinking. To date, there are still several recommendations that have not been implemented.

The Northern Territory made the situation even worse by introducing 'paperless arrest laws' in 2014. The effect wasn't just reducing police paperwork. Such laws have led to more Aboriginal people ending up in police cells for trivial offences. These include swearing, failing to keep a front yard clean, drinking in public, or instances in which police suspected that a person was about to commit one of these trivial offences.[27] This has meant that an Aboriginal person's contact with the criminal justice system has already started unnecessarily, and because they are disproportionately affected by these draconian laws—in circumstances of discrimination. Similarities can also be drawn with another discriminatory area of the law: anti-begging laws, which criminalise poverty.

Stan Grant writes in his book, *Talking to My Country*, that a criminologist told him that Indigenous people are locked up for crimes that would see other Australians walk free, and that once locked up, Indigenous people begin a spiral of reoffending and jail. They are trapped in poverty, mental illness, violence, substance abuse, and unemployment. And tragically one in five Indigenous male prisoners try to kill themselves.[28]

Indigenous Australians are also dealing with intergenerational trauma from what white patriarchal culture has inflicted upon them: the rapes of Indigenous women by white men and massacring of whole tribes, the loss of their land, and the generations stolen from their families. As a result of this unjust history, many live in poverty and despair, unable to relate to a white world that still fails in many ways to acknowledge their trauma and suffering.

We need to act urgently on this issue. Already, half of the children in juvenile detention in Australia are Indigenous,[29] and they are jailed at 25 times the rate of non-Indigenous children.[30] Far too many also return to detention within a year of being released.

Young people

Sadly, we also know that many young people sentenced to youth justice detention centres have past experience in child protection, meaning that they have backgrounds of emotional, psychological, and or physical or sexual abuse. When I worked as a Children's Court lawyer, I saw firsthand how my clients were struggling with a background of abuse and finding a sense of belonging, leaving them vulnerable to joining peer groups involved in crime.

Where there were no child protection issues as such, they still did not have positive role models in their family or schools and were bored. Unlike young people from middle-class and privileged backgrounds, they did not have ready access to nor encouragement to engage in hobbies or interests such as sport or music which would relieve boredom, aid self-esteem, provide the 'adrenaline rush' some were seeking, and allow for personal expression. A few of them needed ongoing therapy as well, and some needed medication for psychiatric disorders and other mental illnesses.

Women prisoners

The majority of women in prison are in there for non-violent crimes and do not pose a risk to the community. Most of them also have backgrounds of family violence and sexual abuse, which are entrenched in a patriarchal society. Many are still traumatised and suffering from various mental health issues. A large number lack secondary education or were unemployed at the time they entered prison. More than half of women in prison have reported sleeping rough or staying in emergency accommodation in the four weeks before imprisonment.[31] A sizeable majority also have substance abuse issues.[32] Some women even find prison safer than their homes—because of family violence. This profile of women prisoners doesn't just apply in Australia.

Journalist Joanna Moorhead interviewed author and consultant Stephanie Covington, who says something must be done about the fact that most women in prison in the UK have committed non-violent crimes such as theft and yet upon release one in two will reoffend within a year, as well as the fact that most have backgrounds of family violence and sexual abuse. She also adds that locking up a mother or caregiver also increases the chances of her children suffering mental health issues and entering the criminal justice system. Imprisonment also makes it harder for a mother to later have access to employment and housing.[33]

Such concerns are significant, especially when the Sentencing Advisory Council in Victoria reported in 2010 what is a continuing trend today—that prison sentences for women tend to be shorter than for men, given the generally lower level type of offending. This may look good at first blush. Even female judges I discussed this with, claim it shows there is no sexism or gender bias in sentencing. But they miss the important point that the mere fact that short prison sentences are imposed instead of non-custodial sentences means our judicial officers are still not properly considering the needs of women and children nor the different reasons for and types of offending among women.

Responsibility, compassion, and sentencing

Whilst the majority of people with backgrounds of abuse and trauma, mental health issues, racial and gender disadvantage, and socio-economic disadvantage do not go on to offend, we cannot ignore the pattern that exists regarding offenders. I by no means suggest that we disregard individual responsibility and accountability for one's actions. And even with greater government investment to address disadvantage, as the 'Harper Review' said, governments can't do everything to solve these problems.[34]

Acknowledging the power to choose and accepting responsibility also helps offenders make the decision to turn their lives around and commit to getting back on track with proper supports to do so. The attitude that those with a background of poverty, abuse, or mental health issues cannot help but commit crimes is also disempowering and unhelpful. And it would be wrong to label all people with such backgrounds as potential criminals. But we still need to show compassion for the circumstances outside of many offenders' control.

Martha Nussbaum, a modern philosopher, highlights in *Upheavals of Thought: The Intelligence of Emotions,* that it is possible to have both compassion and responsibility inform our approaches to the criminal justice system rather than one or the other. It is the compassion that enables us to ascertain the point at which a person accepts full responsibility for his or her offending after appropriate allowance for circumstances that he or she couldn't control. This approach was considered by former High Court Justice Ian Callinan AC in his review of the parole system in Victoria, which I later discuss.[35]

We also need to be open-minded about what compassion looks like in the form of the sentence given. 'Diversion' helps offenders avoid a criminal record by following court ordered conditions—such as undergoing counselling, a rehabilitation or education program, community work, or writing an apology to the victim. Such an approach may be compassionate and in the best interests of a first time offender for a less serious offence or in a few cases for a more serious offence—after careful consideration of several factors. These include details about the offender and the crime and any mitigating or special circumstances that may justify diversion and prevent future offending.

For example, when Tammy was sixteen years old, she assaulted a woman for calling her a 'bitch' when she pushed past her. Tammy was a first time offender, full of remorse, and was struggling with the recent death of her mother from cancer. Through diversion, Tammy apologised to the victim, underwent counselling to deal with her grief and anger management issues, and avoided a criminal record that would have affected her chances of employment. She also engaged with a mentoring scheme, and was able to pursue her studies to become a school teacher.

It could also be said that the most compassionate and wise approach for a more violent and serious offender may be to order a sentence of imprisonment. This is after considering the gravity of the offence and the criminal history of the offender (like a history of escalating violence), the impact on the victim, and rehabilitation of the offender (psychological or psychiatric reports are useful here). Deterrence is also considered as well as sentences for other like cases, and any mitigating circumstances. A judge may decide imprisonment is necessary to not only reflect the seriousness of the violent offence but to prevent further offending, while rehabilitation programs are provided in a contained environment.

Where prison is a last resort and an order involving supervision in the community, such as a community corrections order, is not appropriate, there is no reason why imprisonment could not be seen as compassionate and wise. There may even be an unconscious relief for the more violent offender of facing such consequences for his or her actions and being contained, rather than left feeling out of control or in other cases 'omnipotent'. There are also cases of extremely violent offenders acknowledging that imprisonment, including even a lengthy sentence with rehabilitation programs in prison, saved themselves and others from more serious harm.

Some offenders have also said that prison helped them escape the reach of criminal peer groups to address their violent behaviour and to confront its seriousness. The problem has been where the rehabilitation programs in prison have not been available, are not of high quality, and/or are not delivered when they can make the most impact.

We also know we cannot create a perfect rehabilitation system where no offender re-offends. But on the issue of rehabilitation and crime prevention we can do much better.

There's also one last matter to mention on sentencing. In recent decades mandatory minimum sentencing has been the catch cry of some governments to deter crime. The truth, though, is that evidence for mandatory sentencing is contradictory and there is not much that supports it outright.[36]

Some critics view it as the type of black and white thinking that harks back to ancient patriarchal Greece. It undermines a fair, compassionate, and wise approach tailored to individual cases whilst being mindful of consistency in sentencing. Blanket minimum sentencing instead promotes a punitive 'one size fits all' method that can lead to unjust outcomes.

But others say it is a problem only by a matter of degrees. For example, they believe mandatory sentencing isn't patriarchal and overly punitive if it is only for the most serious violent offences and allows for certain special circumstances to apply—and so hopefully preventing possible injustices occurring. But can politicians truly foresee all possible events when imposing a mandatory penalty?

Many in the legal profession and human rights sector say no. Instead they say fair and wise sentencing means judicial officers must be able to focus on deciding the most appropriate sentence for every offender before them with regard to all relevant factors.

This has been highlighted, for example, where mandatory sentencing prevents courts from considering relevant cultural issues for Aboriginal offenders, which the Koori court process later discussed allows. It also leads to a higher incarceration rate of Aboriginal men and women when their incarceration rate is already too high. In 2014, the United Nation's committee against torture urged Australia to have its states abolish mandatory sentencing laws due to mounting proof that they disproportionately affect Indigenous people.[37]

In the United States, after decades of mandatory penalties, political parties have campaigned to slash mandatory sentences for some crimes, saying the laws are outdated, have led to overcrowding of prisons[38] and unfairly harsh sentences.[39]

But what about governments and some members of the public saying judges are too lenient with the sentences they give? Studies have shown that when lay people are told about all the facts of a case they believe judges generally are getting sentencing right. An area where lay people still would have imposed more severe sentences was in child sex offences.[40] Yet where *manifestly inadequate* sentencing occurs for these and other matters, it can be dealt with through Crown appeals to the higher courts. This includes the High Court as discussed in Chapter Six. Guideline judgements by the Court of Appeal (Victoria's highest court) to guide the lower courts on sentencing for certain types of offences are also helpful.

To have fair and just sentencing we not only need law courses to incorporate a feminist perspective as discussed in Chapter One. Continuing education for judges is also essential just like in other professions. Judicial training through the Judicial College of Victoria and similar colleges around the world can help to ensure that judges address any personal prejudice or lack of understanding of the seriousness of certain crimes. Such training can aid sentencing that is proportionate to the offences committed and takes into consideration all relevant matters. Judicial Commissions that handle complaints about the behaviour of judicial officers, such as where they make sexist, homophobic, or racist comments, also make judges more accountable and mindful about their remarks and encourages them to examine themselves for prejudice.

We also need to have judges from a diverse range of backgrounds, a greater gender balance, and an independent selection process to ensure merit-based appointments. Such measures ensure judges reflect the best in community attitudes, and guard against political appointments.

Yet, interestingly, governments in Australia and overseas have still pursued mandatory sentencing, despite already having a justice system that can deliver severe sentences if warranted. And this is whilst we also know that an important way forward is tackling the underlying causes of crime and providing practical measures to protect the general community and emergency workers (such as police, paramedics, and hospital staff.) This includes the justice reinvestment measures later discussed, and effective strategies to prevent and deter alcohol and drug-fuelled violence. It also includes ensuring all hospitals have specialist highly trained security staff along with CCTV cameras, duress alarms, and isolation rooms for isolating or assessing those who are violent or pose a risk of violence.[41] Significant government investment in emergency workers including police is also critical so that they are always working together in sufficient numbers and are highly trained and resourced.

In the following two chapters, we will look in more detail at alternative approaches to reducing and preventing crime as opposed to the patriarchal view that prison is the only answer.

-3-
Tackling The
Root of Crime

Strolling through the labyrinthine streets of Athens, Socrates happily engaged people around him, encouraging them to question every aspect of their life, their values and assumptions. This radical philosopher was often viewed by those in power as a troublemaker and his ability to attract the youth was seen as dangerous. Hence, Athens turned on him when he was seventy and he was sentenced to death.

I can't help but believe that Athens would have reached far greater heights and perhaps would not have fallen as it did if the Athenians had done two things. Firstly, if they had listened to the radical ideas of Socrates; and secondly, allowed all women to participate in their discourse and in every part of life. Likewise, we need to listen to those calling for a radical approach to prevent and reduce crime. We must turn away from the patriarchal method that focuses purely on punishment—which at least some governments have done (to a limited extent) in recent years. As discussed earlier, this doesn't mean there aren't times when a person may be in that small category needing a lengthy prison sentence. But we must do much more to address the underlying causes of criminal behaviour.

Whilst tackling the root of crime is a radical strategy compared to the patriarchal approach, for many of us it makes perfect sense. It involves embracing a holistic or whole-of-government strategy. This means tackling crime across several government departments including health, mental health, justice, education, employment, and housing. Everything is interconnected and interdependent and forms part of a whole. This approach can be likened to having a serious health problem that has a better chance of being cured through using a number of methods rather than just one—such as a combination of a healthy diet, medication, exercise, other modes of therapy and only resorting to surgery if all else has failed.

We also know that more investment in prevention not only saves much pain and suffering, but costs less in the long run. It isn't only human rights organisations I consulted with as a political advisor, such as Smart Justice, who are advocates for this new direction to reduce and prevent crime. Even the 'Harper Review' into the management of serious sex offenders accepted that a holistic approach was necessary in order to deal with crime, given the overlap between criminality and mental health problems, abuse and social and family disadvantage.[42]

This holistic approach needs to include police more frequently using diversion and cautions or warnings. Continued use of sentences involving supervision and programs in the community to reduce reoffending and the prison population is also beneficial in appropriate cases. Put simply, we really need to divert low-risk offenders. Placing them with high-risk offenders only increases the chances of them not only reoffending but doing so with more serious violent crimes. As a forensic psychologist said to me, in general it's harder to rehabilitate a person once they are caught up in the criminal justice system and are in prison. This is also why 'spent conviction schemes' are also beneficial. They wipe a minor criminal record after a person has completed a period of crime-free behaviour such as 10 years for adults and 3 years for juvenile offenders. This 'clean slate' then makes it easier for people to access employment and insurance. And so it prevents more serious reoffending arising from poverty, social isolation, and mental health issues. Spent convictions schemes exist throughout Australia (except Victoria at the time of writing) and the United Kingdom.

So what else does a holistic approach to reduce and prevent crime include? The following are just a few of the key strategies needed:

1. Early therapy, good parenting, and mentoring schemes.
2. 'Justice reinvestment'.
3. Feminist-centred government policies.
4. A well-rounded education curriculum.
5. Addressing the harms caused by the sex industry, sexist advertising, and sexist aspects of our popular culture.
6. Therapeutic justice (therapeutic courts).
7. Investing in rehabilitation programs in prison and post-release, as well as greater investment in the parole system.

In this chapter we will focus on the first five measures outside of the courtroom.

Early therapy, good parenting, and mentoring schemes

I want to tell you about Theo. Before he was ten years old he was an easy-going, friendly boy. But then he started acting up at school, playing the class clown, craving approval from his classmates. At home he was causing disruption, refusing to follow the house rules his mother laid down. This only made his mother become distant towards Theo, not realising that Theo was trying to get his mother and (mainly absent) father's attention—it was a call for help. Theo's mother did not seek out professional therapeutic support for Theo since it was not something that crossed her mind, nor did she believe in therapy.

Theo spiralled into substance abuse and petty criminal behaviour. Then he became involved in more serious offending and was placed on a supervisory order in the community. He had unresolved grief issues from when his father left to be with a new partner. Having the right therapist would have helped

Theo deal with his grief and would have also identified serious disturbances in his way of thinking. Sessions that included his mother might also have helped to heal their relationship, and enable his mother get in touch with her own pain from the divorce and work through it. Instead, Theo continued being disruptive at home and school and became involved in more crime, so that he ended up in a youth detention centre.

Theo represents what I saw in many of my clients: an underlying distress or trauma that was triggering problem behaviour and offending. Such cases highlight that when children and young people exhibit problem behaviour or signs of distress in school and/or in the home, parents must be strongly encouraged to seek therapeutic treatment for their child and advised of key support and mental health services from a medical practitioner, a school's wellbeing officer, or equivalent adviser. Some parents do not seek such support without encouragement, or may not know how to find a good therapist. And as I said earlier they may even be sceptical about the benefits of counselling and specialist treatment services.

The introduction of mandatory reporting of child abuse also helps early therapeutic intervention happening through the assistance of child protection agencies, for example where a parent or parents are abusing a child. But again, even child protection is an area that requires much greater government investment to increase staffing levels and prevent high staff turnover. This is critical not only because we don't want children to suffer abuse, and where they do, to be left unprotected and without help to recover. But there is another important reason. Psychotherapists working with severely ill, perverse, and violent individuals have said that often their clients have been exposed to violence and moral corruption at the hands of their caretakers, parents or violent couples who inflict their psychosis or disturbance on their children.[43]

And we need to do more to prevent child abuse in the first place. Dr Andrew Scott in his book, *Northern Lights*, says countries like Sweden are leaders in this area, taking a public health prevention approach. This approach guides them in assessing what the risk factors are in families, parenting, and social values so that they can reduce the mistreatment of children. Sweden now has the lowest child injury rates in the world thanks to widespread education programs for safety at home prioritising child safety. There has also been a ban on hitting a child for more than three decades.[44]

Campaigns against family violence and gender stereotyping are also important for child safety. So is replacing the patriarchal view of power resting in domination and control, with one that promotes respectful relationships.

We also have to remember that physical abuse and sexual abuse are not the only things that are harmful to children. Emotional unavailability or rejection is damaging. Researchers have found that if parents or the primary caregivers do not express love and empathy to babies, emotions which are required for 'secure attachment', and don't express this love as a child develops, there can be harmful long-term consequences in their child's mental health and behaviour, requiring therapeutic treatment.[45] It is also concerning that our knowledge in this area isn't recent. John Bowlby first drew the connection between lack of secure attachment and criminal behaviour in 1944.[46] It makes sense that education for new parents must also include the importance of secure attachment for babies and children. They should also be encouraged to access therapeutic supports if they are struggling to provide a loving, warm, and secure environment for their child.

Unfortunately, experts also say that simply engaging in good parenting will not of itself improve a child's mental health issues in certain cases. Dr Anne Salter says, for instance, that there are studies in relation to psychopaths which show that the quality of parenting is unrelated to the number of conduct problems that callous/unemotional children have, and so early therapeutic intervention here is crucial.[47]

This intervention is also crucial as soon as a young person has contact with the criminal justice system. Experts have said for years what the Victorian Parliamentary Inquiry into Youth Justice Centres in 2018 confirmed—that a young offender must be assessed for any physical or mental health issues, cognitive impairment, and substance misuse. And they must have access to appropriate ongoing therapeutic treatment tailored to his or her needs. If a young person then is incarcerated, this intervention should continue throughout incarceration and upon release.

Mentoring programs are critical as well. These should be provided for young people at risk and young offenders as soon as they come into contact with the criminal justice system. An example is the Reboot Crime Prevention Program in Gippsland. Mentors help young people explore their interests, get involved in fun leisure activities, and further their education. We have already seen in Victoria mentoring programs in other contexts, which are extremely successful.

Women and Mentoring based in Melbourne is one such early intervention program. When a woman is charged with a criminal offence she is matched with a supportive female mentor. The program increases the participant's confidence and provides her with skills to cope with her legal matter, access supports, address the underlying causes of her offending, and become more aware of the dangers of self-sabotage. The vast majority of participants have avoided a prison sentence and have not re-offended, moving on to live more positive, vibrant lives.[48] It is a program that should not only be rolled out to all areas of need but can be adapted for young people throughout Australia.

Mentoring programs for boys and girls in school are also important as well as for those caught up in the criminal justice system. AFL footballer Neville Jetta wrote in the *Herald Sun* of the joy and privilege of mentoring young Indigenous youth. He started by running a football program for Indigenous boys transitioning into the TAC Cup. He also became involved in the Good Start program in schools, spreading healthy messages to kids. Jetta has extended his mentoring to help young people reconnect to culture and be involved in leadership programs. He writes that some of these kids are really leading the way and are awesome people in their communities.[49]

Including female footballers, artists, and musicians in leadership programs is also a good idea, as is involving members of local communities who are leaders in their respective fields.

Government funding is also essential for successful programs for at-risk youth such as the Indigenous on-country program, the Yiriman project, in the Kimberly. The program takes young people on trips into their traditional lands with elders in the Fitzroy Valley, providing much cultural healing.[50]

Adapting such programs for non-Indigenous youth would also be beneficial since re-connecting to nature and the environment can help a person become more grounded and centred, as well as more at peace with oneself. Learning more about Aboriginal culture and how it relates to the environment as well would be a wonderful, life-affirming experience.

We also need better relations between police and young people according to youth worker Les Twentyman. Social interactions that have proven helpful include: at-risk kids trekking Kokoda with police, playing cricket matches and baseball games with police officers, and police taking kids on movie outings. These kids learn not to fear police but respect them and see them as mentors. Meanwhile, police officers at all levels develop a greater understanding (and empathy) for young people with difficult backgrounds and how best to connect with them.[51]

Now, let's look at some other ways to create safe and vibrant communities.

Justice reinvestment: long term investment

A silver-haired, conservative Republican helped give birth to an important innovation to increase community safety. Called 'justice reinvestment', it addresses the underlying causes of offending and has already been shown in studies to actually reduce crime. Jerry Madden and his Republican colleagues in the Texas state legislature did something that not enough leaders do: they had open minds and listened to experts around them about what could be done to help keep the prison population down, and then turned these insights into action. They established justice reinvestment programs so successfully in Texas in 2007 that they avoided having to build three more prisons, as the programs led to:

- a fall in prisoner numbers of 1,125 between 2008 and 2010, and
- savings of $443.9 million in 2008-9.

The financial savings were then redirected to more programs and replicated in 27 other American states.[52]

So what is this wonderful thing called 'justice reinvestment'? It's really just a practical, common sense approach of investing in effective drug and alcohol programs, gambling addiction programs, mental health programs/counselling, employment, education, housing et cetera: in essence, programs and measures tailored to address disadvantage and hardship in communities, which in turn reduces crime. A collaborative partnership between governments, service providers, police, and communities is essential for its effectiveness. So is data collection to understand where the problems are and why, and to show which strategies work.

In 2013 an Australian Senate Inquiry into Justice Reinvestment recommended that the Commonwealth adopt a leadership role in implementing this innovative approach through the Council of Australian Governments. Justice reinvestment has already been successful in reducing crime in the town of Bourke in NSW. Here, community-led solutions include a driver learner program to help young people get their licence, police regularly meeting with victims and perpetrators of family violence (and those at risk) and linking them with community services, as well as limits on the sale and supply of alcohol. The 'Harper Review' into sex offenders also recognised that many jurisdictions, including in the United States, are adopting a justice reinvestment approach to increase community safety.[53]

Justice reinvestment in the long run will not only save taxpayers money by reducing construction of costly prisons, but will also create a society that is more fair, positive, and vibrant.

The problem is that to date, whilst some governments are at least turning their minds to justice reinvestment initiatives and putting some in place, we know that generally they are still not investing enough in public housing and are even selling it off to private developers. Nor are they doing enough for affordable housing and ensuring that rents are at a reasonable rate. There is also insufficient investment in drug and alcohol rehabilitation programs, programs to assist gambling addicts, effective services and strategies to address violence against women, mentoring programs, and programs that increase employment.

If you think, *but all of this costs a lot of money*, the savings made from not having to build more prisons through upfront investment in these areas makes it worthwhile in the long term. It then means more money for our hospitals and other areas of public need. In addition, if we had a fairer tax system so that very wealthy individuals and corporations couldn't avoid paying the tax that they should be paying, and paid tax truly proportionate to their income, this would help.

We also need better funding for education to ensure that all children have equal access to high-quality education, regardless of their socio-economic background, and are taught within well-maintained school buildings. This requires a fair, needs-based funding approach.

More specifically in relation to education, we should be incorporating ideas from the successful education systems of the Nordic countries like Finland. Finland has a history of producing amongst the highest test scores in the world and being the most literate nation. But that's not all. Every child has access to high quality education within a creative, playful, warm, and supportive environment that includes less homework and shorter school hours.

Finland's successful, holistic approach to teaching and the personal growth of students shows that there is a better way than privileging the patriarchal focus on competition and pressure. Teachers are also much more highly regarded and better qualified than in many other countries. William Doyle, a lecturer on media and education and a 2015-16 Fulbright scholar, writes of these benefits of the Finnish education system. He adds that even the Harvard education professor Howard Gardner once advised Americans to learn from Finland, as they had the most effective schools whilst doing the opposite of what Americans do.[54] Importantly, Finland does not have the public-private school divide that exists in Australia and elsewhere, or the inequity in education.

On the issue of entrenched disadvantage and joblessness, Dr Andrew Scott provides several helpful insights from examining Nordic countries' positive policy initiatives in his book, *Northern Lights*. Given that Sweden has such low levels of child poverty compared to many other nations, it would be useful to draw on details of successful, local, child health, parenting, and employment programs in Sweden. These details could then inform an Australian approach that is adapted to the needs of particular disadvantaged communities.[55]

Indeed Sweden has extensive employment assistance programs for us to learn from. For example, as soon as single parents of children start to receive government support, they are assisted with planning their future return to the workplace, whilst caring for their children. Dr Scott says this approach contrasts with the Australian experience of cutting their meagre income support to try to push them into paid work. Sweden instead invests in creating job opportunities and provides affordable, accessible, high quality childcare. Job training programs are also provided to help single parents upgrade their skills where needed and overcome any particular disadvantage.[56]

But even where Australia adopted this idea of helping single parents plan for future study and employment, the federal government did so using a patriarchal approach with its ParentsNext Program. Established in July 2018, the program failed overall to treat single parents, who are mainly women, with respect by working collaboratively with them to hear what they may or may not need. Instead the government decided to apply a punitive 'one size fits all' approach.

This program included mandating appointments and activities which parents were already doing but now had the humiliation of having to report on, such as taking children to swimming lessons. Some parents also complained of no consideration being allowed for missing appointments or part-time work commitments due to special circumstances such as a child being unwell. The excessive reporting requirements also made life much harder and stressful for women and their children. And there were instances of women having their single parent benefit unfairly cut off leaving them and their children without food. This led to a Senate inquiry into the program that heard it involved human rights abuses and was unethical. In early 2019 the inquiry concluded the program needed to be overhauled to address barriers for participants finding employment and be fine-tuned for culture and family violence issues.[57] Meanwhile, several human rights and social justice advocates have called for it to be scrapped altogether.

As part of justice reinvestment in a broader context, much greater funding for the mental health sector including community mental health services is also essential. This is to ensure that those with psychosocial disabilities receive the support and care they need, such as life skills training and counselling. It would also help prevent any acute mental health episodes that could put them at risk of harming themselves or others—thus reducing their chances of being caught up in the criminal justice system or having their children caught up in it.

In Victoria, the lack of funding and resources for community mental health services has been a problem for several years. The consequences of this are dire. Highly qualified mental health workers have been leaving the sector amid concerns they are being replaced by less qualified people on lower wages who do not have the skills to deal with complex and acute clients. This is also happening in part due to the rollout of the National Disability Insurance Scheme (a new funding model for services for people with disabilities), that is largely inadequate for people with mental health issues.[58] But this development is not surprising under a patriarchal hierarchical approach by governments and departments who just don't listen or consult enough (or at all). And when crisis point hits, that's when inquiries and royal commissions usually happen—such as the Victorian Royal Commission into Mental Health. And governments suddenly invest more funding in the sector, which some experts argue still isn't at sufficient levels.

Feminist-centred government policies

Like the more feminist social democracies such as Sweden, we need to prioritize valuing women and children and place them at the centre of all policy decisions, along with the quality of life of all our citizens. Such an approach goes against the values of patriarchy which negate the experiences of women and children and are focused on the pursuit of material wealth, status, and busyness, leaving little room for quality of life and time to spend with family, friends, and time for ourselves.

Sweden and the other economically successful Nordic countries have better paid parental leave and shorter working weeks than the OECD average as a result of a feminist-centred approach. Dr Andrew Scott says this points the way to us needing to regulate our labour market to achieve more child friendliness and better work/life balance. This is crucial since Australians are working increasingly long hours and are therefore becoming more anxious and stressed.[59]

Less stress and anxiety for adults through work/life balance means a nourishing environment for adults and children to thrive in and connect meaningfully with each other. This makes children less susceptible to behavioural problems and negative peer groups and therefore less susceptible to turning to crime.

Decision-making that takes into consideration women's experiences and perspectives would also elevate the value and respect for women in our society as well as lead to more just and equitable outcomes. The domino effect would be a great reduction in sexism—a major contributing factor to violence against women.

A well-rounded education curriculum

Investing in high-quality education for all school students doesn't only mean meeting the numeracy and literacy requirements. As with the Finnish model, it also means ensuring access to creativity/arts/music and other means of self-expression, competencies, sport, and access to and an appreciation of nature. The importance of developing a passion and connection to nature is discussed later, in Chapter Ten.

We should include women's voices and experiences in Australian history including feminist activism, emphasising women's rights are very much a part of human rights. This would also enhance respect for women and the qualities traditionally aligned to the 'feminine', such as empathy and compassion, and increase understanding of the impact of a patriarchal view of power and the need to change this.

Respect for and an understanding of Indigenous culture should also be taught in all schools (not just some) and Aboriginal languages. It is important for children to also learn about the devastating impact of the patriarchal, white, colonial culture on Indigenous Australians. Teaching the history of

Indigenous activism is also critical. This education would encourage Indigenous youth to feel proud of their culture whilst learning their history. It would also help all Australian children to enjoy the benefits of Indigenous culture and know the truth of their history—to not only learn of the positives but also the negative side. This is not about shaming the current generation. Instead it is about ensuring that children recognise the damaging effects of the patriarchal view of power in all its forms such as racism. And just as we as individuals must all face our own personal flaws and work on them in order to move forward and be our best selves, so must our society.

Respectful relationship programs should be taught in all schools (they are at least being increasingly rolled out in Australia). The programs must include highlighting the harms of gender stereotyping, pornography, and a sexist culture. Discussions about how toxic masculinity has encouraged boys to view men who are caring and empathetic as not being 'real men' are also essential.

Teaching a healthy approach to masculinity is part of this process. This should also include the importance of becoming a whole person (regardless of gender) through integrating both positive 'masculine' and 'feminine' qualities—which as discussed earlier should evolve to simply being called positive qualities. Mentoring programs such as the Human United Strength Organisation Mentoring program in the United States are also helpful. This is an after school program where high school boys meet to discuss issues that they find difficult to speak of publicly and rethink their views on masculinity—helping them and everyone they interact with.[60]

Secular ethics should also be taught along with empathy training. During my time as a lawyer in the Children's Court, I could see how empathy training would not only benefit students generally but, specifically, some of my children's court clients. I was dealing with a few clients who seemed to lack empathy for their victims. There were those clients who had mental health issues relating to being victims of abuse themselves. For others, it wasn't so clear cut.

One client from a relatively stable background committed a serious assault. When I sat with him in my office preparing his guilty plea, I questioned him, searching for any mitigating circumstances. His eyes were blank, his face a mask. He showed no remorse at all. So I asked him how he would feel if he was the victim in this case, at which point a light bulb seemed to go off in his mind. His face came to life as he replied, 'I never thought of it like that.'

Empathy training has been used successfully in Denmark to teach children from early primary school age to care for each other, be in touch with their feelings, to read other people's emotions, and it has contributed to their happiness and wellbeing so it is well worth investing in.[61]

And it's not just young people who need empathy training: all of us in today's modern world need to work on cultivating more compassion and empathy. It would be useful in workplace training, perhaps as an adjunct to bullying training, and in management training. It should be included in professions such as law, as part of therapeutic lawyering, and medicine, particularly for patient care.

Meditation and mindfulness training would also benefit students in an increasingly stressful, alienating, and materialistic world where serious addiction rates are high. Professor Lea Waters from the Positive Psychology Department at the University of Melbourne says there is already research showing meditation's beneficial effects on student wellbeing, including in reducing anxiety and depression, enhancing social skills, and increasing academic skills. Approximately 7,500 teachers are using mindfulness taught by organisations such as *Smiling Minds* in Victoria. Children learn meditation and mindfulness in wellbeing classes and mindfulness techniques are used to help students prepare for the start of academic classes. Mindfulness moments can also be taught at the start of a school assembly and meditation spaces can be provided in school libraries for students and staff.[62]

The sex industry, ads, and popular culture

If we are truly serious about preventing and reducing male violence against women and girls, we need to address the harms of the multi-billion-dollar sex industry, sexist advertising, and sexism and misogyny in popular culture, since they contribute to the sexist and misogynistic views that normalise this type of male violence. And whilst the impact of these industries on male violence against women and girls is a criminal law issue, we are also dealing with a public health issue, as well as sex discrimination (including sexual exploitation), and gender vilification. And so again we need a holistic approach.

I will spend more time examining the harms of the sex industry only because this is the area where there is the greatest resistance to taking action. Consumers of this industry are predominantly male, and for the purposes of addressing male violence against women, I will focus on them.

Pornography

Pornography was prohibited historically under obscenity law, as it was unfortunately seen only as a problem of morals rather than one focussed on disrespect for women. Over time, the laws around it loosened under the banner of free speech and, for some time, there has been a problem of lack of enforcement.

Interestingly, in the 1960s, Swiss psychiatrist Dr Carl Jung and his associate Marie Louise Von Franz understood the negative impact of pornography on men developing their feminine side and therefore a respectful mature regard for women as well. In the book *Man and His Symbols*, they warned that men who are drawn to pornographic material and strip shows display a crude and primitive way of relating to the feminine. Compulsive viewing occurs when men haven't developed what we now call emotional intelligence, remaining immature or infantile.[63]

Pornography has become even more degrading to women since the 1960s and is very much a tool of patriarchy for women's oppression. A glimpse at what the more 'tame' pornography shows on popular pornography sites reveals that women are often depicted as having an insatiable appetite for sex—depictions harking back to medieval art and literature which (under the authority of the Church) portrayed women as sexually voracious and depraved.[64] Today's pornography though now combines the insatiable appetite for sex with an appetite for double penetrations and gang bangs. Women, as seen through the lens of pornography, also have a voracious appetite for humiliation and degradation.

The standard plotline is well summed up by Anne Manne in her book on narcissism *The Life of I*. A woman is picked up by men in a minibus. They offer her money for stripping naked. She of course agrees, so they ask for sex in return for money and she again agrees and has sex with them all. She is then pushed out of the vehicle whilst the men are holding out the cash. In a final act of degrading her they drive off before she gets hold of it. The effect of pornography on the minds of young male university students is also outlined in Manne's book: viewing women as 'bitches' who get what's coming to them, the view that real women are like those who are depicted in pornography, and the anger when real women say no to them—an anger and aggression fuelled by pornography along with narcissism, the need to dominate and control, and a lack of empathy. This culture also leads to a strong sense of entitlement.[65]

In case you are still not concerned, feminist Mia Doring writes in her blog, *We need to talk about Porn*, that the search terms of pornography on popular pornography site Pornhub (which has millions of viewers daily with access 24/7 from anywhere) include abused school girl, screaming anal, first time anal, teen painal, painal to save her marriage, step daddy, abused teens, abused gangbang, abused anal gangbang, and train abuse (where sexual assault and unwanted groping occurs.) Everything is available, from rape to incest, family violence and more.[66]

This is not surprising given that a pornography producer told journalist Robert Jensen that he showed violence against women because it was what he believed men wanted to see.[67] It's all about putting profits before people, or more specifically before the welfare of women and girls.

Meanwhile, it makes sense that there are experts saying that pornography is a significant factor contributing to sexist and misogynistic views and pointing to studies as well as legal cases confirming its strong links to violence against women. Organisations such as Collective Shout highlight such studies on their websites.

As far back as 1993, the late Dr Marlene Goldsmith MLC, the previous Chair of the Legislative Council of Social Issues in NSW, warned that during the period of 1975–91, when pornography became much more accessible, there was a 90.6 percent increase in rapes.[68]

More recently, the Gold Coast Centre Against Sexual Assault found that the biggest common denominator for the huge increase in intimate partner rape seen by the Centre in recent years was pornography consumption by the offender.[69]

In the United Kingdom, Lord Thomas, who rejected Jamie Reynolds' appeal against sentence for the rape and murder of a teenage girl, told the Commons Justice committee that the case left him in no doubt at all that pornography on the internet had a dramatic effect on Reynolds. Police searching Reynolds's home discovered 16,800 pornographic images, 72 extreme videos, and 40 obscene stories written by him.[70]

A United States Court of Appeals also acknowledged the connection between pornography and male violence against women and girls back in 1985 in the case of *Hudnut*, adding that images of the subordination of women perpetuated subordination and even contributed to women's economic inequality.[71] This particular view of the court is extremely enlightening. It understood how everything is connected. Until we address the harms of pornography and other sexist and misogynistic aspects of our culture, we cannot fully address male violence against women as well as injustices such as the gender pay gap.

Mia Doring says that pornography is not only reinforcing sexist attitudes but creating new ones. While men and boys masturbate to pornography they are rewiring their brains—this means they associate pleasure and sex with the perverse and violent acts they have been viewing.[72] Psychiatrist Norman Doidge also says that men reinforce their addiction to pornography every time they masturbate, and that they wire the images they watch into the pleasure centres of the brain with the rapt attention needed for the brain to change.[73] Doring adds the next stage is wanting to try these acts they watch in real life. She isn't wrong about this.[74]

Dr. Victor Cline conducted research that showed how consumers who become addicted to pornographic materials (including soft porn, which is still harmful by sexually objectifying women) begin to want more explicit or extreme and violent material and end up desiring to act out what they've seen.[75] The serial killer and rapist Ted Bundy was a pornography addict and spoke of how he wanted to act out what he saw, adding that the men he knew who were sex offenders were also heavily involved in pornography.[76] I also found this to be true in the sex offence cases I came across as a lawyer and political advisor.

We are in fact creating fertile ground for more violent offenders in our society because cultural norms are taught through pornography. As highlighted by Collective Shout in a submission on cyber safety, when boys take pleasure in and masturbate to depictions of torture and humiliation, when they are fed porn and sexual abuse, why are we surprised with the crisis of violence against women? They also refer to Dr Michael Flood, an expert in the area, who says pornography is essentially providing rape training.[77]

Mental health experts have also warned there is an epidemic of pornography addiction amongst males including teenagers[78] and even younger children are becoming addicted. (Females are also amongst those who are addicts). Organisations such as eChildhood say that this easy access to pornography by children not only enables addiction but normalises online and offline abuse, and can have significant impact on their development and emotional, physical, mental, and sexual wellbeing.[79] Even in the United States, Utah, South Dakota, and Virginia have declared pornography a public health crisis.[80] We are dealing with a pornographic generation of young people that feminists for decades warned would happen if we didn't act to keep pornography from becoming embedded in our culture.

Also of concern is that Dr Heather Wood of the Portman Clinic in the United Kingdom warns of how men who previously had no conscious paedophilic interests are now seeking out child abuse material after viewing adult pornography for a period of time.[81]

If leading community and social justice advocates as well as some governments around the world can take seriously the strong connection between disadvantage and offending, and so take action to address this disadvantage through measures such as justice reinvestment, why are they so reluctant to acknowledge the strong connection between pornography and male violence against women and children and so tackle pornography? What we watch, and especially what we watch over long periods of time, affects our thinking, and how we think affects our actions. It also affects our very identity.

Given we are dealing with an epidemic of pornography addiction, which we know increases aggression, narcissism, and lack of empathy as well as sexist and misogynistic views, it's within reason to assume that a not insignificant number of our politicians, advisors, business leaders and leaders in other sectors are pornography addicts as well. And so this addiction will be affecting their decision-making.

But what action should be taken to address this serious issue? We again need to take a holistic approach, tackling pornography from several angles.

Firstly, we need to urgently re-examine an internet ban/filter on pornography with the federal government on the basis of pornography being gender vilification or hate speech, the fact that it's necessary to prevent violence against women and children, and in recognition that this is also a public health issue. Such a ban must also have the necessary safeguards to only capture pornography. Given the technological advances we have made, surely we are up to re-examining the feasibility of such a proposal in Australia and the rest of the world.

Iceland's proposed ban back in 2013 is a good starting point and was supported by leading feminists like Gloria Steinem, psychologists, doctors, human rights activists, sociologists, and writers. They praised Iceland wanting to act to protect children and women's right to safety and equality and maintain the integrity of Icelandic culture against the onslaught of an unrestrained industry of sexual exploitation.[82] Iceland has already banned the production and sale of pornography, which we should also do in every state.

Whilst the United Kingdom is at least trialling a partial ban based on age verification to access pornography in order to protect children from it (an important step forward), it does fail to recognise that even adults accessing pornography poses a continued danger to women and children, given pornography's links to sexism, misogyny and violence.

Disturbingly, there are cases of adults deliberately showing pornography to children—whether it be shown by a friend's older brother, a father's friend, or even a father or older brother to the child. You can't rely on a pornography consumer to be responsible and mature about to whom they show it.

A clinical psychologist who works with sex offenders and pornography addicts told me he knew of cases of fathers deliberately leaving the pornography on the computer for their children to see because they had a perverse desire for their children to know what they were looking at. He also said that we need to ban pornography, supports a prohibition on strip clubs, and advocates the Nordic model for dealing with prostitution (which I later discuss) because men need boundaries (just as all humans need boundaries).

Another option is for the federal government to hold Google and other tech giants to account for allowing pornography to be uploaded on their platforms, based on extensive consultation. Our government has already passed laws to penalize them for allowing online content that depicts violent crimes.

We also need laws against gender vilification with the full force of our racial vilification laws. Even the NSW Law Reform Commission has acknowledged that pornography is a form of hate speech.[83] The absence of such laws merely normalises gendered hate speech in all its forms, including pornography, making gendered hate speech acceptable and making it harder to combat violence against women and misogyny. It also reflects just how patriarchal our society is.

Interestingly, in the United Kingdom, at the time of writing there is a growing momentum to make misogyny a hate crime so that police are able to deal with the root causes of violence against women.[84]

We also need well-resourced community campaigns that expose the harms of pornography, like we have for work safety and family violence, to educate both children and adults. Just as men are being asked to call out family violence, they should also call out viewing pornography and switch it off themselves.

Schools and parents must also have expert information on the harms of pornography. The need is so great in the United States that *Culture Reframed* was established. It's an organisation that aims to build resilience and resistance in young people to pornography and hyper-sexualised media. All children should also receive age-appropriate sex education emphasising the importance of consent and that is also inclusive of gay and lesbian relationships, so that no young person feels the need to turn to pornography for sex education.

Sufficient investment in specialised rehabilitation programs for pornography addicts is also needed. Dr Heather Wood adds that therapy should include confronting the perverse aspect of the behaviour.[85] I think it's also crucial that it include: alerting addicts to how pornography increases depression, anxiety, narcissism, and aggression, deceptiveness, a false sense of power and invulnerability,[86] and its links to violent behaviour. Therapists should also discuss with addicts how they view women and power. This should lead to further questioning on how they are treating partners, family members, and others. This is vital since the addict isn't necessarily going to offer information about how they are treating partners and other people, especially women, unless they are questioned on this—and asked the right follow up questions.

David Morgan, also of the Portman clinic, says that the therapy should involve helping the client shift towards love and other positive life forces—such as compassion, ethical thinking and truth, since the perverse activity diminishes these. It should also acknowledge the role that the fear of intimacy and love play, so it is important for the therapist to create a safe space in which they can work on decreasing the client's fears.[87]

Recovery can take anywhere from two years up to twelve years or more and, as one practitioner told me, treatment should ideally include group therapy as well as intensive one-on-one treatment.

Specialist therapeutic services for current or former girlfriends/partners and other family traumatised by the addict's behaviour need significant government investment. Centres Against Sexual Assault should also receive additional government investment to whatever extent is required.

We also must recognise the harm done to women in the pornography industry: rape and violence is not an uncommon occurrence, many women have backgrounds of family violence and sexual abuse, and the industry has strong links to the trafficking of women and girls.[88]

Finally, to be against pornography does not mean advocating for sexual repression or being a puritan, as sex industry advocates claim. Pornography and sexual repression are but flip sides of the same coin: both are extremes, and both place too much emphasis on sex and the body.

Pornography is also in effect filmed prostitution, as Ran Gavrieli said in his Ted Talk *'Why I stopped watching porn'*, and as Dr Gail Dines asserts, it is both the commodification and buying and selling of women and the commodification of sex. As for 'feminist pornography,' Dr Dines says it's an oxymoron—the commodification continues. What we really need to ask is, 'why do we want a society that has a pornography culture?' Why do we think it is fine for a man to view the most intimate body parts of a woman he doesn't know and then move on to the next image and the next?[89]

But then there are more questions I want to ask. Why do we think the rights of men (the predominant consumers) and pornography producers override the rights of women and children? Why is speaking out against gender vilification such as pornography met with an avalanche of protest under 'free speech,' yet speaking out against racial vilification does not provoke the same reaction? Is it because women's rights are still not seen as human rights? Finally, Article 19 of the *International Covenant on Civil and Political Rights* reminds us that free speech is not absolute and may be restricted to respect other's rights, and so this would include respecting the status, dignity, wellbeing, and safety of women and children.

Strip clubs

I have never felt safe walking past strip clubs, which were formally established in Melbourne in the 1990s when more women were entering professions that used to be male-dominated and were entering higher education in increasing numbers. The backlash against equality and respect for women wasn't lost on me, nor were the leering looks of men exiting these places along with adult bookstores, and the irony in calling strip clubs 'Gentlemen Clubs'. I remember that a friend's partner, an advisor with the government at the time, claimed that he and other male advisors and MPs visited one of the newly opened strip clubs, thought such clubs could do no harm, including no harm to the status and safety of women, and so that was the end of the matter.

Strip clubs, like pornography, sexually objectify women—compromising their equality and safety in the general community, not just for those in the industry. Hence Iceland has banned them since 2010. Nicole Kalms, a senior lecturer in the Architecture Department at Monash University, says that strip clubs in effect create no-go zones for women in the public space. Women have reported not feeling safe in club precincts such as King Street in Melbourne, have been sexually propositioned by men thinking they are strippers or women selling sex, and have experienced sexual assault near these premises as men may be expecting women to mimic the behaviours of the sex industry. Kalms says that strip clubs and other sex industry businesses create a social environment that fosters male privilege and dominance and, as feminists suggest, remind women of 'their place' and 'keep them down'.[90]

Like pornography, strip clubs (and women who strip for hire) reinforce and fuel sexist, misogynistic views, which also fuel aggression, narcissism, and lack of empathy—all of which are linked to violence against women. The mere fact they are sexist should be enough to ban them.

Prostitution

I recall visiting Ephesus, an ancient Greek and Roman city in Turkey where there was a secret passageway from the library to the brothel. The men would tell their wives and family they were off to the library and then secretly buy sex with women. I was with a group of tourists and we were told all of this by our guide with a wink and the glib comment, 'The oldest profession in the world.'

What he failed to tell us was that ancient Greek and Roman civilisations had little or no regard for females, and prostitution further entrenched such views. There was no mention of the many women and girls forced into prostitution against their will, or the fact that it's an industry that reinforces misogyny and narcissism. And there was no concern for the wives and children who then had to deal with these men when they returned from the brothel, just as there is no regard for them today, nor for the men's female colleagues, employees, fellow students, and those of us encountering them in public spaces.

There is already research showing that men who buy sex with women are more likely than men who don't to commit violence against women. Clinical Psychologist Melissa Farley and her associates also found that men who buy sex with women have less empathy for prostituted women and are less likely to see its harms to women and the community than other men.[91]

Researchers have compiled a list of attitudes that men have expressed about prostituted women on customer review websites and in interviews. The common thread is that these men view women as mere disposable objects, just 'holes to fuck', and 'perfect whores' if they impose no limits. These commenters see them as servants of men, and even compare them to blow up dolls. A comprehensive sample of these attitudes is at https://www.collectiveshout.org/in_their_own_words.

One former buyer of sex with women said that fifteen years after the last time he did this, his perception about women and sex had changed so much that he believed if there was no prostitution in society, there would be greater respect for women.[92]

Sexism and exploitation are indeed the foundation of the prostitution industry, which is still thriving in Australia. Buyers continue to be almost exclusively men, and women and girls make up the vast majority of prostituted persons. Many of these women and girls have backgrounds of family violence, sexual abuse, drug addiction, and poverty, while the pimps, brothel owners (including female owners) and customers take full advantage without regard for their welfare. And there are many who are trafficked into this industry. In a 2017 report by the Coalition Against the Trafficking of Women in Australia (CATWA), both legalisation and full decriminalisation have failed.[93]

It's worth noting that full decriminalisation also has the real danger of normalising prostitution. If it's just like any other work, which industry advocates claim, should women be told by Centrelink to try prostitution before applying for unemployment benefits? This may seem absurd but in 2005, journalist Clare Chapman reported that Germany's welfare reforms could force any woman under 55 who was out of work for more than a year to take an available job – including in the sex industry – or lose her unemployment benefit. Under these reforms brothel owners were even granted access to databases on job seekers to look for women they wanted to hire.[94] Should school girls be encouraged to consider this as a career? Should women be allowed to work from home in prostitution whilst their children are in the home? Should there be brothels in shopping malls, at the end of our streets, or even next door? And if it's just like other work then what other workplaces demand sexual services for money and stem from a culture of male violence?[95]

But there is some good news in the CATWA report on tackling prostitution. It says that in 1998 Sweden created an innovative and holistic approach to effectively deal with this issue called the 'Nordic model'. This model penalises only pimping, sex buying, and brothel keeping, whilst removing penalties from prostituted persons. In doing so it has been very successful in reducing the demand for sexual services and decreasing human trafficking. This is what an effective approach to prostitution does. At the same time, this model has not pushed prostitution underground as some advocates for the sex industry claim.

The success of the feminist Nordic model has not only been to reduce prostitution. It also helps change negative attitudes towards women and sex and so addresses male violence against women, tackles gender inequality, and requires governments to invest heavily in helping women and girls leave the industry. This effective holistic approach has led to its adoption by Norway, Ireland, Northern Ireland, Iceland, Canada, France, and Israel.

Whilst no model or system for dealing with any issue in our society can be perfect, we have to look at what is best practice. The European Parliament has endorsed the Nordic model as best practice for preventing sexual exploitation, with a view that prostitution needs to be tackled head on rather than viewed as a part of life.[96] This is also in keeping with Article 6 of the *Convention on the Elimination of All Forms of Discrimination Against Women,* which Australia has ratified. It says that nations must take all appropriate measures, including legislation, to suppress all forms of traffic in women and exploitation and prostitution of women.

As for those women who say that they want to be in the sex industry and have a right to participate in it, there is a need to recognise the harm it does in undermining the position, health, and safety of women and children in society. It is no different from people who claim that they want to do work that leads to environmental degradation and destruction or some other social harm. We all want happiness, safety, and to be respected and free from suffering, so we need to work together to achieve this.

Supporters of the sex industry as a whole also claim that they are sex positive and those against it are anti-sex. Firstly, it is difficult to find any aspect of the industry that promotes a positive view of sex instead of encouraging voyeurism and viewing another person as a sex object. Secondly, they do not own the title 'sex positive' since those of us advocating against the industry are also sex positive not anti-sex. We don't have a problem with sex per se, and believe in positive, respectful, kind, caring, playful, and loving ways for consenting adults to relate through sex in which no harm is done to anyone. As for some people arguing that we need pornography in order to celebrate people of different sexualities and body types—what we really need is more mainstream and also art house films featuring intimate relationships between diverse people. Seeing the typical glamorous, Hollywood, heterosexual stereotypes over and over again is boring and un-relatable for many of us. This leads into the next discussion on sexist advertising.

Sexist advertising

In 2017 a coalition of community groups, academics and activists called for the elimination of sexist advertising and for more realistic, positive and diverse representations of women and girls in the media and public spaces. Members of the coalition included Women's Health Victoria and Plan International who made it clear that ads that sexually objectify women and demean them contribute to social attitudes that support and normalise men's violence against women.

We also need to be concerned about the inherent contradiction of images that would be recognised as sexual harassment in the workplace being viewed as acceptable in the public space.[97] They called for a ban on sexist advertising, a ban that feminists had been fighting to introduce for a very long time. This would be combined with guidelines to assist and educate advertisers, and feminist groups working with them to achieve the cultural change needed as well as promoting greater awareness of this issue to business groups.

As I am writing this, Westfield shopping centre is allowing Honey Birdette lingerie stores to use porn-themed advertising in their windows, which normalises the objectification and sex-ploitation of women. Collective Shout are campaigning to pressure Westfield to tell Honey Birdette to remove this advertising. I hope by the time this book is published that they have succeeded. Ideally, there would also be a ban on sexist advertising throughout Australia and the world.

Countries like the United Kingdom, France and Iceland have introduced such bans. Another benefit of a ban on sexist advertising is that advertisers would have to make ads that rely on creative and artistic skill and intelligence—it would in fact allow for greater creativity and innovation.

Popular culture

Our popular culture is rife with sexism and misogyny, including music videos featuring female singers and dancers as sex objects in porn-like poses, and sexist song lyrics in various genres, including country and western and rap and hip hop. The female singers/artists, just like the men, are laughing all the way to the bank while the rest of us have to deal with the negative impact on women worldwide as patriarchy tightens its grip and the violence and inequality continues.

Here is a brief overview of two other areas of our popular culture: R-rated computer games and the film industry, which also highlight the seriousness of the problem we are dealing with.

i) R-Rated Computer Games

The lack of regard by many of our politicians and the gaming industry for the right of women to be respected and to feel safe was once again shown in 2012. It was the year when legislation for R-rated computer games passed our federal and state parliaments. Whilst politicians claimed that the legislation's passage made it a 'great day', that 'adults should be able to view adult content' and that the legislation was 'important to support the gaming industry' which has 'strong potential for creativity', it was an extremely sad day in the fight against male violence towards women and sexism in general. It is also ironic that the bill was introduced in the Victorian parliament by men in the month prior to White Ribbon Day—a day for men to say no to violence against women.

R-rated computer games can not only be extremely violent but some are misogynistic, depicting women as secondary characters and mere sex objects, even taking off their clothes as a reward to the player. Players are also rewarded for murdering women from the sex industry. The fact that gamers can be immersed for hours at a time in these types of games is a concern, as well as the latest development of 3D technology which could be used for such games.

Given that we already know that pornography and sexist advertising reinforce and create sexist views and gender stereotyping, which are linked to violence against women, the legalization of these games should ring alarm bells. The penalty provisions for selling the games to those who are under age also provides a false sense of security. We already know that, like with pornography (even if only made available to adults), children and teenagers can gain access through older siblings, the friends of older siblings, or parents. And penalties if this happens are futile. Who is there to police the home to ensure that this doesn't happen?

It is also no surprise that according to a recent survey in the United Kingdom, one third of women who play video games regularly experience abuse or discrimination from male gamers. Of those, over half have experienced verbal abuse and 10 percent have been threatened with rape.[98] Leena van Deventer, an award-winning game developer, writer, and lecturer at RMIT in Melbourne, has also written and spoken about sexual harassment in the online gaming community, noting that female gamers are forced to identify as male to avoid online abuse from men.[99]

ii) Films

Sexism and misogyny also pervade the film industry which, like its advertising counterpart, cannot be trusted to self-regulate. I don't think I need to say much here in order for the reader to understand the point that I am making. We haven't come very far since Susan Faludi and other feminists criticized the industry back in the early 1990s. A good case in point is the science fiction film *BladeRunner 2049*, which I saw in late 2017. When the film was over, a woman in the foyer turned to me and said with disgust, 'Did you see how many women were killed in that film?' We agreed that it was one of the most sexist and misogynistic films we had ever seen.

Not only were women two-dimensional minor players, not only were they disposable—but one was gutted and left naked in a pool of blood. The landscape of the film is essentially porn land, with holograms of naked women looking seductively at men as well as statues of naked women in sexual poses. The main character has a holographic female servant/girlfriend who lives with him to satisfy his every whim and changes her appearance constantly to ensure that he never gets bored; it reminded me of a 1950s guide on how to be a good housewife that I read during my university days. At the time, my friends and I discussed it incredulously, perhaps too optimistically thinking we had at least advanced from that.

Even if its aim was to show a future that is a misogynistic dystopia, *BladeRunner 2049* did not need to use the gratuitous depictions of women as subservient sex objects or gratuitous violence against women to get the point across. Disturbingly, however, there was no criticism of this misogyny anywhere in the film. This didn't stop the film receiving US and British Academy Award nominations, including for best cinematography and best director in Britain.

It's also concerning that the film was released near the time of the #Metoo campaign. Whilst it's encouraging that Ryan Gosling, the star of the film, supported the campaign, he and other actors need to also stop appearing in sexist and misogynistic films, and writers, producers and directors need to stop making them.

Governments must also start caring about this issue and ensure not only that such films do not receive tax credits (or tax breaks) and government grants, but that sexist films are not shown just as they should prohibit sexist advertising.

Inaction by successive governments to address sexism in our popular culture and advertising as well as the harms of the sex industry has meant that they have been and still are enabling gender-based violence. There is so much more that could be said in this area. But it's time for a change of pace as we take a look in the next chapter at a very different but still important approach to preventing and reducing crime. It is applied when a person is before the courts and is called therapeutic justice.

Note

In order for gender and racial vilification laws to fully address the harm involved, they should take into consideration the context of the systemic oppression of women and Aboriginal Australians when considering penalties for vilification of these two groups. These laws should also exist under both criminal and civil law.

-4-

The Law As Therapy

It was a day like any other in the summer of 1987. At least it would have seemed that way at first to Professor David Wexler of the University of Arizona. He was contemplating his two new law articles. Like his other scholarly work, they reflected his ability to think outside the box in his desire to help people change their behaviour for the better. But as he considered the contents of the articles, he had a sudden revelation. They had something in common that would revolutionise the law.

The first article explored the obligation on a psychiatrist, who knew that his or her patient had made a threat to kill someone, to warn the person at risk. (Psychiatrists were outraged, saying that client confidentiality should come first.) The second article discussed the need for families to gather evidence for a disturbed family member's civil commitment (court-ordered institutionalisation). Both articles appeared to explore very different legal issues. But the common thread was the approach that Wexler used in exploring them.

Wexler had concluded in the first article that the law's 'disclosure obligation' on psychiatrists could enhance the therapeutic relationship with their clients. In the second article, he said that the need for families to gather evidence might make them act in therapeutic ways towards their disturbed relative so that commitment was unnecessary. In both articles he had been looking at *law as therapy*.[100]

Soon after, Wexler coined the term Therapeutic Jurisprudence (TJ), sometimes now referred to as Therapeutic Justice and wrote a book about his visionary insights in 1990. He also teamed up with Professor Bruce Winick and together they developed and expanded TJ. They had an amazing synergy as both were on the same wave length, bringing a sensitive and humane face to the law.[101]

Under the principles of TJ, the law is used to help people avoid re-offending by having a positive impact on their psychological wellbeing. So the law works on a deep level, seeking to address the underlying causes of a person committing an offence. Whilst not every model of TJ is suitable for all offenders, many have benefited from it.

I can't think of anything more dissimilar to the adversarial and purely punitive model that exists under patriarchy. TJ instead focuses on a collaborative, problem-solving approach that has gained momentum in recent years. So it's that holistic perspective again, seeing everything is interconnected. Here, professionals from different backgrounds work together using their different tools to help the individual involved.

The following are a few examples of the types of TJ in Victoria and the United States that I came across during my time as a lawyer and political advisor and are by no means exhaustive.

The Drug Court

In 2014, Bob hit rock bottom. He served a period of remand for his drug-related offending, after having a long history of criminal behaviour that kept escalating. But nothing that the legal system did helped him stop a life of crime. So Bob started on a Drug Treatment Order at the Dandenong Drug Court after remand, recognising that his use of the drug 'ice' had destroyed his family relationships. It had also isolated him from the community and impaired his ability to find employment and access education. So what is the Drug Court that Bob encountered in his final, desperate attempt to change his direction?

This specialised court was first established in Victoria in 2002, based on US practice, to deal with the sentencing and rehabilitation of offenders with drug or alcohol addictions, who had committed the offence either under the influence of these substances or to support their addiction. It doesn't cover perpetrators of sex offences or offences resulting in actual bodily harm.

An eligible offender will be sentenced to a drug treatment order of two years involving supervision and treatment. If a person breaches the order, a short time in custody may occur. Then he or she is released into the program again, hopefully with a greater determination to complete it.

The order uses both rewards and sanctions: rewards include praise and encouragement and decreased supervision when a person is doing well. Sanctions include verbal warnings that can escalate to increased supervision, and periods of incarceration to motivate the person to comply.

Bob says that it wasn't until commencing the DTO that he was able to make the lifestyle and behavioural changes he needed stop using ice. He realised that unresolved grief issues, hanging out with negative peer influences, and boredom had contributed to his offending.

Initially, Bob participated in a detox episode for eight days as part of the DTO. But then he had to spend time in custody for failing to attend his appointments and using drugs again. After his second term of custody, he said the experience had made him feel a greater sense of commitment to graduate from the program, which he did in June 2016. He says that it was the Drug Court that helped him finally embark on a positive path in life.[102]

So how does this translate to benefits to the community? A 2014 KPMG report evaluating the Drug Court found that the program cost one quarter of the cost of imprisonment per year. That's a big saving in taxpayer money. It has also helped to reduce crime. There was a 34 per cent drop in recidivism two years after offenders participated in the program, including a 90 per cent cut in trafficking offences and a 54 per cent cut in weapons offences. There was a 70 per cent reduction for burglary and deception offences; and a 30 per cent reduction for theft from a motor vehicle.[103] Such success led to the statement government's decision in 2016 to expand the Drug Court to Melbourne.

Mental Health Courts: The ARC List

Chris has serious mental health issues that contribute to her running out in front of cars, a violation of the law. This is highly dangerous not only to her but also to drivers.[104] Fining people such as Chris doesn't work since many people like Chris do not have the money to pay fines, nor is there any point placing them on an intensive supervisory type order since they cannot comply.[105] So Chris attended the Assessment and Referral Court (ARC) List in the Magistrates Court, which is likened to Mental Health Courts in other states and overseas.

This is a specialised problem-solving model for those charged with a criminal offence who have a mental illness or cognitive impairment. It does not cover certain violent crimes or sexual offences. The ARC List allows for an informal process where the magistrate sits at the bar table with the participant and their lawyer and ARC staff to discuss the legal matter and the participant's needs. They also work with the court integrated services program. This program provides case management that may include psychological assessment, referrals to various support and therapeutic services, housing, or drug and alcohol programs.

In the case of Chris, a collaborative approach involving police working closely with mental health supports and prosecutors assisted in greatly reducing the number of times Chris ran out in front of cars and helped Chris to act in a more pro-social way. The court allowed Chris to have a voice in what was working for her and what wasn't, as it does for other offenders.

In 2015 researchers collated 6 years of data with the Magistrates' Court of Victoria and found that 57 per cent of participants in the

ARC List program had not reoffended over a two year period. The researchers concluded that this showed the program was worth investing in and suggested areas for further improvement.[106]

The Koori Court

Jimmy was on a suspended sentence when he assaulted another Aboriginal man. It was highly likely that a court would sentence him to imprisonment for the assault. What is important to know about Jimmy, though, is that he and his siblings had been abandoned by their parents, which led to him taking on the role of carer for them all. Then there was the added trauma of them being separated and placed into foster homes. It was Jimmy's gift of being a dancer and his spiritual connection to his land and culture that kept him alive; otherwise he would have committed suicide. Fortunately, Jimmy was able to have his case heard in the Koori Court. Let's take a brief look at the history of this court before returning to Jimmy's case.

Koori Courts were first established as a division of the Magistrates' Court in 2002 in a bid to reduce the over-representation of Aboriginal Victorians in the criminal justice system. They also seek to make the legal system less culturally alienating and more able to deal with the needs of Koori people. This was in line with recommendations by the Royal Commission Into Aboriginal Deaths in Custody and the *Bringing Them Home* report.

The successful initiative resulted in Koori Courts being later expanded to the County and Children's Court jurisdictions and across Victoria. The former Attorney-General, Rob Hulls, said in 2008 that it had led to a 50 per cent reduction in offending compared to those going through the mainstream system, a factor which was instrumental to the rollout of the court.[107]

So what types of offences can be heard in the Koori court? All offences that can be heard in the Magistrates' Court are allowed, except for sexual offences and family violence matters. Again, the magistrate sits with participants, including not only the offender and his or family but also Koori elders and the Koori court officer. Together they discuss the matter.

This meant in Jimmy's case that he was given the opportunity to tell the court about his background trauma and the important connection to his culture that helped him function in the world. During the hearing, one of the Elders asked him where would be a suitable place for him to undertake a sentence such as a community-based order. He said his grandmother's country. Sentencing was adjourned so that Jimmy could re-establish himself there.

On the return date at court, Jimmy said he had been working with an Aboriginal community organisation, a men's group, police, and the local magistrate on his grandmother's country. He was one of the leaders who took Koori men out onto the land and discussed cultural matters concerning them, anger management, and drug and alcohol issues. Jimmy enjoyed doing this not only to share knowledge of dance and other cultural practices, but to give his life meaning and purpose. It had a real healing effect on him. Despite the seriousness of his offending, the magistrate placed him on a community-based order so that he could continue the valuable work he was doing. Jimmy proudly declared his commitment to do so.[108]

The Neighbourhood Justice Centre

The Neighbourhood Justice Centre is an innovative one-stop shop for holistic and community justice to meet all of the accused person's needs to address the causes of his or her offending and to help victims get back on their feet. The Neighbourhood Justice Centre in Collingwood is modelled on neighbourhood justice initiatives in the United States. It works with the local community to address disadvantage, which we know is a significant driver of crime. There is again a collaborative approach used: the police, courts, and corrections and other authorities have the flexibility to work outside their hierarchies to solve problems with the community and help offenders get back on track—whether that be through counselling or other support services. Within just two years this approach led to a 16.7 per cent reduction in reoffending.[109]

The Amherst Gambling Treatment Court

I once had a client who committed social security fraud to support her gambling addiction. I wish there had been a specialist court to deal with her matter so that it could address the underlying causes of her offending. One such court was created in the United States in 2000, the Amherst Gambling Treatment Court.

It is a non-adversarial court where an offender agrees to a contract that outlines sanctions and rewards and involves a comprehensive treatment program. It is monitored by a judicial officer who is both strict and compassionate.[110]

In 2007, there were already encouraging signs that this court was helping many offenders. As of May that year, court staff reported that more than one half of the 100 participants had successfully completed the program and only one was re-arrested—but even this was for an offence that was not associated with gambling.[111]

Back in 2017, there were calls to adapt this model in Melbourne by the Centre for Innovative Justice at RMIT. It has already been successfully adapted in South Australia. The Centre for Innovative Justice suggested introducing a dedicated stream in the Drug Court for problem gambling given that drug abuse and gambling harm often co-exist. The logic was that this would help trial therapeutic gambling intervention using existing infrastructure. Gamblers Help counsellors at Magistrates' courts are also essential.[112]

Greater education for lawyers and judicial officers about gambling addiction and its impact on offending is crucial as well. Widespread community campaigns about the harms of gambling are also needed—just as we need them about the harms of illicit drug use (which is also a public health issue). Governments should also implement tighter restrictions on ads promoting gambling. A prohibition on poker machines should be implemented too—or at the very least restricting them to casinos. Even Joan Kirner, the Victorian Premier who introduced poker machine gambling to our state and allowed the machines into pubs and clubs, later regretted doing so since they are a significant factor contributing to gambling addiction.[113]

Youth Justice Group Conferences

In the last twenty years, there has been increasing understanding of the importance of helping young offenders get back on track and avoid being stuck in the criminal justice system. One way of doing this is allowing in certain cases for young offenders to meet with victims to accept full responsibility for their actions. They hear how their offending impacted on the victim and his or her family, and seek to provide reparation for the crime. These meetings are called youth justice conferences. They are seen to be a form of 're-storative justice' (seeking to repair the harm done) and happen at the pre-sentence stage. The young offender's lawyer and family are also usually present with the victim and his or her family and police informant. The meeting is chaired by a convenor.

There has been both positive and negative feedback about youth justice conferences. A KPMG review of the program in Victoria in 2010 found that overall it was effective and that young people who participated were much less likely to reoffend within 12 to 24 months than those young people given intensive supervisory orders such as probation.[114] But in NSW in 2012, it was found to make no difference to reducing rates of reoffending. This may be in part due to the fact that it doesn't also address underlying causes of offending such as unresolved grief issues, substance abuse, unemployment, or mental health issues requiring treatment. So it has a greater chance of working if complemented by other essential tools, and these can be included in the outcomes plan.[115] The skill of the convenor also plays a critical role in the success or failure of the conference.

Mainstreaming of TJ

Today the mainstreaming of TJ has involved Melbourne Magistrate Pauline Spencer. She developed a TJ blog in order to use social media to reach a wide international audience with the goal of encouraging more lawyers and judges in diverse fields to develop TJ skills and sensitivities and use them in all areas, not just the specialist courts we have looked at.[116]

As a lawyer, I used therapeutic lawyering skills with clients in matters as varied as criminal law, family violence, mental health law, discrimination matters, refugee law, debt matters, and even in an insurance law matter. This involved not only linking clients with various support services but also being mindful that my contact with clients was therapeutic and sensitive to their emotional needs. We cannot under-estimate the benefits of being fully present with compassion and empathy. I could actually see how it was helping clients on the journey to recovery and resolving their legal issues. This also made my work more rewarding and enjoyable and taught me so much.

For young lawyers just starting out, a common sense, intuitive approach is also essential, as you may have a situation where you need to be very firm with someone who is aggressive or manipulative. You have to constantly read the person and situation and must maintain control.

Fortunately, there is an increasing movement towards therapeutic lawyering and making use of therapeutic justice models in the legal profession despite some limited initial resistance—including well-meaning lawyers saying, 'but we're not social workers!'

Now that we have looked at what can help prevent crime and reduce re-offending outside prison, what about when an offender is already in prison?

-5-

Once Inside—Prisoner Rehabilitation

Prisons have historically been dark, grim places full of fear, anxiety, violence, and oppression. In ancient Athens, prisoners were shackled with iron fetters, spoke of physical abuse and suffering and were even strapped to the ground in wooden stocks. The word for prison in ancient Greece was *Desmoterion*, meaning a binding down place.[117]

I've heard it said that if you want to know what a society is like, have a look at what is going on in its prisons—they are a microcosm of our world, our values, and what lies beneath the surface of a polished veneer of respectability and the assertion that 'everything is just fine.'

The exposure of the horrific torture of children in the Don Dale Youth Detention Centre in the Northern Territory recently showed us that everything is not fine. It shone a light on how dangerous the patriarchal thought system is, given that it lacks empathy and so can fuel a false belief that it is acceptable to be cruel to detainees and people of another race (here it was Indigenous youth).

We have established how patriarchy perceives power in the 'might is right' approach—in dominating and even humiliating others. We have also seen how its support for a purely punitive response to crime degenerated into breaking the youth in Don Dale rather than rehabilitating them.[118] The Don Dale case led to calls for radical change to the justice system and the establishment of an independent prison inspectorate to ensure accountability and transparency like that which exists in Western Australia. This also led to calls for radical change in our approach to prisons in states throughout the country.

To prevent re-offending and protect the wellbeing of prisoners, the punishment should always be the incarceration itself with a focus still on fair and humane treatment in prison. This is done whilst maintaining order and discipline for the safety of prisoners and staff. Such an approach allows a shift towards what is most important—prisoner rehabilitation. Again, the best model to use is a holistic model which, unlike the patriarchal approach, understands that everything is interconnected. Therefore, everything has a role to play in this rehabilitation, ranging from prison design, rehabilitation programs, nutrition, education, health care (including mental health care), prison staffing, and so on.

More specifically, rehabilitation programs for all prisoners should be available as soon as prisoners enter prison rather than towards the end of their prison sentence. Rehabilitation should always start as soon as the sentence starts. To assist with this, we need to reduce the numbers of prisoners in the first place. As discussed earlier in this book, this includes methods such as justice reinvestment, addressing the harms caused by the sex industry, and therapeutic justice.

We also know we have to invest much more in evidence-based, high-quality prison rehabilitation programs. This includes specialist treatment programs for all different types of offenders. Whilst we have at least moved from the situation in the early 1990s, during which, I am told, there was basically no rehabilitation offered, there has been a history of insufficient evaluation of and investment in rehabilitation programs across the board in prisons in Victoria. Programs for Indigenous prisoners have also been limited and constantly under pressure.

The 2015 Victorian Ombudsman's report into the rehabilitation and reintegration of prisoners revealed other serious problems.

Prisoners were being denied parole because they hadn't completed rehabilitation programmes due to the waiting list being too long. The report also pointed to a lack of access to rehabilitation programmes for those on remand waiting to be sentenced. Insufficient supports and specialist beds for those with mental health issues or cognitive impairment was also exposed.[119]

Group therapy came under scrutiny as well. The Ombudsman found that there was little recognition that group therapy on its own may not be sufficient to address the underlying causes of an offender's behaviour and prevent him or her from reoffending. Offenders may require one-on-one therapy, which, due to the size of the prison population, seems impractical to provide in person. But here's a chance for governments to be innovative by using cyber counselling, whereby a specialist anywhere in the state or country could provide sessions to a prisoner using online technology.

Prisoners also complained to the Ombudsman that group-based therapy left them exposed to bullying and violence by prisoners who found out about their personal experiences and backgrounds. They also felt they could be more honest with one-on-one therapy.[120]

So what else is needed for prisoner rehabilitation? Investment in education and vocational skills for prisoners cannot be underestimated. Even the 'Harper Review' recognised the importance of investing heavily in testing the literacy and numeracy of prisoners and providing educational training. (It's worth noting that university-level education provided for free in prison should also be for free for everyone else in a fair society.)

Classes in skills such as cooking and budgeting are also important, as are art classes and art therapy for personal development and growth, self-expression, and creative thinking. In the United States, some imprisoned sex offenders even attend classes on Jane Austen's novels. Professor Devoney Looser writes in an article for *Salon* of her experience of teaching these classes and how interested the men are in learning about stories told from the point of view of intelligent, though disempowered, women as they struggle for a meaningful life in a world of injustice.[121]

Other innovative approaches include detainees at Don Dale Youth Detention Centre being taught how to care for horses and ride them. This new program started in October 2018. It helps these young people learn through interacting with horses, how their actions can affect others. It also enables them to understand the importance of respect, caring, and responsibility as well as providing them with employment opportunities post release.[122]

Drama therapy has also been shown to benefit prisoners. For example, the *Somebody's Daughter Theatre Company* works with female prisoners at the Dame Phyllis Frost Centre to give performances that help them discover who they really are as human beings and feel a sense of accomplishment.[123]

Music also has an important role to play. Neuroscience research has demonstrated the benefits of music in raising our spirits and energy, as well as having a calming effect, so it should be used for prisoner rehabilitation. This could involve singing, chanting, playing instruments, or listening to Mozart or meditation/ambient music, for example.[124]

The role and training of prison staff is important as well. If we look first at the world's most humane prison, Halden in Norway, prison officers have completed a two-year university course on ethics, human rights, and the law (unlike training in Britain and Victoria, which only last a number of weeks—although recruits may have relevant life experience and have undertaken other forms of useful study). Halden prison officers are also encouraged to mingle with inmates. They talk to them, counsel them, and provide role modelling, rather than exhibiting the patriarchal 'us and them' mentality. It is a profession that the Halden prison guards can truly be proud of.[125]

A thorough screening process for prison staff is also critical to ensure as much as possible that people who would abuse power towards other staff or prisoners are not hired. They must receive, as well, high-quality mental health and disability training, since so many prisoners have mental health issues ranging from depression to psychopathy, as well as addiction issues. Debriefing sessions and counselling wherever needed should be provided to staff due to the inherent difficulties of such an occupation—this is beneficial not only to their wellbeing but also to the wellbeing of their families and the prisoners. Sufficient numbers of prison staff is essential too, just as sufficient staffing levels are also essential in other areas, such as hospitals and schools.

A daily process of self-examination is critical for staff whilst working on their underlying fears (just as it is for all of us) and setting respectful boundaries with inmates. How this can play out is shown in the example of John, who worked in a medium security prison. When he began work at the prison, he received all sorts of insults from the inmates. Rather than reacting with anger or seeking revenge, John went home and reflected on what had happened, realising that the inmates had responded to his own fears and had sought to regain some sense of power that they had lost due to being detained.

John then chose to let go of his fears of the aggressive inmates and not buy into their power play. Upon his return to work, he again encountered the bullies. But instead of lashing out or being fearful he focussed on his desire to be of assistance. He then established respectful relations with these and other prisoners for the next several years that he worked at the prison.[126]

On the topic of women's prisons, the author and consultant Stephanie Covington says if we can't bring about a change in imprisoning women, we should at least be training staff to have a trauma-informed approach that takes into consideration that so many female prisoners are trauma victims rather than 'bad'. Such an approach would make prisons safer for everyone, with less assaults and fights between prisoners and a decrease in self-harm. Since the trauma-informed method recognises that prison re-traumatises many women prisoners it should be incorporated into how prisons are managed and how staff interact with female prisoners.[127]

Meanwhile, in Brazil there is a very radical approach to prisons that has elements we can learn from. It is used by the Association for the Protection and Assistance of Convicted Persons ('APAC') prisons and is gaining attention around the world. *Dateline* reporter Evan Williams spent one week inside an APAC prison in São João Del Rei. Whilst there, he was astounded to learn that the re-offending rate when prisoners leave is as low as 5 per cent and that it costs one quarter of what it does to run a mainstream prison. He also discovered that there are no guards and no weapons, and that the prisoners have keys to the prison.[128] Basically, the prisoners help run the prison even though inmates have been convicted of robbery, murder, and rape, some serving terms as long as 24 years. Participation in education and rehabilitation are compulsory, as is a practice of faith or spirituality. It doesn't matter what faith a prisoner has just as long as he has one and commits to daily prayer/meditation.

This is reminiscent of the twelve step program of Alcoholics Anonymous, which requires the belief in and surrender to a higher power greater than ourselves in the hope that it can help restore us to sanity. Critics of APAC have only been able to focus on the requirement of faith, but this is an integral part of why APAC works—it helps prisoners avoid feeling that the situation is hopeless or that they have to rely solely on their own self to help them rehabilitate, knowing just how vulnerable they are—instead, they connect to a power beyond themselves (some would even call it a higher Self) and it is this commitment to faith that is also very humbling whilst they still undergo the work of self-examination and discipline.

There are several other factors which make APAC work. The prisoners are given the responsibility of cooking, cleaning, and enforcing prison rules. If they see someone breaking a rule they are encouraged to intervene. They work together collaboratively, helping each other every step of the way. It is this responsibility and trust that helps them learn to be dignified and honest men.

The prison is also light-filled and close to a forest. The oppressive, mainstream prison can also be seen above them as a constant reminder of the importance of not trying to escape or seriously breaching any rules at APAC, as otherwise they will be sent there. The oppressive, mainstream prison is very much like hell in comparison. All APAC prisoners have come from that prison first, and some say that APAC works because of the stark contrast. In the mainstream prison, which is at 172 per cent capacity, prisoners are crowded together in small cells, sleeping on mattresses on the floor. The prisoners lack sunlight and there is rampant violence and drug abuse. There are few rehabilitation programs, prison guards are heavily armed, and only those prisoners who are well-behaved are then able to serve the rest of their prison sentence at APAC.

When they arrive at APAC, they are often shaking, their spirits defeated by the shouting, squatting, slapping, violence, and humiliation of mainstream prison. The APAC prisoners then help the newcomers work on being free from their addictions and get back on track, understanding that none of them are fully recovered yet but are in the process of recovering.

There are elements of APAC we could incorporate here without having to use the contrast of a hellish, mainstream prison to keep prisoners committed to rehabilitation. For example, giving prisoners greater responsibilities such as cooking, and allowing them to assist with delivering rehabilitation programs is worth considering. Former prisoners who have turned their lives around could also assist with rehabilitation programs and mentoring. Prisoner involvement in ensuring rules are obeyed is also helpful, and education and rehabilitation programs must be available to all prisoners. The fact that the APAC prison is light-filled and close to nature also contributes to its success and should be considered for our prisons.

We also know from examples like Norway's Halden prison and other prisons in Europe that those which resemble the world outside, rather than being large, dark institutions, create higher chances for prisoner rehabilitation and later reintegration back into the community. Prison design is an extremely important factor in the prisoner rehabilitation process. Prisons like Halden use soft, natural colours, include trees and nature in the environs, and don't use the standard concrete walls for buildings.[129] The entire notion of erecting large maxi prisons that are essentially warehouses for prisoners is antiquated and not helpful.

Transition Centres are also extremely effective for prisoner rehabilitation and re-integration, since re-offending rates are significantly lower than for prisoners who do not exit prison via such centres.[130] Prisoners stay in Transition Centres towards the end of their sentence and are given daily access to the community with the supports and knowledge needed to develop their skills for full reintegration. Yet at the time of writing, there is only one prisoner transition centre in Victoria, and it's only for men. It does not make sense that governments have not invested more heavily in transition centres for male and female prisoners for decades if they really want to tackle crime and help offenders get back on track.

For many of us in the community, it also doesn't make sense that governments have allowed for privately-run prisons if they truly care about prisoner rehabilitation and reducing crime. Let's have a brief look at this issue.

Private prisons

There is increasing concern here and overseas about the use of private prisons. It is difficult to fathom how allowing private prison operators could be perceived as ethical since private enterprise is about making a profit. How do you justify making a profit out of the misfortune of others, and how do you focus on the public interest and wellbeing of prisoners in light of the profit motive?

Whilst private prisons are generally cheaper to run, a recent audit of Victoria's three private prisons found that the prison operators are not always meeting the state's expectations for key safety and security measures – particularly in relation to assaults in prison. And whilst new contracts have introduced a tougher performance regime (they had to because the performance regime wasn't high enough) the audit also found that there is limited public reporting on private prison performance. This undermines the transparency of the system. Nevertheless, the audit also found that whilst private prisons have violence reduction strategies to reduce assaults, there is a lack of evaluation of these strategies, and the methods for investigating serious incidents need to improve.[131]

Meanwhile, in the United States, private prisons have also not avoided controversy. A department audit of the nation's first private prison in Ohio, in 2012, found that it had violated several of the state's standards, including overcrowding prisoners, poor sanitation and meals, and extremely poor hygiene. Journalist Leigh Owens says that such findings confirmed *City Beat*'s research on private prisons, which found numerous violations of state standards. A study by researchers at George Washington University also showed that private prisons have significantly higher inmate-against-staff assaults and inmate-on-inmate assaults due to the lower standards from keeping costs low and profits high.[132]

As Donna Red Wing wrote in an article on this issue in 2012, private prisons are big business. In the for-profit incarceration industry, rehabilitation is simply bad news. In the US, the industry protects its profits by lobbying for harsher sentences and against immigration reform (since immigration detention centres in the US, as in Australia, are largely privately operated).[133] But then all of this makes sense in a patriarchal society where compassion, accountability and transparency, and focusing on shared public interest are not high on the agenda.

Another important area in our discussion on prisoner rehabilitation and reintegration lies outside the public/private prison system. It's called parole, and in Victoria it has been the subject of much debate and scrutiny.

The parole system

Parole is seen generally as a useful system to help prisoners make the adjustment back to life in the community under supervision when they have completed a minimum term of their sentence. In many cases, this is better than a prisoner being left without the aid of supervision when exiting prison. Exceptions are serious sex offenders and serious violent offenders who may have continuing supervision at the end of a full sentence.

For the parole system to work, though, like all aspects of the justice system, it requires significant government investment, up-to-date departments, and the acknowledgement that not every offender can be nor is willing to be rehabilitated.

In Victoria, there was an extensive review of our parole system in 2013 by former High Court Justice Ian Callinan AC in light of the tragic rape and murder of Jill Meagher by parolee Adrian Bayley, who had breached his parole beforehand after serving a sentence for a series of rapes. In his review, Mr Callinan emphasised the importance of facing the unfortunate truth that there do exist incorrigible offenders who, despite great attempts to rehabilitate them, must be seen as habitual, serious offenders.[134]

He made several significant observations about the parole system at the time which included:

1. our Parole Board was vastly under-resourced, could not cope with the ever increasing workload, and thus needed major investment,

2. there was an unacceptably high staff turnover in the parole system,
3. the Board and staff needed a new comprehensive electronic database that included up-to-date information about offenders,
4. a specialist panel of the Board for more serious and violent offenders should be established,
5. community safety must be paramount in all considerations for parole,
6. applicants for parole must not be granted parole unless they have undertaken all required programmes (I add here that the government must then invest in the programmes to ensure they are available to all prisoners and rehabilitation starts as soon as they enter prison), and
7. the risk assessment test then in place for offenders was not appropriate and a different test or tests needed to be used.

To date, many reforms have occurred based on recommendations from the review in part or whole as well as other reforms related to breaches of parole. I won't critique these but will say it beggars belief that the system was left by successive governments to be run into the ground, particularly under the banner of being 'tough on law and order' and 'community safety.'

Whenever a system has so tragically failed our society, we must also ensure that tightening it up with higher standards doesn't inadvertently lead to an unfair system for those who do the right thing. More specifically in relation to parole, we must ensure that prisoners who would qualify for parole and parolees who do not pose a risk to the public, are not disadvantaged by blanket, tighter restrictions. Otherwise their rehabilitation can be undermined, putting community safety at risk.

Sufficient investment in post-release supports for prisoners is crucial too, such as access to stable ongoing and affordable housing, health care, employment, and continuing rehabilitation programs to prevent re-offending. All of these are interconnected. Without the secure housing, it makes it harder to near impossible for prisoners to obtain employment and undergo rehabilitation. Alarmingly, in 2015 the Victorian Ombudsman reported that 40 per cent of female prisoners were homeless upon exiting prison.[135] And a 2018 national study found that 54 per cent of prisoners expected to be homeless upon release.[136]

Supervising officers should also work in a collaborative as well as authoritative manner with prisoners leaving detention. A few years ago, I spoke with a senior member of an organisation that helps women prisoners access housing and employment post-release. She pointed out a major barrier a few of the women faced: when the corrections officer wanted to meet with them as part of their supervision, it often interfered with their work, and there was no allowance for the contact to be outside work hours. These women then had to give up their jobs, which threatened their ability to get back on track, have stable housing, and not re-offend.

And again there was the difficulty of obtaining parole in the first place, due to the lack of accessible housing. Meanwhile, homelessness amongst the general population (including older women) is increasing rapidly as well. This is unacceptable.

–6–

Kicking Them While They're Down

Situations beyond our control can make us feel at times that we are prisoners in our own minds; our negative thoughts weigh us down and we feel small and vulnerable rather than expansive and free. When I practiced mental health law, I visited women and men in psychiatric units to discuss their involuntary detention, medical treatment, and legal rights. I also represented some of them before mental health review board hearings seeking their release. On the surface, they had different personas, appearances, and mental illnesses. But beneath this surface, I discovered a general pattern, especially for the women. The pattern was contained in their medical files: time and time again I found references to a background of sexual abuse and/or family violence. I'm not saying that this was the sole cause of the mental health problems, but such trauma has been known to be a significant contributing factor.

Whilst not all victims of such abuse end up as psychiatric in-patients, we know that the impact of abuse is still far-reaching, leaving many suffering from mental health issues ranging from low sense of self-worth and even self-hatred to depression, anxiety, post-traumatic stress disorder, disassociation, and self-harming and suicide. This type of trauma can also lead to substance abuse as well as undermining victims/survivors' access to education and employment and their ability to maintain employment. It can also impair their ability to experience enough trust to enter into relationships or sustain them, and to care for their own children.

Perpetrators come from a range of socio-economic backgrounds and ethnicities, though they are predominantly male. Some also have backgrounds of abuse. They carry out their crimes in a patriarchal society that disrespects women and children and instead embraces gender stereotyping, sexual objectification, and eroticises violence. It also promotes a toxic masculinity that includes narcissism, a sense of entitlement, aggression, lack of empathy, and intense shame and even self-loathing for any personal vulnerability. And again there is the belief that power lies in dominating, controlling, humiliating, and destroying others.

Perpetrators can be extremely manipulative and deceptive, even carefully crafting a saint-like image in some cases. More specifically in relation to sex offenders, whilst some plan the abuse beforehand and even groom their victims, others are opportunistic. And most perpetrators of sexual abuse are people that victims know rather than strangers.

It's important to keep in mind that it is not helpful to call perpetrators monsters, which the tabloid press often do. Such labels make it harder to identify them, since they often present as likeable everyday people. The term 'monster' also undermines attempts at rehabilitation and may make it harder for some victims to recover.

Violence against women and children is prevalent, as shown by the following statistics: intimate partner violence is the leading cause of death, disability, and injury for women between the ages of 18 and 44 in Australia.[137] One woman a week is killed by a partner or former partner in Australia.[138] One in three Australian women has experienced physical violence since the age of 15 years. One in five has experienced sexual violence since the age of 15 years.[139] Meanwhile, in the United States one in four girls and one in six boys will be sexually abused before they reach 18 years of age.[140]

It's also no surprise that victims of sexual abuse and family violence have by and large been treated appallingly by the justice system—hence the title of this chapter. They have in reality been kicked while they're down, re-traumatised over and over again. Whilst law reform has been occurring in this space especially since the late 1980s/ early 1990s, it has been incredibly slow and very incremental due to sexism in the law—amongst lawmakers, the judiciary, and law enforcement agencies.

Sexual abuse and the law

For centuries, the law in relation to rape and all forms of sexual abuse has been informed by patriarchy and its views of human relationships and sexuality whilst silencing women's voices and women's perspectives. This disregard for the collective experience of women and also the needs and sensitivities of child complainants has occurred whilst focussing on the rights of the accused.[141]

Several myths abounded and continue to be spun, such as women and children are inherently unreliable and lie about sexual assault. The truth is that men are more likely to be raped than be falsely accused of rape—in fact they are 230 times more likely to be raped than falsely accused of this offence.[142]

Other myths include the idea that the accusation of rape is easily made, but difficult to challenge, and that women cannot be sexually assaulted by their spouse, even though throughout the 1980s various Australian states removed a husband's immunity from the law of rape. The myth that some sexual assaults are more serious and damaging than others continues, as well as the idea that non-consent must be verbally articulated, evidenced by struggle, and universally results in physical injuries. There is also the false assumption that a true or genuine victim of sexual assault does not delay in reporting.[143]

These myths played out in the courtroom during my university years and at legal profession functions. I also saw a general lack of sensitivity and understanding about sexual assault and its seriousness.

For too long, it has been too traumatic for victims of sexual assault to go through the criminal justice system due to the process involved. The adversarial nature of our law courts is derived from the Greek warrior tradition, which is all about winning.[144] It encourages an aggressive approach to justice that is devoid of sensitivity and empathy. So it is not surprising that this battleground has proven too traumatic for victims.

But that's not all. Until very recently, there has also been little support available for victims, and a failure to inform them of what is involved at each stage of the criminal justice process, which exacerbates their trauma. When I was working at a Centre Against Sexual Assault as part of a clinical placement as a law student back in the 1990s, victims were not actively encouraged to go through the criminal justice system due to the likelihood that the trauma would be too great for victims to deal with. Today, we are still dealing with a situation where it is too traumatic for many, and even when victims decide to pursue the matter, only 23 per cent of sexual offences reported to police get to court according to the Victorian Crime Statistics Agency. Meanwhile, as reported in *The Age,* the United Nations statistics put the rate of rape in Australia at about twice the international average,[145] and yet the prospect of conviction in our courts is still too low.

I have met male lawyers, even in the social justice sector, who dispute that there has ever been a gender bias or sexism in the law in dealing with sexual abuse. So let's go back. Firstly, it wasn't until 1991 that we had laws to make it irrelevant whether a victim struggled or sustained an injury, restricted the admissibility of a woman's sexual history, and increased the rape penalty to 25 years to reflect the seriousness of the offence. Courts were only then given the power to allow children and complainants with a cognitive impairment to give evidence via closed circuit television. But it also doesn't make sense that this wasn't made a right for all complainants of sexual abuse at the time.

It was only in 1991 that judges were also prevented from saying to a jury that complainants of sexual abuse are an unreliable class of witness. And judges finally had to warn a jury that delay in complaining didn't mean the allegation was false. Similar laws were enacted in other Australian states. And yet...

In 1993 Judge Derek Bollen of the Supreme Court in South Australia directed a jury in a rape case that it was acceptable for men to use *rough handling* of their wives in order to have sexual intercourse, and that experience has taught judges that there are cases of women making false allegations of rape and sexual attack. Fortunately, one of Australia's leading female judges at the time, Elizabeth Evatt, who was also the then President of the Australian Law Reform Commission, condemned the remarks, as did other women, saying it was an example of the judiciary not being in touch with society.[146]

In November 1992, Judge Norman O'Bryan in the Supreme Court of Victoria imposed a lenient sentence on a rapist who beat a 17-year-old girl unconscious and slit her throat—because the judge argued the girl was unconscious and therefore not traumatised by the rape. On appeal, the sentence was increased, but the case provoked widespread criticism in Australia.

Then, in April 1993, Judge John Bland in the County Court of Victoria told a youth who had pleaded guilty to raping a 15-year-old girl in a hay shed: 'It does happen, in the common experience of those who have been in the law as long as I have anyway, that 'no' often subsequently means 'yes'.'[147]

The majority of the Victorian Court of Criminal Appeal in 1994 also described a rape in which the woman was knocked unconscious, beaten, raped anally and vaginally, and held captive for two and a half hours as *not very grave*, which led to renewed media focus on gender bias or sexism in the law.[148]

I recall in the early 1990s attending a law function where the then-Commonwealth Director of Public Prosecutions, Mr Michael Rozenes (who later became Chief Judge of the County Court of Victoria), gave a presentation on Commonwealth offences. During his presentation, he strayed into the area of sexual offences (a state matter) saying that in effect the sexual history of the victim was relevant for sentencing since for instance 'raping a nun was worse than raping a prostitute.' I couldn't believe what I had just heard and felt a mixture of distress and shock. I looked around the room and saw the sea of mainly male faces from the legal profession including a prominent Supreme Court judge in the audience. There were very few women in the room, and I couldn't help but wonder what else would have been said if we were not present.

Only one person in the room spoke up to disagree and said the comments were unfair to women: a man in the back of the room. Some of the attendees refuted his comments. I wanted to speak up but thought that I would be accused of being the typical 'hysterical female' and something inside me said *wait, your time will come.* At the end of his speech, I spoke to Mr Rozenes privately of my dismay. An ABC reporter then asked him to repeat what he had said for her tape recorder to which he refused, but I had my tape recording and gave it to the ABC reporter. She then reported the comments, and the next day they made media headlines. The Commonwealth Attorney-General Michael Lavarch requested that the DPP apologise, which he did.

Unfortunately, the gender bias and blatant sexism didn't end back there in my law school days. For example, in 2016 a County Court Judge Christopher Ryan, who heard the case of a children's court security guard having sex with a 14 year old girl, described the girl as *worldly, nubile,* said that she *would have been difficult to resist* and that the security guard was *not made of steel.* The judge was in effect shifting blame onto the teenage girl. He only gave the security guard a 2-year good behaviour bond and placed him on the sex offenders register for 15 years. The Chief Justice of Victoria at the time rebuked him for making such comments, and the Court of Appeal did decide that the sentence was manifestly inadequate.[149]

In other cases, judges have made comments that seem to reflect the seriousness of the sexual abuse. But then they surprise us by imposing manifestly inadequate sentences, showing how little they have in fact understood the seriousness of the crime and the traumatic impact on victims and their family.

This failure by judges was highlighted in the case of Dalgliesh (a pseudonym), where the trial judge continued a disturbing trend by other judges in passing down a sentence that failed to reflect the gravity of incest. He thought it appropriate to only sentence 'Dalgliesh' to three and a half years imprisonment for impregnating his 14-year-old stepdaughter. The Director of Public Prosecutions ('DPP') appealed to the Court of Appeal, saying the sentence was manifestly inadequate. The Court of Appeal agreed but said that it couldn't alter the sentence because it had to follow current sentencing practice in Victoria, which did not reflect the gravity of such offending.

Fortunately, the DPP then appealed to the High Court, which said the Court of Appeal had got it wrong and must impose a sentence appropriate to all the circumstances of the case and one that is just. It was wrong to elevate 'current sentencing practice' to be the most important factor considered at sentencing—the court must still address the gravity of the offending. The High Court also said that earlier decisions of the Court of Appeal to the contrary were wrong and should not be applied.[150] This is a good example of the appeals process to the High Court working well.

The alleged sexual assault of then eighteen year old Saxon Mullins by Luke Lazarus in NSW in 2013 highlights continuing problems with the law on consent. It is clear that judges need further education and training in this area, and widespread public education on consent, respectful relationships, and the dangers of toxic masculinity is a necessity. We need to move from a patriarchal society to one where gentleness, kindness, and caring for another's wellbeing are signs of true strength and call out sexism and misogyny wherever it exists.

The ABC's Louise Milligan undertook an in-depth investigation into the Saxon Mullen case. Whilst Lazarus was initially convicted of rape, on appeal a different Judge, Robyn Tupman, acquitted him, saying that whilst Saxon had not consented, it was not clear that Lazarus knew that. This was despite Saxon's evidence that Lazarus said he was taking her to a VIP section of a nightclub and then instead took her out into a dark laneway on her own, ignoring her protests to return to her friend inside. Saxon alleges that Lazarus suddenly changed from the nice guy he had appeared to be and ordered, 'put your fucking hands on the wall,' after which he tried unsuccessfully to have anal sex with her and complained that she was 'tight'. She responded that she was a virgin. He said, 'Oh shit, really?' He then told Saxon to get on her hands and knees in the gravel and arch her back. Lazarus tried again to have anal sex which then occurred. Saxon said she was in effect too frozen by fear to try to physically resist or scream: something not uncommon for victims of sexual assault. At trial Saxon also alleged that she had told Lazarus to stop. He says she didn't.

Afterwards Lazarus asked Saxon for her name so he could enter it into his phone, which he explained to the court was to add to the trophy list of women's names. When Saxon found her friend at the nightclub she was hysterical. Later at her sister's house she was bleeding and in pain. Lazarus the next day was texting a friend saying he 'took a chick's virginity, lol….so tight. It's a pretty gross story. Tell ya later.' Saxon was taken to a Sexual Assault Service, where she was examined by Dr. Freedman, who told ABC's Four Corners that it had been difficult to examine Saxon because she was in pain and had sustained a number of painful grazes around the entrance to her anus.

Whilst Judge Tupman, hearing the appeal, accepted that Saxon did not consent, she did not accept the prosecution's argument that there was no reasonable basis for Lazarus to believe

that Saxon was consenting. She added that she found it difficult to reconcile Saxon's police statement where Saxon said she
thought at some point she told Lazarus to stop, with her saying
at trial she told him to stop, and so believed Lazarus denying
this. The judge failed to understand that it is not uncommon for
victims to have discrepancies between what they say to the police
and in court due to the nature of their trauma.

The Judge also referred to the concept of 'contemporary morality' and how it applied to anal sex in light of the testimony of a
female friend of Lazarus who said she had engaged in anal sex on
several dates.[151] This is troubling, given our previous discussion on
how pornography (which heavily features women subjected to anal
sex) is dictating social norms or contemporary morality and such a
matter is considered to help determine if a woman consents or not.

The reference by the judge to a lack of questioning Saxon during the trial as to why she stayed with Lazarus and did not leave
also highlights the importance of judicial training on how victims of sexual assault may freeze, a matter raised by the Institute
of Criminology of the University of Sydney in its submission to
the NSW Law Reform Commission for its review on the laws on
consent.[152]

The Court of Criminal Appeal rightly ruled that Judge
Tupman had erred by failing to take into consideration in her
judgment what steps Lazarus had taken to ensure whether Saxon
was consenting as required by law. But the Court ruled out a third
trial, saying it would be too oppressive given that five years had
already passed and Lazarus had already spent eleven months
in prison.[153] It is unfortunate that the Court of Criminal Appeal
did not consider that it would be too oppressive for Saxon not
to have a third trial given the seriousness of the alleged offence,
and to ensure public confidence in the justice system given Judge
Tupman had not applied the law correctly on appeal, leading to
her acquitting the accused.

This case also highlights the importance of laws on consent

being absolutely clear that a person initiating sex must take reasonable steps to ensure consent is freely given, and that the other party communicates her or his consent. This is instead of being able to rely on a presumption of consent unless the other party takes action to refuse.

In Australia, at the time of writing, Tasmania has rigorous laws on consent using a communicative/affirmative model. Likewise, Victorian law not only says there must be free agreement to have sex, but also lists among the many circumstances in which a person does not consent—*where the person does not say or do anything to indicate consent to the act*. The 'explanatory memorandum' (a document that explains every clause in a bill of parliament) confirms that this means *the person must have clearly communicated her or his consent.*

So far there have been no concerns raised that the Victorian or Tasmanian provisions have led to innocent persons being found guilty of rape. They have successfully moved away from a patriarchal approach to a more fair and just one.

This continued in Victoria with changes to the law over recent years that further emphasised the importance of a person's capacity to consent and that a person can withdraw consent at any time. Judges can now also better address the possible misconception for juries that complainants must be able to remember all the details of an offence and describe it consistently every time, and say that experience shows that people may react differently to sexual assault—there is no typical or normal response.

Wonderful as these changes are, governments to date have unfortunately refused to listen to calls by victim advocates that such jury directions should be mandatory where relevant rather than left to either party to request that they be given. This is because legal counsel may not request these directions when they should.

We also need widespread education campaigns about what constitutes consent and highlighting the seriousness of rape and all forms of sexual abuse. For example, a Scottish education campaign includes posters saying:

Drinking is not a crime. Rape is.
No matter how drunk, no matter what she is wearing,
no matter if you have already kissed – sex without con-
sent is rape.
If there is any question over whether a woman has
drunk too
much to give consent, assume she hasn't given it.
Responsibility for rape will always lie with the rapist.[154]

As Professor Patricia Easteal says in her submission to the NSW Law Reform Commission's inquiry into consent and sexual offences law, legislative intent must also be reflected in the media. This is essential if we want our society to develop enlightened views on consent and stop victim-blaming.[155]

Another step forward has been the introduction of laws against grooming in Victoria and other states in Australia. Such laws recognise that some perpetrators 'groom' their victims, deliberately building a close relationship of trust to facilitate sexual abuse. The grooming can range from showering children with gifts, to taking them on outings, and giving them alcohol or showing them pornography. Perpetrators can also groom parents, showering them with gifts for example in order to gain access to their children. It's important though that such laws, just as those in other areas, are not so broad as to pose the danger of inadvertently charging innocent people who are simply being friendly with a child with the crime of 'grooming'—a single offence without sexual assault. They are also a reminder, though, to teachers, coaches, mentors et cetera of the need to keep healthy, firm boundaries with children whilst also giving support and encouragement.

Family violence and the law

Family violence is another area where much-needed changes have occurred in recent years. So what exactly is it? Family violence is any violent, threatening, coercive or controlling behaviour that happens in current or past family or intimate relationships. So it's not restricted to physical injury. Instead family violence also includes direct or indirect threats, sexual assault, and emotional and psychological torment. Economic control, damage to property, and social isolation are also forms of family violence as is any behaviour which causes a person to live in fear.[156]

This broad definition helps us to increase our awareness of what constitutes violence and to take non-physical violence as seriously as physical violence. The term 'family violence' also helps encapsulate the terror and life-threatening danger of it rather than calling it for example 'abuse in the home'. But we still need widespread public education about what it is and its seriousness.

When I was growing up and throughout the 1990s, it was known that family violence was prevalent—as it certainly has been throughout the world since patriarchy began. Yet some male and female members of the judiciary and legal profession were astounded by the Victorian Royal Commission into Family Violence's finding in 2016 of how widespread it is.

In the 1990s and earlier, family violence comprised a significant number of police call outs (and still does), and yet police often took little or no action. As a result, some feminists preferred to call it 'criminal assault within the home' in order to encourage law enforcement to take it more seriously—though this terminology didn't take into consideration the other forms of violence often involved. There has also been a significant failure by police to act on breaches of intervention orders (also known as apprehended violence orders in NSW).

Too many members of the judiciary did not understand the seriousness of family violence as well, and this continued into the present day. Courts in recent years were struggling to cope with the ever-increasing rise in family violence cases before them whilst higher numbers of women were being killed by current or former partners. All of these factors contributed to the establishment of the 2016 Royal Commission into Family Violence in Victoria.

The Commission's 227 recommendations contained no surprises for reform, given that advocates had long called for them. They include:

- family violence training for the judiciary,
- the state rolling out specialist family violence courts,
- the creation of support and safety hubs for victims and perpetrators to access services,
- that Victoria Police establish a 'family violence centre of learning' to improve family violence training and education at all levels of the organisation,
- an urgent blitz to rehouse women and children forced to flee their homes due to family violence (this must be safe, secure and stable accommodation),
- stronger perpetrator programs,
- an independent Family Violence Agency to hold government to account.

All 227 recommendations must be fully implemented on an urgent basis and be well-resourced. Unfortunately, we have a long way to go for changes in our approach to family violence to take effect, partly because education and training is lagging behind. In 2018 Judge Susan Cohen of the County Court referred to jealous rages that turned violent on three separate occasions by footballer Shannon Grant against his then partner, as not being about deliberate aggressiveness. Instead she said they were more to do with loss of control. Journalist Sarah Farnsworth reported that Judge Cohen also said that the underlying cause was Grant's excessive drinking.

This was despite the royal commission saying that violence against a partner is underpinned by repeated coercion, control, and domination and that negative attitudes towards women and a tolerance for violence were key factors. Whilst alcohol was likely to 'fuel or exacerbate' violence, it is not a cause. In light of the Judge viewing alcohol as the heart of the problem and saying on three occasions that Grant 'simply lost control'—including when he wrestled his partner to the floor and stomped on her with his foot, and on another occasion left her so bruised she couldn't leave the house for a fortnight—she overturned Grant's 6-month jail time. Instead, Judge Cohen imposed a two year community corrections order.[157] Clearly this judge needed judicial training on family violence. But she is not alone.

The High Court in 2016 also had to rectify a decision by the Court of Appeal involving family violence in the case of the Queen v Kilic. When the victim began her relationship with her attacker, she most likely had dreams of a future of love and happiness together. Such dreams were in tatters when she first suffered violence from him. Then, when she was pregnant, he doused her with petrol and set her alight. She nearly died from the horrific burns. But her torment didn't end there.

The Victorian court decided that a trial judge's sentence of 14 years imprisonment was manifestly excessive for the defendant— despite his history of family violence, the details of the horrific attack that nearly killed the victim, and the long term prognosis that had led to the termination of her pregnancy. She is left with permanent scarring on her face, breasts, and other parts of her body, and will require ongoing medical care and mental health care for the rest of her life. Still, the Court of Appeal said that 14 years was not in keeping with current sentencing practice and reduced it to 10 years. But thankfully, the High Court ruled that the Court of Appeal were wrong and said that the court had in effect failed to fully understand the seriousness of the victim's injuries.[158]

When I think of misogyny and the law, I think of where it played out overtly in Victoria, as it has elsewhere, under the partial defence of provocation. That defence allowed men to have their conviction for murder reduced to manslaughter by arguing they were provoked to kill their wife or girlfriend due to jealousy or fits of rage, such as her ending the relationship or having an affair—affronting male honour. The defence was finally abolished here in 2005 and should have no place in any state or country.

Another blow to patriarchy's hold on the law came in 2015 when law-makers sought to increase understanding of family violence and its seriousness. Changes were made to jury directions in Victoria for situations where victims of family violence attack a partner in self-defence. Judges can now direct juries that family violence is not limited to physical violence (as discussed earlier), and that it is not uncommon for a person who is subject to family violence to stay with an abusive partner after the onset of the violence or to leave and return. But again, such jury directions should be mandatory when relevant to the case.

More positive changes happened this time in family law matters. The federal government in 2018 introduced laws to prevent perpetrators of family violence from cross-examining their victims in court. But why did it take so long? Women's advocates had been campaigning on this issue for several years. And many years ago the state government banned under criminal law self-represented litigants cross-examining a complainant in a sexual violence or rape matter.[159] These are not difficult law reforms to make.

But at least the changes have happened and more will come. Let's take a brief look at a few other areas of reform that assist victims/survivors.

Other reforms for victims/survivors

Victim impact statements

In 1994, Victim Impact Statements were introduced to help judges order appropriate sentences and give victims a voice in the justice system. Some victims have reported that reading out the statement to the court is therapeutic, as it provides them with the opportunity to let the court and the defendant know how the crime impacted on them and their loved ones. (This is similar to victims being able to let the offender know how the crime impacted on them under restorative justice processes.)

Greater use of closed circuit television

In 2006 the Victorian government created a right for complainants in sexual offence cases to give their evidence via closed circuit television, finally recognising the need to ensure that the use of such arrangements is routine. This assists all complainants to give the best evidence they can with as little trauma as possible.

Intermediaries and privacy for complainants

Only recently in Victoria has legislation been introduced to provide support for complainants through 'intermediaries'–expert advocates who can support and help guide them through the court process. They are already being used in Britain as part of a holistic approach to help complainants. And in early 2017, a teenage girl who withdrew from a rape prosecution due to being re-traumatised by the system, highlighted the fact that further reforms were necessary. Not only had she called for the introduction of intermediaries in Victoria but also asked that explicit details of an alleged sexual offence be automatically subject to a suppression order to protect complainants from re-traumatisation.

Time limitations

In 2015, the Victorian government introduced laws that removed time limitations for claims of injuries suffered from sexual abuse, physical abuse, or psychological abuse arising from physical or sexual abuse of a minor. The law finally acknowledged that due to the trauma of abuse, victims may not seek immediate legal redress. And so they should not be barred from seeking compensation through the justice system in the future. Other states have also made similar reforms.

Victims of Crime Commissioner

The creation of a Victims of Crime Commissioner in this state in 2015 and in other jurisdictions is another significant reform. The Commissioner's role is to make sure that both service providers and the justice system meet victims' needs and include their participation in the system. Victims deserve and need support and also have much wisdom to give to help improve the criminal justice process. This should never be about revenge or vengeance but about making sure the justice system is effective and fair, that it assists rather than damages the healing process for victims, and that perpetrators are held accountable for their actions.

Judicial training

Any improvements in the way that cases of family violence and sexual abuse are handled have in part been due to judicial training. I recall a conversation with a newly appointed Supreme Court judge in 2001 where I asked him what training was available for newly appointed judges. He looked at me with incredulity and said firmly, as if to put me back in my place, 'We don't need any training. Our experience as barristers is all we need.'

Fortunately, this Supreme Court judge's view did not prevail. In 2002, the Judicial College of Victoria began running training sessions to keep judicial officers in touch with the community, aware of pressing social issues, in tune with technology, and up to date with the latest developments in all areas of the law. Training has covered areas as diverse as family violence, sexual assault, unconscious bias, sentencing, therapeutic approaches to addiction, Koori cultural awareness, dispute resolution, and dealing with self-represented litigants.

It is crucial for all members of the judiciary to engage in ongoing judicial training to fulfill their role to the highest standards, to engage in continual self-examination for prejudice, and to enhance their wellbeing and enjoyment of their work.

More specifically, the heads of each court and tribunal must (where they have the power to do so, as in Victoria) direct all judicial officers to undertake up to date training in family violence, sex offences, and sexual harassment. This is necessary to increase sensitivity and understanding of these matters that come before them. The training should include the seriousness of such cases, how victims may respond to violence, how perpetrators operate, and the drivers of such violence.

This also means that governments must invest sufficiently in the necessary numbers of judicial officers to permit the time away from the courtroom needed to undertake training.

Restorative justice

As discussed earlier restorative justice is another way for justice to be delivered outside of the adversarial context. It usually involves a meeting between the offender and the victim whereby the offender seeks to repair the harm done. Whilst it has a place for certain offenders and victims, it is mostly inappropriate for sexual abuse and family violence matters.

Nevertheless, restorative justice has been hailed by some as the answer to the criminal justice system being too difficult for victims of sexual assault to engage in. It has also been put forward by some lawyers to avoid making necessary changes in the law to address the unfair bias in favour of the accused that has made the system so traumatic and unfair to victims.

And whilst some people are of the view that using restorative justice just depends on a victim's willingness to participate, there is a lack of understanding and sensitivity to the real danger of a victim meeting with a perpetrator and becoming re-traumatised. There is also the possibility that the perpetrator has no real remorse—particularly where they may be sadists or psychopaths. It is not just a case of victims being 'willing' but also of needing to protect their wellbeing and not damaging their recovery from trauma.

In the recent situation of a teenage girl who was allegedly raped by three adult men (strangers to her) and was unable to proceed with the trial due to being too traumatised, a vocal male supporter of restorative justice said that this was a perfect case for its application. I could not understand how this form of justice was suitable given that the three alleged perpetrators were not admitting guilt, had tried to sell their story to a newspaper to make money, and given the traumatised state of this young girl. How could she be expected to meet with them? What other form of restorative justice could apply? She did meet with the Premier and advised him of law reform changes needed, which would have been somewhat therapeutic, but this is not restorative justice strictly speaking.

We also have to remember that restorative justice is not meant to replace the criminal justice system but to sit alongside it. And whilst it is more accessible for non-sexual offences, it has had limited application for certain cases of sexual offences. For example, it appeared to work well for a victim of sexual abuse by a distant family member wanting to attend a family gathering but without the perpetrator being present. Through restorative justice, her counsellor helped her disclose the abuse to her family and she was then supported to attend the gathering without the perpetrator present. It has also applied, seemingly successfully, in other cases of sexual abuse where, for example, a teenage girl wanted support and assistance to let her father know how harmful the incest was to her. She received that assistance to talk to him about it whilst he was in prison for the offences; though he seemed somewhat unresponsive, it appeared to help her move on.[160]

Many feminists have long argued that restorative justice involving victim and offender meeting in a family violence context is also inappropriate given the power imbalance involved and the threat to the wellbeing of the victim. They are also concerned that outcomes of such meetings are not subject to court scrutiny and the concept of fairness.[161]

But despite these concerns, the Victorian Royal Commission into Family Violence recommended that a framework be established to offer restorative justice to victims in a way that places them at its centre. Victims must also make a fully informed choice to want the process, perpetrators must admit guilt and take full responsibility for their actions, and there must be strong safeguards in place that include international best practice and experts.[162] The very real danger of re-traumatising the victim is ever present, so these cases need to be carefully selected, scrutinised, and evaluated.

So is there just one way for restorative justice to happen? No. There are different ways to suit the needs of each case. Restorative justice may be done through group conferencing, or a victim impact panel where the victim/survivor can talk to a specific audience (including family violence perpetrators other than the perpetrator in her case) within a structured format. Or it could involve a conversation with the perpetrator.[163]

We need to remain cautious here: where perpetrators are directly involved in the restorative justice process, we have to remember that they can be very manipulative and deceptive. And whilst an offender may express real remorse at a point in time, they may later slip back into projecting hate and blame onto others, including their victims, which is why expert screening/assessments of these offenders is essential.

Again, though, where restorative justice can be healing for victims/survivors by allowing them to have their voices heard, feel empowered, and move beyond the grief and trauma towards experiencing inner peace, this is progress. At the same time, it is not essential for all of them to undergo restorative justice in order to experience healing.

This is highlighted by the example of Clarissa Dickson Wright, one half of the popular TV partnership, *Two Fat Ladies*. She relates in her autobiography *Spilling the Beans* that virtually all her life, her main resentment was against her father, who whilst a brilliant surgeon was also a perpetrator of family violence. Clarissa held much rage and hate against him. But she knew that she needed to let these go and forgive him so that she could forgive herself for the things she regretted having done in her life. To facilitate this, she underwent a Gestalt process. This involved her sitting facing an empty chair and imagining her father sitting in it, wearing his black jacket, pinstripes, bow tie, and stiff collar. When Clarissa started to speak to him, she was surprised by what she said, but I wasn't. I imagined that it was what so many survivors of family violence wanted to say to perpetrators. She told her father that all she and the rest of the family had wanted to do was love him and have him love them. After saying these words Clarissa burst into tears and felt a dam was breached which helped her heal, later moving into a space of forgiveness.[164]

Victims and organisations

It says a lot that in our society we are at a point where some people perceive organisations apologising to victims of abuse as innovative. We would be easily forgiven for thinking that organisations apologising is just basic human decency and should happen as a matter of course.

This also applies for victims in other areas. In one particular case of discrimination I handled at the Victorian Civil and Administrative Tribunal, I represented a client with a complaint against a high-profile venue. I managed to obtain compensation for her and when I spoke to the other party's lawyer afterwards, he was stunned when I said this matter could have ended a lot earlier if his client had apologised and if that apology had been sincere.

The failure of organisations to act ethically and responsibly by apologising sincerely to victims (and taking necessary swift action) as soon as they discover that any of their staff or members caused harm was most evident during the Victorian Parliamentary Inquiry into the *Handling of Child Abuse by Religious and Other Non-Government Organisations* in 2013. The *Betrayal of Trust* report issued by the Committee handling the inquiry found that organisations were aware of criminal abuse in the past but their responses were motivated by self-interest and the protection of the organisation rather than the safety and rights of the children.

Silencing children who were criminally abused is abhorrent as is the abuse itself. The approach was a patriarchal one, devoid of empathy and concern for the wellbeing of the most vulnerable whilst concern for prestige, status and the protection of reputation/honour was paramount. It allowed for a system of domination and violence to continue unabated.

The approach by these largely religious organisations hold up a mirror to all organisations, whether they be workplaces, aged care homes and disability homes, universities, and even the family unit; reflecting how the less powerful and vulnerable are sometimes abused and left to fend for themselves. They are silenced and treated as if they are the ones who have done something wrong—in other words, they are kicked while they're down.

I highlight this further in the following two chapters, which discuss patriarchy and law enforcement, the prevalence of sexual harassment, and the way it is handled by employers and the justice system.

-7-

Policing the Police

It's a cold Autumn evening in 2017. A woman with red hair and a feisty and warm demeanour is speaking from a podium in a crowded hall. I hear small gasps in the aisle where I am sitting. The couple in front shake their heads. I'm frowning at what I'm hearing, even though it isn't a surprise to me. At least not the details of this speaker's time spent as a police officer in Victoria Police in the 1980s to the present day. She is talking about her memoir *To Hell and Back,* the title of which aptly sums up her 30 years in the police force. This is what surprises me: that she survived for so long in a workplace where a supervisor said to her that if she wanted a good reference she had to be naked on his desk, a workplace where she suffered character assassination and was even framed for speaking up about bullying and sex discrimination. Caroline Pethick's integrity and gutsiness was what Victoria Police needed and still needs.

For too long the sexism, homophobia, racism, and lack of accountability and transparency in policing have been covered up. Patriarchy has been staunchly defended even though it crippled Victoria Police, turning it—like police and military organisations throughout the world—into a toxic workplace. This doesn't mean there aren't men and women in such organisations with integrity. There are. But this toxicity just makes it harder for them to stay and also to be recognised for promotion.

So how do you overcome such toxicity? It takes more than one person to do this. And what impact does this have not only on staff but in terms of policing? Let's take a look at some of the answers to these questions as well as what attempts have been made to clean up Victoria Police to see if patriarchy is on the way out or not.

At first it appeared as if things could change for the better in the early millennium. During 2003 and 2004, allegations of sexual harassment by predatory police officers towards female colleagues did manage to come to light. As a result, an external private consultant was hired to conduct an investigation. Dark cornerstones within the organisation were turned over, uncovering a serious problem with sexual harassment. The consultant recommended various reforms for Victoria Police. But not much changed for the organisation. Firstly, the reforms that the consultant recommended should've been subject to independent oversight and follow-up monitoring. Secondly, greater, far-reaching reforms needed to be implemented with a complete overhaul not only of management but the whole culture and structure of the organisation. The giant octopus of patriarchy had Victoria Police in its tight grip and wasn't giving up—at all.

But hope came in November 2014. The then Victoria Police Commissioner Ken Lay asked the Victorian Equal Opportunity and Human Rights Commission ('VEOHRC') to investigate sexism, sexual harassment and predatory behaviour in the police force. The investigative team had their work cut out for them, uncovering a systemic culture of sexism and a high prevalence of sexual harassment, including a few cases of sexual assault. Too many cases were covered up and perpetrators were simply moved to other sections of the force, others even promoted, whilst some resigned with an unblemished record. Not surprisingly, there was also a highly gendered breakdown of the workforce in terms of rank / level, nature of role performed, and place of work.[165]

One interviewee said that the organisation was run by men to suit other men and that women get excluded, intimidated, and spoken over every day due to their gender.[166] Women were also commonly regarded as sex objects.

The review heard of many and varied victim-blaming attitudes for sexual assault. Most commonly, they heard the view that the victim invited the behaviour because she was sexy or promiscuous or was drunk or socialising inappropriately. Female interviewees made it clear that many of their male colleagues and superiors did not understand violence against women, the drivers behind such violence nor the impact. They often referred to complainants with disrespect and accused them of making false reports. Jokes about rape were made and if women 'flaunted themselves' they were viewed as 'asking for sexual assault'.[167]

The review also heard that women were often regarded as less competent than their male colleagues and constantly needed to 'prove themselves'. If they managed to get promotions, they were accused of sleeping their way to the top, being like blokes, or being part of the 'lesbian mafia'.[168] Those who reported sexual harassment, including sexual assault, were often perceived as disloyal to the team, ostracised, and physically and emotionally abused for making a report and not fitting in.

Interviewees said as well that male officers would sit around the muster room and watch pornography while females were expected to be unfazed by this.[169] Officers would also show off images of pornography on their mobile phones regardless of females being present.[170] Not surprisingly, sex discrimination and sexual harassment were widely regarded as non-events within Victoria Police. Gay men and gay women also had an elevated risk to be targeted for harassment.[171] And as in the case of perpetrators of child sex abuse, perpetrators of sexual harassment in the police force were found to have multiple targets,[172] and tended to be in a more senior position.[173]

The impact of a sexist culture, including sexual harassment, on policing was summed up by one female interviewee. She said that you have to address violence against women in the police force if you want to address it in the community. The violence within Victoria Police could even be equated with family violence since the police force can be regarded as 'family'.[174]

Fortunately, the newly appointed Commissioner of Victoria Police, Graeme Ashton, accepted the wide, sweeping reforms recommended by VEOHRC in 2015, and apologised to all victims of abuse. His commitment to radical change in the organisation also came within the context of public scrutiny and oversight by VEOHRC—including monitoring the organisation over the next few years with two more audits. These audits were aimed at ensuring that the necessary changes happen in various areas including management, structure, training, and career pathways for women. Reforms to complaint handling were identified as crucial too as was the establishment of a reparations scheme. It's a long road, though, to radical transformation.

The audit in 2017 praised Victoria Police for its work towards implementing all of the 20 recommendations from the review. But, it also found the organisation was still embedded with sexism, sexual harassment, and a rigid adherence to gender stereotyping. And so it had to widen its sexual harassment and sex discrimination training to all staff.

Not surprisingly, the resistance to reform by many members of the organisation continued. In 2019 the final audit found that Victoria Police still has unacceptably high levels of sexual harassment and discrimination. It also said that police officers are still not being protected, and that a victim-centric complaints system that was recommended back in 2015 has still not been established. But it also found that the gender pay gap has narrowed and more women are being promoted.[175]

This is an important crossroads for Victoria Police. There is still the potential for them to achieve gender equality and to become a best practice model for workplaces. But this can only happen if the whole organisation steps up and further cements its commitment to radical reform well into the future, and if the government ensures that there is external oversight for all serious police misconduct as later discussed. This would be a significant contribution to the community as well as beneficial for all staff.

A conversation I had with a recruit undertaking academy training recently helped me reach this conclusion. Her enthusiasm was contagious as she said they learn about the independent review into sexual harassment and undergo in-depth sexual harassment training. There is zero tolerance of any inappropriate behaviour (whether it be sexist, racist, or homophobic) nor bullying of any kind. Instead a warm, professional, and caring environment is provided. Recruits are engaged in rigorous training that involves working collaboratively with each other rather than in competition. They are also trained not to view all criminals as simply 'bad' but to understand the underlying causes of crime. This approach should be embedded throughout the organisation.

Patriarchy's impact on policing

The long history of patriarchy's grip on Victoria Police has serious ramifications for our society. It is borne out in the way in which police (like the law, our courts, and the judiciary) have handled sexual abuse and family violence complaints. This is not only shown by the comments of female officers to the inquiry into sexual harassment. For example, the Ombudsman's review into police handling of sex crimes back in 2004 raised concerns about some of the officers handling such matters. In one case, an experienced detective blamed a 12-year-old girl for sexual abuse by a sixty-three year old man. Children in a country town were also left at risk due to the failure of the sex crimes squad to adequately investigate allegations in 1999 that two men were molesting schoolchildren. One investigation, centering on an allegation about a Melbourne commercial television executive, was limited to a detective ringing a family member.

Anti-child abuse advocates, Dr Reina Michaelson of The Child Sexual Abuse Prevention Program (CSAPP) and Bravehearts founder Hetty Johnston, called for the Ombudsman report to be made public and also alleged that a highly organised paedophile ring involving Victorian police and former politicians had been operating in the state since the 1970s.[176]

In 2011, a study by criminologists of sexual assault files with Victoria Police found that if complainants were between the ages of 31-40, they were less likely to have their matter investigated and this was particularly the case if they were drunk, drug-impaired, had a cognitive impairment or mental illness, or worked in prostitution. If there were multiple offenders involved in an alleged sexual assault and/or an offender was alcohol or drug-affected themselves, it also had a bearing on cases failing to go forward. It appeared from the study that young and old victims are easier for police to deal with.

Carolyn Worth, from the Centres Against Sexual Assault Forum, said in addition that, 'I suspect what happens in the 31 to 40 age group is that they are seen as being out socialising, having a few drinks and maybe not regarded as "real victims".'[177] It also appears that excuses were made for offenders if they were affected by alcohol or drugs.

In the meantime, police inaction on call outs to family violence incidents and failing to act on pleas for help for breaches of intervention orders also continue to be a serious problem. This issue was brought to a head with a recent lawsuit launched against Victoria Police alleging that they failed in their duty to protect a victim of family violence and her family on at least six occasions. The allegations include police mistakenly informing the victim an intervention order was in place, allowing an intervention order to be revoked by the court despite the man being a repeat offender, and failing to inform the family that it had been revoked.[178]

But it's not all bleak. There are also reports that members of Victoria Police have acted diligently on cases of child sex abuse by Catholic Church clergy. This includes their handling of the matter of Cardinal George Pell, who was accused and convicted for the historical sexual abuse of two choir boys. (Cardinal Pell's appeal to the Court of Appeal failed and so he may appeal to the High Court at the time of writing.) Victoria Police also recently launched a five year strategic plan to better tackle cases of family violence and sexual abuse—an important step forward.

Police brutality and corruption

Patriarchy's impact is also seen with police brutality and corruption. In the year leading up to July 2017, more than 80 Victoria police employees were charged with criminal matters. These included not only alleged offences against members of the public but also fellow police officers. In one case, a police officer was later found guilty of assaulting another officer whilst she was off-duty and intoxicated in Ballarat. The victim was lying face down in a police cell handcuffed, stripped of her pants and her underpants, when she was kicked with force. She received a large payout from Victoria Police due to the seriousness of the assault and her degrading and inhumane treatment.[179]

Then in 2018 Victoria Police officers were caught on camera punching, beating, and dousing a disability pensioner with mental health issues in capsicum spray and with a high pressure hose. The Victorian Premier's response at the time was to rush to the defence of Victoria Police and simply say that Victoria Police is the nation's best police force; that they act with professionalism and in his experience 'proportionate to the risk that they face.' The Police Association's Mr Gatt said that one thing he knew after 20 years of policing is that '*there's always two sides to a story.*'[180]

Such comments are not helpful to the public, the man subjected to such violence, nor even to the police. They have also been used for centuries in an attempt to invalidate and silence the voices of victims of family violence and sexual abuse and have no place in the discussion of such violent actions by police officers.

Acknowledging the seriousness of the matter and concluding that an investigation is needed would be helpful instead. As it stands, the Independent Broad-based Anti-Corruption Commission (IBAC) charged three of the police officers with unlawful assault and all three responded by saying they would fight the allegations that they used excessive force.[181]

The issue of police brutality and mishandling of police complaints also made headlines back in 2014. The United Nations delivered a decision that highly criticised the Victorian Government and its police force saying it had breached the International Covenant on Civil and Political Rights (ICCPR). This is because of the failure to compensate Ms. Corinna Horvath for being viciously bashed by police in 1996, and left spending 5 days in hospital to recover. None of the officers who beat Ms. Horvath lost their jobs at the time-in fact, they were all promoted.

When Ms. Horvath was originally awarded compensation of $300,000 by the Victorian County Court, the Victorian government appealed, claiming it could not be held vicariously liable because the officers acted outside the realm of their duties. The state won and Ms. Horvath was left uncompensated.[182] Yet, a few months after the United Nations criticism of the matter, then-Chief Commissioner Ken Lay apologised to Ms. Horvath on behalf of all police members and paid her compensation.[183]

Rather than being defensive or trying to play down misconduct and corruption like so many organisations, Victoria Police and all police forces should show leadership in this space. This means welcoming external oversight and scrutiny, and incorporating a history of police misconduct and corruption into the curriculum for police recruits to remind them of the dangers of it. They've already done this on the issue of sex discrimination and sexual harassment, so there is a precedent.

Former FBI Director James Comey, in his book on leadership and ethics, *A Higher Loyalty*, says he included in the curriculum of the FBI's training academy the history of the FBIs vicious and unchecked campaign of harassment and extralegal attack on Dr. Martin Luther King and others. He wanted them to remember that well-meaning people lost their way, (though I'm not convinced that all were well-meaning to begin with), and reflect on the FBI's values and their responsibility to always do better. Trainees must also visit Dr. King's memorial as part of their training and read his penetrating insights into humanity, racism, and justice, such as his quote: 'an injustice anywhere is a threat to justice everywhere.'[184]

Where police try to justify any brutality for the purposes of interrogating suspects, including terrorists, Comey points out that the FBI had concluded long ago that coercive interrogations were of no utility and that the information obtained was largely unreliable or useless. So they perfected the art of 'rapport-building interrogation' instead. This amounts to forming a trusting relationship with those in custody and led to the FBI obtaining life-saving and timely information from terrorists, serial killers, and mobsters.[185]

It is not surprising, though, that generally Victoria Police, like other police forces, has a problem with integrity. In a recent report by IBAC, (following a series of investigations into police corruption that were substantiated by IBAC in 2017), 46 per cent of survey respondents feared some form of personal repercussion if they reported corruption within the organisation. One respondent summed it up: 'You ask yourself – is this career ending?'[186]

And in November 2018, the High Court of Australia said that the conduct of Victoria Police in turning a criminal law barrister into a police informant was reprehensible. Some of the criminals she informed against were on her client list, such as drug lord Tony Mokbel. The Court said Victoria Police were involved in allowing atrocious breaches of the sworn duty of every police officer to discharge all their duties faithfully and according to law without 'favour or affection, malice or ill-will.'[187] This is the patriarchal 'the ends justifies the means' approach, with its emphasis on being purely 'result driven' that too easily leads to abuse of power, misconduct, and corruption. Consequently, a royal commission was called to investigate police management of informants.

Independent oversight of complaints against police

For decades, lawyers have said that police forces cannot handle complaints against themselves as there is an inherent conflict of interest. This issue was raised yet again when a parliamentary inquiry in 2018 heard that Victoria Police often failed to properly investigate allegations of police misconduct or assault, proving the need for an independent investigative body. Robinson Gill Lawyers said in their submission that IBAC would refer 90 per cent of complaints about misconduct back to Victoria Police, which created a clear risk of a conflict of interest. Many clients had been awarded compensation through the legal system after Victoria Police investigators dismissed their claims as 'unsubstantiated'. The need to establish a new independent complaint body, or a separate body with IBAC that is fully resourced to investigate allegations of police misconduct was clearly made out.[188]

Flemington Kensington Community Legal Service have also long advocated for the need for an independent body to oversee allegations of police misconduct. The police force is no different from any industry or organisation where time and time again we have seen that self-regulation and self-oversight does not work. The public understand this, but many politicians and organisations do not, including The Police Association, who denied the need for independent oversight and told the inquiry that they had faith in the status quo for handling complaints.

Fortunately, the parliamentary inquiry thought differently. It said the current system for complaint handling wasn't working and recommended a new, dedicated Police Corruption and Misconduct Division within IBAC. This would ensure that serious misconduct must be investigated externally and never by Victoria Police unless exceptional circumstances apply. The inquiry also proposed a new definition of misconduct to include wrongful arrest and serious assault, and said that where less serious complaints are addressed within Victoria Police, investigators must be free of conflict of interest. Tamar Hopkins from the Police Accountability Project added further reforms are needed: removing the exemption of IBAC complaint handling from freedom of information requests and creating judicial review.[189]

Caring for the wellbeing of police officers

In rejecting a patriarchal approach to policing, police forces have to do more to help employees suffering from post-traumatic stress disorder (PTSD) and other mental health issues due to workplace bullying, sexual harassment or through trauma-related work. Mental health training including prevention strategies against PTSD from trauma-related work, is also essential. So is appropriate debriefing and counselling—which should be widely available as well for other emergency workers, members of the military, and other workforces where relevant.

This means sufficient resources must be given to police psychology units in all police forces. These units should consist of psychologists and social workers who provide not only counselling, training, and coaching but also a 24-hour on-call service. Police officers, like other emergency workers, must also be able to access Workcover payments much faster than is currently the case. This has been a problem for a very long time in Victoria and whilst our state government finally said in late 2018 that it would tackle the issue, it is a shame that it has taken this long for any government to make a commitment to do so.

The increase in police suicides in recent years has further highlighted the fact that more must be done to care for police members' psychological needs. And as expert Dr Gilmartin says we should recognise that law enforcement is a career that challenges people tremendously and takes its toll on them emotionally and physically.[190] This is not a sign of weakness or not being tough enough. Such macho patriarchal views only compound the problem.

Thankfully, Victoria Police is undergoing a process of major transformation, though resistance is strong. The completion of this process will hopefully happen in the not too distant future—as long as there is continued commitment to radical reform, independent oversight and scrutiny of all serious police misconduct, and constant vigilance. The improvements so far in Victoria Police with the assistance of VEOHRC show us the power of independent investigations, oversight and monitoring, which is highly relevant to the next chapter on sexual harassment.

-8-

Turning a Blind Eye

'If this ever happened to me again I don't know what I would do given how badly my complaint was handled by management and human resources—who happened to include women by the way.' (Anonymous interviewee)

We know that sexual harassment is a systemic problem that is not confined to Victoria Police; they hold up a mirror of it being a systemic problem in our society that is not handled well generally. Yet surprisingly, the authorities back in 2015 didn't say that given it's so prevalent in Victoria Police it's likely to be prevalent elsewhere and a major social problem. Indeed a 2008 Senate Inquiry into sex discrimination had already been told that it was.

Despite the creation of the *Convention on the Elimination of All Forms of Discrimination Against Women* in 1979, and several countries' introduction of sex discrimination or equal opportunity laws, sexual harassment is a worldwide problem predominantly done by men to women. This is very much an issue of gender-based violence.

I'm mindful, though, of the few cases I know of where men, particularly young men, have been victims of sexual harassment, including sexual assault, from male employers and senior male colleagues in areas as diverse as small businesses and construction sites. And I have heard of a few cases of female perpetrators of sexual harassment.

Perpetrators are not confined to one industry or profession. They include business owners, scientists, military officers, lawyers, doctors, surgeons, fire-fighters, customers/clients, factory workers, office managers, male sexual harassment officers, social workers, human resource managers, CEOs, lecturers, politicians, and the list goes on. They also tend to be in a more senior position than their victims and include mentors.

The law on sexual harassment

In Australia we have Chris Ronalds AM to thank for ensuring that we have laws against sexual harassment. Whilst she was drafting the *Sex Discrimination Act 1984*, Chris insisted that it include making sexual harassment unlawful. It was the first legislation in the world to use the term 'sexual harassment' and was based on her own personal experience of being sexually harassed as a law student and in her first job as a lawyer.[191]

Sexual harassment is currently defined under the *Sex Discrimination Act 1984* as any unwelcome sexual advance, request for sexual favours, or conduct of a sexual nature. These are done in circumstances where a reasonable person would have anticipated the possibility that the person harassed would be offended, humiliated, or intimidated.

Many people don't realise it's such a broad term ranging from leering, wolf-whistling, and sexually suggestive jokes right through to requests for sex, sending sexually explicit emails or texts and all forms of sexual assault, including rape.

Do we need any changes to this definition? A medical practitioner who works extensively in this field told me that this definition is too broad—sexual assault is not harassment as such. So it is more appropriate for equal opportunity and sex discrimination laws to refer to 'sexual harassment and sex offences' with separate definitions, and then enforce the same complaint handling and prevention regime for both. The complainant still has the additional option of seeking help through the criminal justice system for sex offences such as sexual assault and indecent exposure. Such a reform to the definition of sexual harassment would better reflect the different types of unlawful conduct.

There are also calls for the impact of sexual harassment under the law to be broadened. This is because a person may not be humiliated, offended, or intimidated but still want the sexual harassment to stop. The perpetrator's actions may still create a 'hostile work environment' or interfere with complainants doing their work and so the law should reflect this.[192]

What are the causes of sexual harassment?

The causes of sexual harassment lie with a patriarchal society that promotes a power imbalance between men and women, gender stereotyping and narcissism, a sexist culture as highlighted in Chapter Three, and a patriarchal view of power that focuses on humiliating and triumphing over others—rather than the true power explored in Chapter Thirteen.

Unfortunately, despite how serious and damaging sexual harassment is, it is difficult to get politicians and business people to address the causes of it until they see its economic impact. So we need to point out to them the larger payouts of compensation by employers from litigation proceedings in recent years, higher staff turnover from victims leaving the workplace (and taking with them expertise and knowledge that will take time to replace), and the cost of victims being on stress leave, leading to higher insurance premiums.

Do victims usually report it and who are they?

Sexual harassment is under-reported, as victims fear losing their job. They know in many cases it is career suicide to speak up, and also fear not being believed. If they do raise it with their workplace, it is often dealt with internally under a shroud of secrecy rather than externally through the Human Rights Commission or the courts. A recent survey by the Human Rights Commission found that 71 per cent of Australians had been sexually harassed at some point in their lives, with women (85 per cent) far more likely to experience it than men (56 per cent).[193]

The women are usually young (although it certainly happens to older women) and have not been in the workplace for very long. Victims are distributed throughout all industries, in part-time and full time work, from Anglo-Australian backgrounds to those with multicultural backgrounds, Indigenous Australians, and migrant workers.

Those in less senior positions and less secure employment are particularly vulnerable, as well as those who are not officially on the books through cash in hand employment and workers with disabilities. In addition, lesbian women have been sexually harassed by men who claim they can 'convert them'.[194]

Also of concern is that across most sectors, there is a lack of understanding of the rights of victims of sexual harassment and confidence in asserting those rights.

And then of course there is the sexual harassment of women outside of the workplace, but that's another area that needs to be addressed by governments and society as a whole. Whilst this chapter focuses on workplace sexual harassment, it should be prohibited in any area of life (or at the very least any area of public life). It is also worth noting that Belgium penalises sexual harassment in public spaces.[195] And in London, targeted weeks of action by extra uniformed and plain clothes police on public transport have been effective to send a message to harassers as well as increasing the number of arrests.[196]

Meanwhile, in the workplace context, the current legal framework has many flaws. Let's look at this more closely, seeing how sexual harassment affects victims and how they are treated in the current legal landscape.

The impact on victims and how they are treated

Based on my experience as a lawyer in the field, and interviews with victims and other professionals in this area, organisations cannot be trusted to handle these matters in a way that prioritizes the welfare of the victim.

Instead, similar to the organisations in the Betrayal of Trust Report and Victoria Police as highlighted by the independent review, many victims are treated without compassion and understanding. They are not given the necessary supports either to assist their rehabilitation back into the workplace after an internal investigation has found the perpetrator guilty. Often victims are told to keep quiet, and any compensation that they obtain is via a confidentiality agreement to silence them and protect the reputation of the organisation. Perpetrators are simply moved elsewhere within the organisation, or if they leave, it is with the support of silence about the sexual harassment so that they can easily obtain employment elsewhere with the support of colleagues.

There is a culture of victim-blaming even in the legal profession, and by human resource departments who in effect act as 'the department of cover-ups'. This victim-blaming and covering up is done by both male and female staff/management—so there goes the idea of a sisterhood. Victims also fear not being believed—a valid fear where colleagues prefer to sustain the myth of the perpetrator really being as charming and helpful as he seems to them.

In her book, *Generation F: Sex, Power, and the Young Feminist*, Virginia Trioli highlights the negative impact on women of speaking up about sexual harassment including sexual assault. She refers to the two complainants of alleged sexual harassment by the master at Ormond College at the University of Melbourne back in the early 1990s. Both women were subjected to unfair criticism from certain feminists like Helen Garner and members of the legal profession for making the complaints and seeking police help. Along Collins Street, lawyers were heard saying that the two complainants would never get work in Melbourne. They were furious these women could do this to one of their own.[197]

These lawyers revealed what many in the profession and other occupations still think whilst they over-identify with their roles, their male bonds—their 'in group', so to speak—and develop a sexist, patriarchal view lacking empathy and compassion. They embrace a desire to punish women who speak up and assert their legal rights, and have a strong 'us and them' mentality. One of the women in the Ormond College case had to leave Melbourne and complete her legal studies elsewhere, such was her distress. And more recently, female lawyers have alerted the federal Sex Discrimination Commissioner that sexual harassment is still prevalent in the legal profession.

In one case, an Australian victim of workplace sexual assault underwent a harrowing internal investigation where the perpetrator was eventually found guilty. But he was allowed to resign under a shroud of secrecy and with an unblemished record, rather than be dealt with by way of public dismissal. He then took up a position as a lawyer elsewhere. Concerned that he could still do harm to others, the victim contacted a peak legal body and was told that, whilst not trying to silence her, she needed to consider how speaking out on this issue would affect her legal career.

The impact of sexual harassment is far-reaching. Victims often require treatment for serious mental health issues such as depression, anxiety, adjustment disorders, and post-traumatic stress disorder. Some even end up on stress leave under Workcover or Comcare regimes whilst others leave their workplace fearful that any Workcover involvement will make it harder for them to find employment elsewhere.

If there are few jobs available in their line of work, victims may have to relocate to another state to obtain employment. This happened in one case not only because the victim worked in a niche area but also because the perpetrator blackened her name with the few other firms in Melbourne in her field, where the managers were part of the perpetrator's network.

It is also difficult for victims in rural and regional areas where there are not as many employment options for them. They fear that if they make a complaint of sexual harassment, many in the community may shun them. Victims who leave their workplace due to sexual harassment wherever they are, also face distressing questions about why they left their previous workplace in interviews. They also deal with underlying fears about whether they will be safe in the next workplace. As a result, many struggle to rebuild their careers.

Victims/survivors are often viewed wrongly by men and women as being weak as well. There is the disturbing belief that victims were targeted because they were not 'strong enough'. 'They just need to learn how to be strong and examine how they ended up in this situation in the first place,' some say. Such attitudes are not only unhelpful, untrue, and unkind, but they dismiss the courage and strength of these women, and in few cases men, in being able to keep going in the workplace the best they can, as well as where they have come forward to make complaints and endure the legal processes involved.

Too many people also feel sympathy for perpetrators on the basis that 'these poor men must be overwhelmed by their attraction for these women and can't cope with that attraction.' They are also worried about these men losing their jobs, without thinking about the victims having to leave their jobs and/or having their careers jeopardized or ended.

Victims of sexual harassment in all its forms should be viewed as whistle-blowers when they speak up and be rewarded and supported for doing so as well as compensated for the trauma they have suffered. In line with this, a reparations scheme to compensate victims of sexual harassment should be considered. It could be funded by government with employers based on extensive consultation. This would help survivors who have not received compensation due to it being too traumatic to pursue litigation or sign a confidentiality agreement. The problem of such agreements is later discussed.

If we want to see more women in positions of power and gender equity we need to eliminate sexual harassment as it is very much a barrier to women building their careers, as well as reaching their full potential in general. We also want to ensure that this doesn't happen to men, either.

Problems with the complaint-based process

i) Taking legal action

Conciliation and hearings

In Australia, we have a two-tiered system for taking legal action against the organisation involved and the perpetrator, under the Sex Discrimination Act and state and territory equal opportunity laws. There is a conciliation process (like mediation) at the state or federal human rights commissions to try to reach an agreement that resolves the matter without going through a legal hearing. If that fails a tribunal hearing at the state level or a federal court hearing at the federal level may occur. Despite conciliation not requiring the parties to have lawyers, employers tend to use them and so due to the power imbalance and the stress on complainants it is also crucial they have legal representation.

And so complainants bear the burden of seeking legal advice and representation on top of their distress or trauma. But many also do not have the financial means to pay for legal advice and representation for conciliation, let alone for litigation in a court or tribunal. Whilst there are free legal services that handle these matters, governments must ensure there is sufficient funding for them to provide timely advice and representation for cases with merit and not apply means tests that are too tight. No-win no-fee firms are another option for complainants seeking affordable legal representation—but that doesn't mean that a complainant with limited funds won't still incur certain costs or fees.

But nor do complainants want to attract the publicity that such cases receive. Despite the sensitivity, seriousness, and nature of these proceedings, the complainant is not de-identified as a matter of course. For example, complainants of sex offences in criminal prosecutions are de-identified, so there is no reason why they can't be in sexual harassment cases.

Complainants are also often too traumatised to endure a court or tribunal hearing—they are not only dealing with the abuse on a personal level but on a public level—their whole career is at stake and litigation is extremely stressful. In one case that went to a tribunal hearing, the complainant succeeded. But due to the trauma of the sexual harassment, coupled with the strain of litigation, she ended up in a psychiatric unit to recover. Whilst some complainants have had success in the courts and tribunals and have not 'been broken' by the system, problems remain. The strain of the current process, the fact that the complainant bears the burden of seeking legal representation and taking legal action, and the lack of anonymity still needs to be addressed.

Do our judges really understand?

It has only been in the last few years that the courts have also started to recognise the far-reaching impact of sexual harassment and have awarded higher damages, due to a landmark Federal Court decision in 2014. A female employee of the technology giant Oracle was sexually harassed by a male worker for six months. The original judgment awarded the woman $18,000 in damages, but the Full Court increased it to $130,000, in part because of changing community understanding of the damage and loss of enjoyment of life harassment could cause.

However, this 'change in community understanding' is perplexing. A high percentage of the population (particularly women) have known for too long of the damage and loss of enjoyment of life that the sexual harassment can cause. Once again the courts and our lawmakers have lagged greatly behind community attitudes, and as such have incorporated their patriarchal perspective into their application of the law.

Meanwhile, in the United States, judges have dismissed cases where supervisors groped women, called them whores and sluts, and repeatedly asked them on dates. Such acts were not viewed by male judges as creating a hostile environment to work in, at least not for the 'reasonable' person.[198]

Fortunately, in Australia, when the reasonable person test was wrongly applied by Justice Einfeld in 1988 in the case of Hall v Sheiban, his decision was overruled the following year by the Full Federal Court. Unlike Justice Einfeld, they did not take a patriarchal view. The Court understood the importance of acknowledging women's perspectives and how distressing sexual harassment can be including where the doctor in this case unzipped a nurse's uniform, and pulled her onto his knee to try to kiss her. The Court found sexual propositioning and all forms of sexual misconduct unacceptable. It was also unacceptable that Justice Einfeld was of the view that women of 'normal life experience' would not find the unwanted advances in the case such as the doctor constantly pressing his ardour as distressing.[199]

The Court also understood that a woman may find it difficult to complain at the time of unwanted sexual advances because she fears losing her job.[200] So the importance of the context of what was happening was recognised by the Court. This is similar to how in sexual assault cases in Victoria juries are warned that evidence that a person did not resist is not sufficient to argue there was consent.

Unfortunately, though, the perception of what is 'reasonable' is still problematic in Australia. So is the proper examination of the context of allegations. An example is the Geoffrey Rush defamation case, which included allegations that Mr Rush made comments that constituted sexual harassment to fellow actor Ms Norvill, as well as groping gestures, and touching Ms Norvill's breast. During the trial, Justice Wigney said in response to the allegation that Mr Rush called Ms Norvill *'yummy'*, that whilst he wouldn't say yummy or scrumptious in his workplace, he was a boring lawyer whereas Mr Rush is an actor. Justice Wigney added that 'this is a theatrical workplace where people use florid language...'[201]

It shouldn't matter which workplace a woman is in, she is entitled to professional, respectful language towards her.

When Justice Wigney later found Mr Rush not guilty of sexual harassment and therefore decided in favour of his defamation claim, he said in effect that he did not find Ms Norvill to be a credible witness. Yet Justice Wigney did not sufficiently examine the context of some of the issues that led to him disbelieving her. For example, this was shown when he raised concerns that Ms Novill didn't say anything adverse against Mr Rush when promoting their play *King Lear* and instead said she was privileged to work with him et cetera. The context of the need for actors to promote their films and plays as part of their employment obligations, including to refer glowingly to their colleagues, and indeed to do so to ensure future work is worth highlighting.

Nor did Justice Wigney examine within the context of their professional relationship that it is often difficult for victims of sexual harassment to reconcile a highly regarded person, even a mentor or someone they look up to, with a predator. And so they are often torn and in conflict about this, and therefore can act in seemingly conflicting ways. This makes sense when understanding the nature and context of the relationship and who is in the position of power.

Whilst Justice Wigney raised the issue of discrepancies between the evidence given by Ms Norvill during the trial and what was contained in her formal statement, the context again was not examined enough in my view. Discrepancies between legal statements and evidence given during a trial by complainants of abuse are not uncommon as highlighted in Chapter Six. This is due to the very nature of the trauma allegedly involved and the nature of memory generally. This could have been explored by Justice Wigney before making his finding for or against Mr Rush.

Justice Wigney also viewed a certain text sent by Mr Rush to Ms Novill as a throwaway line or joke as Mr Rush said it was. The text message was that Mr Rush thought of Ms Norvill *'more than is socially appropriate'* and with an emoji of a face with a tongue hanging out.[202] Many people I know would see this as a sexual advance.

ii) Internal grievance procedures

Internal investigations can be harrowing and brutal, just as a court or tribunal hearing can be. This can depend in part on the expertise and skill of the private investigator conducting the investigation. Complainants can feel at times as if they are on trial and be further traumatised where investigators do not keep them up to date with the processes of the investigation, as dealing with the unknown merely exacerbates their trauma. This is similar to complainants in the criminal trial process not being kept informed about each stage of the process.

There have also been instances of investigators taking their frustrations about the case out on complainants, further traumatising them. This is compounded by an absence of external oversight or scrutiny of the investigation and insufficient skills and expertise of some private investigators hired to conduct such investigations. I also know of a high profile investigator questioning a complainant over the phone for the details of a sexual assault when she had just come out of a counselling session in tears, deeply distressed, and unable to talk properly. This is clearly inappropriate. Such questioning should always be in person.

The fact that a person can make a private career out of workplace sexual harassment, including sex offences, raises ethical issues as well. These cases should really be handled by a government agency just as police and the Office of Public Prosecutions handle cases of sexual abuse, and WorkSafe deals with workplace injury. But the problems don't end there.

There is no monitoring of the organisation in question after sexual harassment investigations to ensure the complainant is looked after and any recommendations arising from the investigation, such as regular bullying and sexual harassment training for all staff, takes place. In addition, recommendations by investigators have also failed to mention the need for support, rehabilitation, and reintegration of complainants back into the workplace, including for victims of sexual assault.

The 'Rolls Royce' investigation by the Victorian Equal Opportunity and Human Rights Commission into sexual harassment in Victoria Police also had the benefit of thorough findings and extensive recommendations. It also allowed for continued monitoring and review of Victoria Police implementing those recommendations. Unfortunately, other workplaces do not have the benefit of such high-level investigations occurring and with the necessary oversight and monitoring afterwards. This is not justice.

iii) Lack of access to expert counselling

There is a lack of access to free, independent expert counselling for complainants. I have known of employer-referred counselling programs which have not been able to provide sufficient help nor diagnose the victim with PTSD or other relevant mental health issues as needed, and have refused to co-operate with any investigations into sexual harassment.

iv) Confidentiality agreements

Complainants of sexual harassment have had to sign confidentiality agreements that bar them telling anyone about the unlawful conduct if they wish to settle the matter without a court or tribunal hearing and receive compensation. This is even where the perpetrator has admitted the sexual misconduct or has been found guilty by an internal investigation.

It's also alarming that if complainants seek to have the matter dealt with externally through a state equal opportunity commission or the federal human rights commission through a conciliation or mediation process, they can still be required to sign a confidentiality agreement in order to settle the case. It is in effect a state-sanctioned practice of silencing the victim.

This is a concern not only due to the unequal bargaining power between the parties. Silencing victims in this way only serves to further disempower them and puts the legal industry and mental health experts at odds with each other. Mental health experts rightly say that such confidentiality agreements jeopardise the recovery of victims, can re-traumatise them, and are highly inappropriate in such cases.

Broad confidentiality agreements can also prevent complainants from accessing support, whether it be from family and friends, co-workers, future partners, and employers. I have even known of cases where the agreements have sought to be so wide as to include non-disclosure to health practitioners. Employers have also sought these non-disclosure agreements where the sexual harassment includes criminal offences. At the same time, law firms have been paid well for drafting these agreements, including at least one of them which is speaking out now about the problem of sexual harassment in the legal profession in Melbourne.

Non-disclosure clauses in these agreements also make it harder for complainants to protect their reputation. There are cases of supporters of the perpetrator making false comments to harm the reputation of the complainant, but these people aren't covered by the agreement. Even if the agreement covers other employees or people outside the workplace, it is difficult for the employer to provide oversight. So complainants are left not only finding it harder to recover due to being silenced by the non-disclosure clause but also finding it extremely difficult to protect their reputation and find work elsewhere in their industry if supporters of the perpetrator have blackened their name.

Back in 2008, I appeared before a national Senate inquiry into the effectiveness of sex discrimination laws, giving evidence on sexual harassment, the problems with the complaints-based system and confidentiality agreements. I argued that such agreements attached to payments not only silence victims and jeopardise their recovery, but prevent accountability and transparency. This prevents us from accurately gauging how sexual harassment is being handled, its prevalence across different organisations, and how to ensure a fair and effective system to address it and prevent it. Despite raising concerns about these agreements, the flawed complaint-based model, and reforms needed including a positive duty on employers to eliminate and prevent sexual harassment—nothing was done.

The problem of confidentiality agreements and organisations being left in charge to settle matters using them also came to a head in 2018. The media discovered that a complainant of sexual harassment against a member of the AFL (Australian Football League) had received compensation in return for signing a confidentiality agreement that did not allow her to discuss the matter. It led to calls for the AFL to ban these non-disclosure agreements in return for cash payments, and if it did it would lead the way and put pressure on other organisations to follow suit. We should have a system where victims should be compensated without being silenced and still have their privacy and reputation protected under the law.

The Sex Discrimination Commissioner, Ms Kate Jenkins, also entered the debate, writing in an article for *The Age* that we need to 'stop talking about so-called "hush money" and refocus our attention on the basic values of fairness and justice.' I take an alternate view. It is the 'hush money' that goes against the values of fairness and justice. We already saw this with the way that religious organisations have dealt with child sexual abuse by using such agreements. This has allowed perpetrators to not be held to account and to continue the abuse elsewhere. The same is the case with workplace sexual harassment.

Ms Jenkins also argued that these confidentiality agreements can be agreed to by all parties and are often to the benefit of the complainant and the other parties involved. She also said that confidentiality agreements on mutually agreed, confidential terms feature in many alternative dispute resolution processes, including those at the Commission.

But the very nature and sensitivity of sexual harassment means that confidentiality agreements containing clauses that in effect silence a complainant are inappropriate. And as for agreement by complainants to such agreements, there is not much choice (if any) given to them if they want to obtain compensation. We should not apply a standard legal practice of non-disclosure to such cases.

The Sex Discrimination Commissioner also said the focus should be on how to reduce the rates of sexual harassment for the AFL.[203] But the reality is that allowing these types of confidentiality agreements means that it is harder for all organisations, including the AFL, to reduce and prevent sexual harassment and act with integrity on such matters. The silencing of victims sends the wrong message.

Not surprisingly, after the Sex Discrimination Commissioner announced she was delighted to hold a national inquiry into workplace sexual harassment for 2018/2019, she had to ask employers to allow a limited waiver of confidentiality obligations in non-disclosure agreements to allow complainants to make submissions to her inquiry. Unfortunately, not many employers did this.

At the same time, the Commissioner's decision to hold this inquiry is very much in the public interest and at least there will be people who are survivors and legal experts who are able to contribute to the consultation process, though perhaps not as many survivors as we would like.

But the recent AFL scandal also raises other areas of reform needed. We cannot leave any organisations in charge of investigating these matters themselves and monitoring outcomes due to an inherent conflict of interest.

v) Victimisation

Despite victimisation of complainants being prohibited under federal and state legislation there is evidence this remains a problem. One complainant informed the then Human Rights and Equal Opportunity Commission's (HREOC) Listening Tour back in 2008 that the victimisation that took place after she complained about her boss's sexual harassment of her was even worse than the sexual harassment itself.[204]

In the case of Lee v Smith, when the complainant attempted to report the sexual harassment which included rape, her position of employment was placed in jeopardy and she was criticised for bringing personal problems to work.[205]And we have seen with the 2015 inquiry into Victoria Police that complainants have been shunned, ostracised, and even emotionally and physically abused for making a report.

Sexual harassment law should also fully address the victimisation of a person for rejecting sexual harassment, for example, where a woman is bullied by her boss because she has refused his requests for sex or where she is overlooked for promotion.

Bystanders who intervene to support a victim or a support-person assigned to a complainant during an internal investigation can also be subjected to victimisation by other staff so they require protection too.

vi) Lack of rehabilitation of victims

State and federal legislation in Australia and worldwide should impose a clear obligation on employers to take all reasonable steps necessary to prevent and stop victimisation in all its forms as discussed, but also to ensure the rehabilitation and reintegration of victims in the workplace. Severe penalties for non-compliance must apply.

The case of Imogen highlights the importance of this. When Imogen informed her employer that she had been a victim of sexual assault by a senior colleague, her employer asked her to undergo an internal investigation so that they could protect the other women she worked with. Imogen agreed despite knowing the investigation would re-traumatise her. After a gruelling investigation, her complaint was upheld and the perpetrator resigned under strict confidentiality agreed to with the employer. Imogen had no say about this. The perpetrator left quietly, telling other staff he simply had a disagreement with management.

But the problems didn't end there. Upon Imogen's return to the workplace, the employer thought it was appropriate to allow a farewell party to be held by staff externally for the perpetrator with the women Imogen fought to protect also attending that party. Imogen was told by management that she 'just had to deal with it.'

Management also made statements that allowed people to think Imogen had done something wrong whilst also silencing her—saying that she wasn't to tell anyone what had happened to her. A senior member of the organisation also shouted angrily at Imogen when she broke down crying at work—accusing her of trying to cause trouble. This person also said that a victimiser, who was shunning and ostracising Imogen, was simply being honest. Not surprisingly no action was taken against the victimiser. The employer also placed Imogen on standard, high-pressure professional duties with additional unfamiliar duties despite knowing she was traumatised. Nor did they offer Imogen the supports and rehabilitation she deserved and needed, including informing staff that she was traumatised and should be supported and eased back into work. Consequently, she completely broke down with chronic post-traumatic stress disorder.

In addition, when Imogen first raised the sexual assault and after the investigation, at no time did her employer advise that the matter should be referred to the police and that they would support her with this—even if it was to only make a report.

Independent investigation and oversight

External oversight of workplaces by an independent body is essential to properly address sexual harassment. It's time to get radical and create the following model or one similar to it: we should establish a division attached to our state or federal human rights commissions or WorkSafe to focus on sexual harassment with well-resourced and highly trained specialist investigators across Australia. They would investigate these cases in all organisations, large or small and have extensive powers necessary including access to all relevant documents, premises, and witnesses.

There also needs to be an obligation on employers to report sexual harassment to this body (as well as complainants having the opportunity to report directly). And where the matter involves criminal conduct such as sex offences, the employer must advise the complainant of her right to have the matter reported to the police and to do so as soon as possible whilst making it clear that they will help her do this. If the complainant chooses to contact the police, she may decide to make a report but may not seek a police investigation, or may make a report and seek a police investigation. Many complainants may not wish to pursue the latter course due to the stress involved and the higher burden of proof applying ie *beyond reasonable doubt* rather than the *balance of probabilities* test that applies in an internal investigation or a civil hearing.

The independent body handling sexual harassment will have the power to investigate, make findings and recommendations (including ones that are binding), assist with a resolution, enter into enforceable undertakings with the employer, and monitor outcomes. It can also prosecute the employer for any breaches of the law such as not taking all reasonable steps necessary to prevent the unlawful conduct. This high level of transparency and accountability would also help the body or commission to be fully appraised of the amount and types of sexual harassment and sex offences in workplaces with adequate data collection. It would also assist in developing prevention strategies. In addition this body must ensure that support and rehabilitation for victims occurs with the additional powers to issue compliance notices and take legal proceedings where an employer refuses to comply. High penalties should also be in place for non-compliance.

Whilst all sexual harassment is serious, due to its prevalence and possible resourcing issues, if necessary the more minor incursions can be dealt with by an organisation/employer as long as they report both the incident and how they dealt with it to the independent body. This independent body must also have the power to question the complainant on whether she views the outcome to be satisfactory.

It must also be able to conduct its own motion inquiries and investigations into any workplace where it reasonably suspects sexual harassment is happening and is not being addressed.

Overview of Prevention Strategies and Other Reforms

If we want to prevent workplace sexual harassment and also better address it, we need to employ an approach that tackles it from different angles and sees everything is interconnected. This is a complex area that requires detailed consultation with experts and the public, as well as changes to not only anti-discrimination laws but also other workplace laws. As already discussed, a few of the many reforms and strategies include amending the definition of sexual harassment as well as the following:

1. **Addressing sexism:** We must address sexism in our culture in all its forms through measures already discussed in Chapter Three including a ban on pornography, addressing the other harms of the sex industry, and banning sexist

advertising. We should also introduce laws against gender vilification. Furthermore, we need nationwide campaigns against sexism and efforts to raise awareness of its seriousness, recognising it wherever it manifests and speaking up against it.

2. **Education campaigns and training**: We need nationwide education campaigns against sexual harassment targeting the public as well as workplaces. This should also occur in schools, universities, and religious institutions. Sexual harassment is still not fully understood or taken seriously, nor is there sufficient information on what victims should do and the complaint mechanisms available. Victims will also often tell a family member, friend, or work colleague first and so the initial reaction a victim receives will influence whether a formal complaint is made then or not.

   Regular, up-to-date sexual harassment and bullying training is essential in all workplaces and it must be compulsory for all staff. This training must be in person rather than online and tailored to the needs of the workplace, for example if it is a large or small business, with the assistance of WorkSafe or the Commission. The training should also include contact details for free legal services to provide advice. Sexual harassment and bullying policies and training should also be given to all volunteers as part of their induction.

   I know of a case where a victim missed out on receiving the training as she had to help out with the case load of a colleague who was ill, and subsequently was sexually harassed over a period of time. If she had undergone the training, it would have helped her identify the abuse early on and act on it. Given that the perpetrator was a trusted supervisor, she found it difficult to distinguish the split between mentor and perpetrator.

Extensive judicial training on sexual harassment and its impact is also necessary to ensure that judges are appropriately handling these cases as mentioned in Chapter Six.

3. **Management training**: A zero tolerance of sexism should also be incorporated in all management training as well as a thorough examination of how to deal with sexual harassment and the importance of empathy towards complainants.

4. **Obligation to prevent sexual harassment:** The law must require every employer to take *all reasonable steps necessary* to prevent all forms of sex discrimination and sexual harassment—including sexual harassment by customers and clients. This obligation should exist regardless of whether incidents of sexual harassment or discrimination occur. There also needs to be a legislative obligation to promote gender equality. (Similar laws exist in the UK.)

   This means there must be zero tolerance by the employer for a sexist culture, regular sexual harassment training as discussed earlier, and the employer (wherever possible) must bring more women into management or supervisory roles—who also provide ethical leadership. I say this given that we know of some women who, like many men in power, have not handled sexual harassment complaints well and have been sexist. Severe penalties for failure to comply with these obligations are necessary. Detailed guidelines and binding codes of conduct should be provided by the Commission or WorkSafe.

5. **Independent oversight:** As discussed earlier, we must ensure that no organisation can secretly deal with sexual harassment. This could be achieved by using an oversight investigative model based on what is described in this chapter or similar to it, which includes mandatory reporting to this body and findings of guilt following the perpetrator, and appropriate data collection by this body

and a research/educative function. Annual reports to parliament by this body should be considered to aid transparency and accountability, and there should be a review on the effectiveness of this new oversight/investigative model within for example 5 years.

6. **Counselling:** Supports must also be in place for complainants to obtain independent, free counselling (and not simply a few sessions) through a therapist with expertise, rather than being referred by the employer to a counselling service where the therapists don't have the necessary skills nor independence from the employer. This is to ensure that complainants are evaluated and treated for post-traumatic stress disorder, depression, and other serious health issues arising from workplace sexual harassment or sex offences.

7. **Remove time limits:** A complainant of sexual harassment may be too traumatised or fearful to make a complaint immediately or soon after the event. Time limitations for making the complaint to state and federal human rights commissions/discrimination boards and seeking legal redress should therefore be removed. It is not appropriate to allow time limits even with a discretion for them to be waived—as this still creates uncertainty. If this is not accepted by government, then alternatively a six year time limit should be considered instead of the current 6 months at the federal level and 12 months at state level as they are completely inappropriate and unjust for such cases. Six years is the time frame for other employment matters, and frivolous or vexatious claims can still be struck out.

8. **Legal services:** Governments must ensure sufficient funding for free legal services to whatever extent is needed so that victims can assert their rights. This will also make employers take sexual harassment more seriously.

9. **De-identify complainants and protective costs orders:** Complainants should also be de-identified in all

conciliations and court and tribunal hearings to protect their privacy and prevent as much as possible further trauma. They must also have protection from costs orders against them unless their case is frivolous or vexatious. Otherwise complainants with valid claims who wish to litigate may fear doing so, and we must remember these matters do involve the public interest—particularly given the prevalence of sexual harassment.

10. **Conciliation:** Complainants should always be allowed to bypass conciliation and go straight to a court hearing. There are situations where the employer is not interested in any meaningful resolution of the matter at conciliation which only further traumatises a complainant, and a complainant may not wish to sign a confidentiality agreement to settle.

11. **Confidentiality agreements:** Confidentiality agreements which contain clauses to silence complainants must also be prohibited. However, laws must be in place to allow the negotiation of agreements that protect the privacy and reputation of the complainant. It should also be unlawful for employers to tell complainants that they cannot tell anyone what happened to them.

   In addition, employers must be prohibited from entering into confidentiality agreements with perpetrators found guilty by an internal investigation or who admitted guilt, where such agreements prohibit employers from making any comments or taking action that could suggest or imply to anyone that the perpetrator committed any unlawful conduct.

12. **Victimisation and rehabilitation:** We need laws that make it clear that employers must take all reasonable steps necessary to prevent and address all forms of victimisation as discussed earlier. And secondly, to provide rehabilitation and reintegration of victims back into the workplace

after an internal investigation. High penalties for failure to comply are necessary for both breaches. This would signal to staff that such matters are taken seriously and that victims who speak up will be supported rather than shunned or silenced. This is essential to help prevent sexual harassment. If the victim is too traumatised to return to the same workplace, then financial assistance and all other necessary assistance must be given to help her or him seek work elsewhere.

13. **Dysfunctional workplaces:** Employers/managers must ensure that no misconduct in the workplace is tolerated and that healthy professional boundaries are enforced at all times. Perpetrators thrive in a dysfunctional workplace—it helps them assume the mentor role, for example, with the young women employed whilst other managers and staff are not acting professionally and getting away with it.

   Employers must also ensure that the people they promote and hire as managers and supervisors have both the necessary expertise in their role and are approachable so that perpetrators are not given as much opportunity to groom potential victims. Nor would victims be left in a situation where they need to seek the perpetrator's assistance with their work, so they are then better able to keep their distance and make a report of sexual harassment.

14. **Other workplace laws:** Employers must be backed by workplace laws to take strong disciplinary action, including sacking an employee not only in relation to sexual harassment but also other serious forms of misconduct, such as employees downloading pornography at work or bringing hardcopy pornography into the workplace. This sends a clear signal to staff that no unlawful activity or serious misconduct will be tolerated.

15. **Audits:** Workplaces should be subject to unannounced audits, which would include examining their strategies to

eliminate and prevent sexual harassment and all forms of sex discrimination, promoting gender equality, conducting sexual harassment and bullying training, and handling of complaints.

16. **Reparations:** There should be a reparations scheme established to compensate survivors of sexual harassment.

17. **Power:** We need to change our patriarchal concept of power, as discussed in the last chapter on true power.

Note: All changes to the law must also ensure a fair process for respondents to allegations of sexual harassment as well.

The national inquiry into sexual harassment will hopefully lead to major law reform and public education on this issue. But again, none of the problems here are new—they have been raised by myself and other advocates with previous Sex Discrimination Commissioners, in state equal opportunity reviews, as well as with the *National Senate Inquiry into the Effectiveness of the Sex Discrimination Act 1984* back in 2008.

It is a shame that it is taking this long to gain more serious attention and movement on this issue—a shame that it has taken celebrities in Hollywood calling out sexual abuse and igniting the #MeToo movement in order to help create a cultural shift when every day women have been speaking out for so long and have been silenced.

We also have to recognise the role that traditional media and governments play in this; the huge momentum of the #MeToo movement was not only due to celebrities being involved. It was also due in part to women around the world finally finding a way to get their voices heard. They found a media platform to speak of the prevalence of violence against women and pointing out that the legal framework for handling complaints was sometimes ineffectual and even causing more harm.

-9-

Patriarchy, Race, and Culture

'We took the traditional lands and smashed the traditional way of life. We brought the disease, the alcohol; we committed the murders; we took the children from their mothers; we practised discrimination and exclusion, it was our ignorance and our prejudice. And our failure to imagine that these things could be done to us.'[206]

It was the 10th of December 1992, and our Prime Minister Paul Keating was the first political leader who spoke the truth of what happened to Indigenous Australians under white patriarchal colonial rule, acknowledging the injustices perpetrated beginning with dispossession. Telling the truth and bearing witness is extremely important; we have understood this for victims and survivors of South Africa's apartheid, we have understood this in relation to inquiries and the royal commission into child sexual abuse in Australia, and more recently with a national inquiry into sexual harassment. But white Australia still has a problem with bearing witness for Indigenous Australians—to fully confront the fact that Australia was invaded by white colonialists, not 'just settled', and that as Stan Grant says, we have much work to do to find solutions to the problems that beset the first Australians.[207]

I remember when the High Court in the case of Eddie Koiki Mabo v Queensland struck down the doctrine of *terra nullius* six months prior to Paul Keating's speech. It was a doctrine which said that Australia was uninhabited when the white man came and that Aboriginal people had no rights. The fact that such a legal doctrine was allowed to exist is mind-boggling and abhorrent. It attests to a legal system devoid of empathy, compassion, and integrity, and one underpinned by racism. And yet still there were certain politicians and media critics, such as former Victorian Premier Jeff Kennett, who claimed that the High Court's decision was a danger to our society and meant that our backyards would be taken away. Of course they have been proved wrong.

The racism that underpinned the doctrine of *terra nullius* also underpinned Aboriginal Australians not being given the right to vote in Australian federal elections until 1962, when the Menzies Liberal and Country government legislated for it. They also weren't granted citizenship status until 1967 via a referendum. It's a sobering thought that the first people who lived here and who cared for the land far more than white people weren't even considered citizens until then.

Child sexual abuse is another area where racism as well as double standards came to light towards Aboriginal people. White Australia was quick to react with outcry concerning revelations of child sexual abuse in Indigenous communities during the Howard government era that led to the *Intervention* (coercive measures, including welfare quarantining, that some people argue were overall ineffective[208]). But no such outcry or quick action was taken against white perpetrators of sexual abuse of aboriginal children in Nhulunbuy in 2004 when the issue was raised by aboriginal elder Bakamumu Marika with the Northern Territory Police. Germaine Greer reveals in her book, *On Rage*, that the situation was even highlighted in the report of the Northern Territory Board of Inquiry into the protection of Aboriginal children called

Little Children Are Sacred—the same report that triggered the government's *Intervention*. And still no action was taken.[209]

When juvenile prostitution for white men finally made the headlines in 2008, local magnate Galarrwuy Yunupingu said it was known by everybody to have gone on and it was about time an authority stamped it out.[210] These aren't isolated incidents, either. Greer writes that according to Judy Atkinson, Professor of Indigenous Studies at Southern Cross University, Aboriginal adolescents are abused in every state, while prostitution and suicide were unknown in pre-contact Aboriginal societies.[211]

Just when we may have thought that we had heard everything about the damaging impact of white patriarchal society on Aboriginal people, another shocking revelation came to light in 2018. It was reported in the media that children who had been made wards of the state had also been given a criminal record for this. Such injustice has had a disproportionate impact on Aboriginal children. Until the early 1990s, the Children's Court did not differentiate between the handling of child protection and criminal matters it dealt with. Taungurung elder Uncle Larry Walsh was one such victim of this injustice. He told NITV News that the criminal record he had after being stolen from his family when just a toddler had serious consequences for the rest of his life.

'In court, I'd say "come on your honour, 1956, I was two and a half years old, how can I have a criminal conviction from then?" But nobody would answer that question, and every time I argued with them, it would only make my record worse. Another time, a judge called me a disgrace to my race, because of, again, that thing of having a conviction since 1956.'[212]

The Victorian government recognised how reprehensible this injustice was and knew that it had to act fast. Not long after the revelations, it introduced laws to prevent historical care and child protection orders from being treated as a finding of guilt or conviction.[213]

Yet despite all that I have told you, some white Australians still question the need to look at the impact of white patriarchy on Indigenous Australians. They may even ask, 'But didn't white Australia apologise recently for the racism? Haven't our governments spent enough money already to solve the problem of Indigenous disadvantage?'

On the 13 February 2008 the then-Prime Minister Kevin Rudd did apologise on behalf of white Australia for the generations of Indigenous Australians stolen from their families and placed with white families and in institutional care. This apology was an important step in the right direction. However, successive governments have failed to eliminate the systemic inequality and poverty faced by Australia's First People.

According to a 2017 Closing the Gap report, the Indigenous employment rate was 48.4 per cent, compared with 72.6 per cent for non-Indigenous Australians. It also showed that Australia is not on track to close the life expectancy gap by 2031, or halve the employment gap. Disparities also remain in child mortality rates, family violence rates, and education levels. According to the Productivity Commission, in the past 17 years the adult imprisonment rate has increased by 77 per cent.[214]

Patriarchy and Aboriginal women

Celeste Liddle also highlights the additional problems faced by Aboriginal women due to white patriarchy in her 2014 article, *Intersectionality And Indigenous Feminism: An Aboriginal Woman's Perspective*. For many years, Aboriginal people were not paid at all for their labour and Aboriginal women in particular were strongly affected, as they often worked as domestic servants. Liddle says that their wages were in many cases held in trusts by governments and so their stolen wages claims are ongoing many years later.

Liddle also refers to how Aboriginal women have not only had to deal with white patriarchy but also 'black patriarchy.' This is comprised of patriarchal structures inherited through colonization by mainstream culture, and secondly through traditional Indigenous practices and how they view and assign gender roles.

There is also the adoption of white patriarchal cultural practices to try to enhance Aboriginal pride, when in fact such practices further entrench gender inequality and sexism. A prime example is the Miss NAIDOC pageants. Liddle says beauty pageants make the statement that a woman's physical attractiveness is her most important attribute, and so Miss NAIDOC pageants reinforce this for Aboriginal women. This is extremely disappointing since Liddle explains that Aboriginal culture values age and wisdom, thus affording greater value to older Aboriginal women. Yet older Aboriginal women are excluded when it comes to beauty. A major problem with our white patriarchal society is that we don't value wisdom or our elders enough, and here is yet another example of where it would be better for us to learn from positive Aboriginal practices rather than Aboriginal people incorporating our white patriarchal ones.

Liddle also highlights that Aboriginal women are dying from intimate partner violence ten times as often as other women and yet this barely rates a mention in our society. In addition, racism towards Aboriginal women and Aboriginal people in general underpins our legal system. In an article for Eureka Street, *Police Still Failing Aboriginal Women*, Liddle says this is seen in the case of Linda. Rockhampton journalist Amy McQuire and human rights advocate Martin Hodgson uncovered that police cared so little about the murder of this Aboriginal woman that they failed to investigate it properly, leading to the imprisonment of an Aboriginal man, Kevin Henry, for 26 years despite the fact that he has always maintained his innocence. And despite bringing to light evidence of a coercive confession and other critical shortcomings, no public outcry has occurred.

Then there is the brutal rape of Lynette Daley, who was left to bleed to death by two men. The NSW Director of Public

Prosecutions failed twice to take the perpetrators to court, arguing there was insufficient evidence to do so. Due to the perseverance of Lynette's family members and two influential Aboriginal women pursuing the matter, the case was eventually heard in court, where it took the jury only 32 minutes to deliver guilty verdicts due to the strength of the evidence against the two men.[215]

Reforms needed

So what are some of the solutions to the problems faced by the first Australians? Change the Record, a coalition of leading Aboriginal and Torres Strait Islander, human rights, and community organisations, have done much work in this area. They released a blueprint in November 2015 for closing the gap in imprisonment rates of Aboriginal and Torres Strait Islander people and reducing the disproportionate violence that the groups, especially women and children, experienced.[216] This has involved calling for a whole-of-government approach at the state and federal levels that includes:

- justice targets to reduce imprisonment rates
- ensuring that all laws to close the gap have a human rights approach,
- investing resources into strengthening communities with a justice reinvestment approach, as discussed earlier in this book,
- ensuring local community input,
- community-oriented policing,
- prohibiting mandatory sentencing,
- eliminating unnecessary imprisonment,
- prioritising rehabilitation for offenders, and
- ensuring that all policy solutions are underpinned by the principle of self-determination and respect for the culture of Aboriginal and Torres Strait Islander people.

It is also important that treaties are fully established with the First Nations people throughout Australia in close consultation with their elders.

Dr Hannah McGlade, Senior Indigenous Research Fellow at Curtin University adds there must be support for Aboriginal Healing centres, respected elders and traditional healers, as well as men and women's groups and healing on country.[217] She also says that paternalistic welfare policies, such as the cashless debit card, are not helpful and in fact do more harm. Applying such policies to whole Aboriginal communities in response to the few perpetrators of child sex abuse does not make sense, and there have been reports of cashless debit cards being traded in for cash, which makes households poorer. When children are left so hungry and deprived, they are more vulnerable to child exploitation by criminals.[218]

In relation to the high child mortality rates amongst Aboriginal children compared to non-Aboriginal children, Dr Andrew Scott looks again to the Nordic countries for assistance. Whilst they also have Indigenous populations, there is little sign of significant health problems amongst them compared to non-Indigenous children. In addition, experts in the field have said that Australia's high child mortality rate for Aboriginal children is probably due to social rather than medical factors. And so countries like Sweden should be studied for solutions. They also say that reducing inequality and investing in the early years of life enhance children's wellbeing.[219] To this I add that we also should be consulting more with Aboriginal and Torres Strait Islander communities and hearing from them what is needed.

We also need to acknowledge where governments and non-government organisations are getting it right—for example investing in educational scholarships for Indigenous students for secondary, university, TAFE and registered training organisations (RTOs). Some workplaces also have internships or clerkship programs for Indigenous Australians along with a reconciliation and Indigenous employment plan. Investment in programs targeted specifically to meet Indigenous people's needs, including those living in remote areas, are helpful as well.

But we also can't run from fully acknowledging our dark past. Jens Korff on his resource website about Australian Aboriginal culture called *Creative Spirits*, questions the denial of contemporary white Australia of the massacres and genocide of the Aboriginal population. He says that Australians may be afraid of their shadow side that used to 'hunt' these people, poisoning and slaughtering them.[220] It's a shadow side we need to face and learn lessons from before we can truly move forward.

Clearly much more work needs to be done by us as a nation for reconciliation that achieves equality for Indigenous Australians whilst we join with the values of truth, love, and kindness.

Asylum seekers

The devastating impact of patriarchy isn't only seen on Indigenous Australians, it is also seen in the treatment of asylum seekers, who are also viewed as the 'Other' without a common humanity and shared interests. Mandatory detention policies, indefinite detention, and offshore detention have led to the re-traumatisation of detainees, including some engaging in self-harm and suicide ideation.

In March 2009, the United Nations Human Rights Committee recommended that Australia should abolish the remaining elements of its mandatory detention policy, but our government didn't listen, pursuing a patriarchal hardline approach devoid of empathy and fairness.

Under our immigration system children, women, and men have been detained behind barbed wire, and laws were in place until 2009 allowing our government to charge them for the costs of detention.[221]

Our immigration system has treated asylum seekers like criminals when they haven't committed a crime, and subjected them to ongoing neglect despite criticism from the United Nations Human Rights Committee and reminders that these people are seeking asylum from persecution. And whilst our successive governments have wrongfully said that asylum seekers arriving by boat are coming here illegally, in 2018 an independent body of human rights experts that are part of the United Nations Human Rights Council condemned Australia for the illegal indefinite detention of refugees and asylum seekers without charge.[222]

Such concerns were raised within Australia many years ago. I recall a meeting between Department of Immigration officials and lawyers like myself, mental health professionals, and case workers and social workers for asylum seekers in 2006. We told Department officials of the problems of mandatory detention and indefinite detention. It was an abusive system in violation of international law. But we also explained what successful humane alternatives existed in countries like Sweden where asylum seekers were dealt with on a case by case basis and lived in the community with appropriate supports. Community-based care not only had a high compliance rate, but there were large savings in costs as well by not using the mandatory detention regime. So it also made economic sense to dismantle it. Some of us hoped that the government would swiftly take action, but we were to say the least disappointed.

People also weren't being told the whole truth as to why asylum seekers who breached a visa condition ended up in a detention centre. They were viewed as serious law breakers who had to be punished. And yet they included asylum seekers (one of whom was my client) who sought menial jobs in breach of their visa conditions because they could not survive solely on the assistance they received from charities and felt ashamed about this. The fact that such people were detained because they took action to stop themselves from starving was reprehensible.

Fast forward to 2017, and *The Guardian* revealed that confidential documents from inside Australia's offshore detention centre on Manus island showed brutal conditions inside. This included persistently high rates of self-harm, repeated suicide attempts, regular violent and sexual assaults, and warnings of an emerging culture of drug use by staff and detainees.[223]

In 2018, 1,369 people were still held at key sites being Villawood, Christmas Island, and Yongah Hill, with some spending more than two years in detention. Many were detained because they came by boat, despite the fact that most asylum seekers arriving by boat are found to be genuine refugees by a rigorous and stringent system of assessment in Australia.[224] And we still have children in detention facilities at the time of writing.[225]

The situation worsened on the 5th of October 2018. After almost one year of working on Nauru, the Australian government told Medicins Sans Frontieres (Doctors Without Borders) that their mental health services were no longer needed and that they should leave the island within 24 hours. The medical organisation rightly responded by condemning the indefinite, unfair, offshore detention of refugees and asylum seekers, saying that the mental health problems of detainees were beyond desperate. Children were suffering from traumatic withdrawal syndrome, unable to eat or drink or even walk to the toilet due to being so distressed. Some of these children had been on Nauru for four years. This appalling situation led to a growing call to end both mandatory and offshore detention.

Such a cruel, inhumane response to adults and children fleeing persecution is the sign of a society gone mad—but that is what patriarchy is, an insane thought system that leads not only to a lack of compassion, empathy, and sensitivity but also to brutality.

I would not be surprised if we at some point had a royal commission into Australia's treatment of asylum seekers and refugees, although it would come too late. We have had royal commissions and inquiries into so many other areas where cruel and inhumane treatment has occurred. At the very least there will need to be a national apology.

But as I write this section, our federal parliament passed the Medical Evacuation Bill to allow refugees on Manus Island and Nauru to come to Australia for medical treatment, although it was opposed by the government. Perhaps this will eventually lead to Australia's current policy towards asylum seekers and refugees being replaced with one that is humane and fair? Unfortunately, I am not hopeful at this stage.

Migrants

The desire to dominate, control and humiliate others has manifested in racism towards migrants in Australia and the rest of the world. The abusers fail to realise or don't even care that these migrants are also dealing with the added stress of the unfamiliar, and trying to start a new life and belong. They have come here seeking better opportunities, better job prospects, to be reunited with family, and in some cases seeking freedom from persecution, war, and other trauma. They share our insecurities and anxieties and, like us, want to be happy and free from suffering. They are in fact our brothers and sisters.

Some migrants have also been racist towards citizens of countries they settle in and towards each other. Prejudice is in all of us if we are truly honest, and this can include racism. An unfounded fear is also at the heart of this prejudice—fear of the 'Other', of difference that one does not understand, and the projection of all our own guilt and hatred onto the 'Other', which only increases our fear. Let's look briefly at examples of this in Australia with migrants and consider whether or not any positive changes have occurred.

During the gold rush era, racism was directed towards Chinese migrants trying their luck in our vast country. Authorities made them pay unfair taxes that left them in massive debt, having to work like slaves to pay it off whilst also suffering from racist abuse. Fortunately, some prominent Australians, like the passionate social justice advocate Caroline Chisholm, criticised this racism. But often this fell on deaf ears. In 2017, the Victorian Premier made an apology to the descendants of these Chinese migrants as we come to terms with our racist past and learn from our mistakes.[226] We could see where prejudice and unfounded fear leads—to the abuse of others.

The history of racism in Australia includes the White Australia Policy that was in force from Federation to the mid-twentieth century when it was gradually phased out. This policy was based on our fear of other races and cultures and was designed to keep Australia white and British. Each time relaxations in the policy were made such as in the 1950s to allow non-British migrants to enter Australia, some racist resistance was encountered.

For example, in the 1950s, Greek Cypriots and other migrants were discriminated against, even though the Australian government wanted them here to help build our post-World War II economy. The discrimination occurred not only in the workplace but with everyday interactions. Some were told to *sit at the back of the bus or else,* and Australian men picked fights with them, calling them *dirty wogs* and worse. Children in school yards hurled racist slurs whilst migrant children desperately tried to fit in. There were no laws against race discrimination then. Fortunately there were also many Australians who weren't racist but were instead welcoming and kind to these and other migrants. And yet, racism by some of the population continued with each new wave of immigration, including Asian and Middle-Eastern immigration.

On the other hand I know of Anglo-Australian women who were not accepted in the past by all members of the migrant communities they married into because they were of a different race and culture. As a consequence, they had to deal at times with being put down and shunned. Anglo-Australian women and girls were also viewed by certain members as 'sluts' due to racism and the sexist resentment of their greater social freedoms. And I knew when growing up that in Europe and other parts of the world, there was a history of racism based on the idea that 'purity of the race' was something to be proud of—so mixed race marriages were easily frowned upon (unless of course they involved aristocratic alliances). But again we must also remember that most members of migrant communities welcome Anglo-Australians.

We also have the shameful history of some Australian men who were serial sponsors of Asian women, abusing them in horrific circumstances, and then disposing of them to be replaced by another. This was an issue of racism, sexism, and exploitation that marred our image of embracing multiculturalism. It also highlighted that patriarchal authorities at the time failed to understand that migrant wives are particularly vulnerable to abuse.[227] Fortunately, this began to change when in 1994 laws were introduced to make it illegal for anyone to sponsor more than two people on partner visas in a lifetime—the second application must be at least five years after the first.

Meanwhile, a 2017 survey on racism commissioned by the broadcaster SBS with Western Sydney University had both good news and bad news. The good news is that it found strong community support for cultural diversity and action against racism. But unfortunately, it also found that racism is still a serious problem. People from non-English speaking backgrounds reported the highest rates of racism in the workplace (54.1 per cent) and education (55.8 per cent). They also reported high rates of racism in every day interactions including shopping.[228]

There are some Australians who still long for the White Australia of old, who cannot embrace the vitality of multiculturalism, and are also on the look-out for vulnerable groups to project their hate onto. This is why it is so important that in Australia we have laws against race discrimination and racial vilification at the state and federal levels. Nationally, the *Race Discrimination Act* was introduced in 1975 and laws against racial vilification added in 1995. These laws have to some extent helped to combat racism and make it clear it is unacceptable though more work is needed to reduce it. Community education campaigns promoting ethnic diversity and our media reflecting more multicultural images have also played an important role to reduce racism and still do.

Since the end of the White Australia Policy we have increased our understanding of the harms of racism and the value of multiculturalism—accepting the very best in our diverse races and cultures, respecting Australian democratic values, and remembering our common humanity. We are all interconnected and part of one whole. The global rise of nationalism, the far right, and terrorism, are a serious threat though to mutual respect, understanding, and safety and so we must be vigilant.

Culture

When I was at secondary school, my legal studies teacher posed the question as to whether a person's cultural background should be taken into consideration when they commit an offence and lessen the sentence because in his or her culture the behaviour might be acceptable. I remember the sick feeling I had in my stomach at the time, of thinking how could we ever say it is justifiable to afford women and children less protection under the law from abuse due to men of more patriarchal cultures justifying their actions on cultural grounds. It was where my mind immediately went. Fortunately, our law does not do this.

I recall a case of incest and physical abuse when I undertook a work placement with the Sexual Offences section of the Office of Public Prosecutions. The victim, a teenage girl, was sexually abused by her father over a long period of time, and in addition he would throw her onto the floor and kick her repeatedly. When it came to sentencing the father, he argued through his lawyer that the physical abuse he inflicted upon his daughter was appropriate discipline in his European culture—that this was acceptable in his home country and so his actions should be dealt with leniently. Fortunately, the Judge hearing the matter made it clear that such arguments were inappropriate and that the father would be tried according to Australian law and Australian standards. It was also highly improbable that in his culture such abuse would be seen as acceptable and even if it was, it was irrelevant here. This was a win for the rights of children and women everywhere.

But such enlightened views did not exist throughout the legal profession. This became apparent when I worked on deportation cases as a junior lawyer. If such matters involved men who committed rape in Australia but came from a more patriarchal culture than our own, my supervisor thought it appropriate to argue as a defence that in the client's home country it was part of his culture to view and treat women poorly. I refused to put such arguments.

We have also had to enact laws in Australia to prohibit misogynistic cultural practices that occur in other countries, such as female genital mutilation, and strengthen laws prohibiting child marriage. These are important examples of ensuring that all females, regardless of their cultural background, should have protection from abuse and that all perpetrators are equal before the law and held to account.

But after focusing on patriarchy's impact on the lives of people through the justice system and our cultural landscape, what about its impact on our relationship to nature and animals? Are there justice issues here that the law needs to address and does this have implications for our economic model? And how does the fact that patriarchy underpins our economic development and technological advances influence our wellbeing?

-10-

Nature, the Economy, and Technology

Fiona Stafford has a poetic eye for the beauty of trees and forests. She writes of the translucence of trees after rain, of thick dark foliage and sunny leaves, of peeling skins and fresh smells and sap.[229] Their histories and myths abound in her book *The Long Long Life of Trees*, including a 2000 year old Kauri tree that is the God of the Forests, son of the sky and earth in the Maori culture. Called the Tana Mahuta, it stands tall in the Waipoua Forest.[230]

The writer John Fowles loved forests, too. They nourished his creativity and spirit as he wandered along trails not knowing where they would lead, ever curious and open to the serenity and peace of the towering trees shielding him with their great canopies. But John Fowles also knew that nature was in danger. He spoke of how the tree itself is crucified in the modern world instead of Christ, as we are consumed by greed and stupidity.[231]

Our growing loss of the poetic enchantment and beauty of nature has plunged us into a crisis. We must confront patriarchy's denigration of our environment and the impact that this has on us. The narcissism and aggression fueled by this thought system is destroying our natural world and threatens our very human existence. Ecofeminism, which emerged in the late 1970s and early '80s, sees the inextricable connection between the exploitation of women and the exploitation of the environment within the context of patriarchy. It understands that we need a new approach to save our natural world and ourselves. We must radically change our attitudes towards nature and our way of life—leading to changes in our economic model, the law, and even how we regard technology. This is an important justice issue where the wellbeing of humans, animals, and the environment are interconnected and so all are at stake.

One of the world's most pre-eminent elders and scientists, David Suzuki, also understands that we are facing the eleventh hour. His book *The Legacy*, published back in 2010, makes lucid points on this issue and the way forward. Much of this chapter draws on Suzuki's ideas and those of feminists and mental health professionals as they complement other points on patriarchy in this book and also the later discussion on where true power lies.

In the beginning....

Our ancient indigenous ancestors were not the unintelligent savages that many people assume, says David Suzuki. Anthropologist Claude Levi-Strauss even believed there was no reason why there wouldn't have been those with the minds of the calibre of a Plato or Einstein, although applying their minds to the solution of different problems at the time.[232]

Experts tell us that our ancestors had a profound understanding of the natural world and their place within it, as well as a reverence for Mother Earth. This knowledge and reverence has been carried through indigenous cultures right up to the present day.

From what we know from Australian Aboriginal culture in 1788, their management of the natural world was not passive but rather active and required much expertise. Bill Gammage writes in his book, *The Biggest Estate on Earth: How Aborigines Made Australia*, that Aboriginal people were alert to season and circumstance, committed to a balance of life achieved through caring for all their country. The law was an ecological philosophy that was enforced by religious sanction and ensured that a systematic and scientific approach was used in managing the land, one that provided for a myriad of practices to deal with an uncertain climate and nature's restless cycles. The law also required that people leave the world as they found it.[233]

Their chief management method was fire and knowledge of the life cycles of native plants to ensure plentiful wildlife and plant foods throughout the year. Consequently, Aboriginal people did not require as much time and effort as Europeans to acquire food and establish shelter.

Gammage writes that what plants and animals flourished related to their management. Land was managed at a local level and detailed local knowledge was crucial. Each family knew their own area intimately and cared for it whilst also knowing well the ground of their neighbours and clansmen. They could therefore share larger management or assume additional responsibility of land if need be. The sheer scale of the enterprise was massive and breathtaking. And people still, generally, had plenty to eat, few hours of work each day, and much time for spiritual practices and leisure.

Three rules directed management by Aboriginal people. Firstly, they needed to make sure that all life flourished. Secondly, plants and animals had to be made abundant as well as convenient. Thirdly, Aboriginal people acted local whilst maintaining a universal perspective and way of thinking.[234]

Australian Aborigines truly saw themselves (and still do) as protectors of Mother Nature.

An environment teetering on the edge

Fast forward to the 21st century and Australia and the rest of the world are dealing with a myriad of environmental problems. Instead of working with nature, Suzuki says that we have as a species single-handedly been altering the biological, chemical, and physical properties of the planet at an explosive speed.

This has been accompanied by costs we haven't foreseen due to our primitive knowledge of systems, such as insecticides reducing bird populations and even high levels of DDT found in the breasts and milk of women.[235]

Alarmingly, research by Rachel Carson also found a connection between synthetic chemicals such as DDT and cancer. Heidi Hutner speaks of Carson's work in her TED Talk in 2015 on *Eco-Grief and Ecofeminism*. Hutner also discovered further research showing connections between toxic chemicals and this disease. She says that one in four men and one in five women in the US will get cancer at a time when there is increasing environmental pollution, and babies today are born with hundreds of chemicals in their bodies.

Meanwhile, we have been burning fossil fuels at unprecedented rates and, as Suzuki and other scientists warn, adding to greenhouse gases more than any other time in human existence. This contributes to climate change and its corresponding catastrophic ecological damage. In nature, everything is connected, so as more heat-trapping gases are added to the atmosphere, polar ice melts and oceans warm and expand. Animals and plants have had to relocate from temperature changes, altering ecosystems which are fundamental to our basic needs.[236]

And yet we live as if the ecosystems don't matter. Their web of life is continually damaged in various ways, such as thousands of species being driven to extinction annually. Scientists now say one million plant and animal species are set for extinction in the next ten years.[237] Our destruction of ecosystems is happening through our de-forestation of vast tracks of land and other forms of environmental damage.

And what is happening in our oceans? Unfortunately, marine biologists warn that if we do not radically change our fishing practices by 2048, there will be no commercially viable fish species left in the sea.[238] The rise of industrialized fishing, with super trawlers taking massive quantities of fish, is having a negative impact. So is the pollution of our oceans as plastic and garbage tossed into them are later being found in the stomachs of sea animals.[239]

In Australia we are still continuing in the tradition of many of the new white settlers who had little regard for nature. They were, as Professor T.G. Strehlow said, acting on an unrestrained lust of killing for its own sake and living by the adage, *If it moves shoot it, if it doesn't chop it down*.[240]

We are also grappling with the significant impact of climate change on Australia's water security. As rainfall patterns have been shifting, the Climate Council of Australia says that the severity of droughts and floods has increased. They predict that the risk to our water security will worsen unless we have rapid and deep reductions in greenhouse gas pollution.[241]

The world is also grappling with relentless population growth whilst there has been a decline in food production and the area of agricultural land has shrunk. Scientists say Canada, like other nations, is using immigration to keep the numbers and the economy growing but the ecological cost is not factored in.[242] This is happening in Australia, as well. In December 2018, the Prime Minister of Australia met with state Premiers and Territory leaders to finally discuss population growth and how best to deal with it. But whilst this included assessing the impact of such growth on infrastructure (which is very important), there was no mention of the impact on our ecology—a highly critical issue.

If we don't change our approach, scientists warn that science and technology may not be able to prevent irreversible degradation of the natural environment and continued poverty for much of the world.[243] The Swiss psychiatrist Dr Carl Jung also believed that if we do not take moral responsibility for overpopulation and environmental problems, nature may seek a resolution though a violent response such as accidents, illness, or disease.[244]

A New Direction

We can't keep living like this. We have reached our own 'rock bottom' as a society and need a new direction that encompasses the following:

1) Listening to people who want action on climate change

Many people, especially young people, understand that we are facing an environmental crisis that threatens our future. Thousands of school students in Australia even went on strike on the 29th of November 2018 as part of the Strike 4 Climate Action movement. The purpose was to voice their concerns over governments in Australia and worldwide not taking the issue of climate change as seriously as they should and failing to introduce measures required to tackle it. More student strikes also happened in 2019 due to the urgency of the situation. Australia's Coalition government had already thought it appropriate to bring a lump of coal into parliament to make light of the issue in 2017, whilst refusing to have effective climate policies that included phasing out coal usage. Then in 2019 Pacific Island nations said Australia must do more as they face rising sea levels which threaten their survival. In response, our Deputy Prime Minister said Pacific Islanders would survive with rising sea levels because many of their workers 'come here to pick fruit.' This is the patriarchal mentality we are dealing with. Not surprisingly, the Fijian Prime Minister called these comments very insulting.[245]

2) Listening to our elders and their wisdom

We need to listen to the elders in our society, including the elders of Indigenous communities, to change our way of living, our approach to our environment, and learn sustainability. Elders such as the late Ecofeminist Grace Paley and Inuit Elder Annette

Helmer remind us the earth is our wealth[246] and we must respect all living things, embrace non-violence, and be caretakers of earth for future generations to enjoy.

Elders also help us know what was in the past and what should be now. They tell us abundance was the norm and that is how we should be measuring progress. For example, Suzuki says whilst a person who fishes may think all is well because a 200-pound sword fish was caught all the way up at Newfoundland, a much older fisherman recounts that he used to fish just 6 miles out of Boston and would throw back anything under 200 pounds. Both are fishers with very different perspectives of what is a healthy baseline.[247]

3) Protecting our environment makes good economic sense

Business people and politicians need to understand that looking after the environment and reducing greenhouse gas emissions is necessary for economic prosperity. And the environment must never be subservient to the economy if we are to survive.[248] Suzuki says we are not immune to the laws of nature and our most fundamental needs come from the biosphere, so raising the economy above this is in fact suicidal.[249] We need clean air, clean water, clean soil, healthy crops, and protection from extreme weather conditions to live.

The late feminist lawyer and environmentalist, Marie Byles, also said we can't keep stealing from Mother Earth fixed on the old profit motives. Instead we must look after nature, recognising that humans are not the centre of the universe but that we are closely connected to the environment, as well.[250] Because of this connection, both humans and nature thrive when the environment is cared for.

Whenever business and governments say that they need to put the economy above the environment, they also fail to realise that governments should be factoring in 'nature's services' to be economically responsible, when considering any development. Nature's services include water filtration, flood control, waste treatment, providing habitats for wildlife, climate stabilization, and recreation. Suzuki says that while ecosystem services are in effect priceless and keep the planet healthy, it is possible to show some monetary value for them. His foundation did this in a study called *Ontario's Wealth, Canada's Future*. It estimated that $2.7 billion worth of ecosystem services was obtained annually in the 1.8 million hectare greenbelt of land surrounding Toronto. Meanwhile, developers would provide a one-time injection of money only.[251]

Economists, governments, and business people also need to see other ways that sustainability and making money can go together. Environmentalist Tony Juniper wrote in *The Guardian* in 2013 of research already showing that pharmaceutical companies make billions of dollars from the genetic diversity of wild species found in forests. The carbon capture rate that is achieved through halving the rate of deforestation by 2030 is equated into trillions of dollars. And bees and other animals provide services that contribute to agricultural sales in the billions per year. Not to mention the large sums of money from tourism in forests and wildlife parks and reserves.[252]

Meanwhile, we are becoming increasingly aware in Australia and overseas that there are jobs in efficient renewable energy and alternative technologies in which governments should be investing heavily. Looking after the environment and providing jobs for people can and should go together. Even some business people and former politicians on the right of the political spectrum embrace renewable energies and protecting our natural world. They include former Liberal Party leader Dr. John Hewson. It makes sense to invest in energy that is cheaper to run, more efficient, doesn't pollute our environment or put it at risk.

So what else needs to be done to protect nature, address climate change, and ensure our economic prosperity? A reasonable tax on carbon emissions and setting meaningful renewable energy targets are also essential. Closing coal-fired power stations must happen whilst transitioning the workers of such stations to other employment such as in efficient renewables. A prosperous economy also requires sustainable farming practices that preserve the environment and even enrich it. We already know for example the harm that intensive dairy farming has done by polluting waterways in New Zealand.

The time of listening to patriarchal men who deny climate change and the need to care for the environment for our economic prosperity and for our very survival, such as the Trumps, Putins, and Tony Abbotts of the world has got to be over.

4) Change our approach to the economy

Suzuki joins other environmentalists and ecofeminists in advocating for an important radical approach—that consumption should no longer be the driver of the economy. It has led to products being deliberately made not to last, discarded so that they return to the planet as waste. In addition, nature cannot replenish renewable resources such as trees, fish, soil, et cetera at a rate needed to keep up with our level of consumption.[253]

If consumption is no longer the driver of the economy, this provides us with the opportunity to place the environment and people's wellbeing at the heart of the economy instead. But some economists need to be convinced of this, especially where they see no barriers to the constant expansion of the economy and our level of consumption. They need to listen to other experts, such as physicists, who say that relentless growth is impossible in all systems.[254]

Suzuki adds that we must question whether or not growth really should be the goal of our economy and look at both the context within which it occurs and its impact.[255] We also need a different way of measuring progress that tells us what we really need to know: are we improving our quality of life? The GDP can't do this. But there is already another method we can consider that measures what is truly important to us. The GPI (Genuine Progress Indicator) can tell us about income distribution, the value of household work, higher education, volunteering, the cost of crime, resource depletion, pollution, environmental damage, and disposable goods. Suzuki says that the GPI tells us the reality (that governments don't speak of)—that the majority of us are working harder and longer with no improvement in our quality of life or time spent with family, community, and expressing other important aspects of ourselves in hobbies or other interests.[256]

Feminist Eva Cox wrote in 1996 in her book *Leading Women* of the danger in us not prioritizing relationships and community in our economic model that is so focused on the profit motive.[257] But our governments didn't listen. We shouldn't despair, though. There are signs of change. In New Zealand, Prime Minister Jacinda Ardern's government delivered a 'wellbeing budget' for 2019 that focuses on policies to improve the wellbeing of its citizens, especially the vulnerable. Significant investment is made in the following key areas: tackling mental health, child poverty, and family and sexual violence. We can build on this approach not only with the proposed reforms discussed in earlier chapters, but also with a radical change in our approach to the economy and the free market outlined in this chapter. But experts say we must act now.

5) A non-patriarchal economy

We need to leave behind a patriarchal, materialistic, and mechanistic approach to the economy. And embrace one that understands the connection between the environment and the mental health, wellbeing, and survival of humanity as well as economic prosperity. It's not one or the other. This fundamental shift in our thinking includes the following:

a. Considering future generations

In the past, it was understood that we had a sacred duty to pass onto future generations a world that is as rich or richer than the one we came into. North American Aboriginals traditionally considered their ancestors when making a decision and then thought ahead to how their decision-making might affect the seventh generation after them.[258]

Imagine if our community and business leaders and politicians made decisions thinking beyond the short term and their own self-interest and towards future consequences and impacts on future generations...

b. Everything is connected: the holistic approach

Governments need to understand that everything in the world is connected and interdependent. What we do has an impact on others and our environment and so we must make more responsible, considered decisions based on respect, love, and preservation.

So what does this mean in practice? Examples include all policy decisions by governments addressing any environmental impact including impact on the biosphere and wildlife. And just as we need a holistic approach to tackle crime including violence against women, we need a holistic approach to deal with protecting and working with nature.

We can no longer approach the environment as a machine, focusing only on examining the parts separately without the context and the fabric of inter-dependence. To do so, Suzuki says, loses sense of the whole, and also means that when focusing on one section you are not addressing underlying root causes of our environmental problems but rather treating the symptoms only.[259] More specifically, as we place aspects of nature under separate government portfolios, we are fragmenting a single interconnected system, that without seeing the whole picture we can never manage sustainably.[260]

c. Reverence for nature and the unity of all things

We need to have a reverence for nature that we have lost. Suzuki says that Aboriginal people speak of the earth as their mother and say that we are created by the four sacred elements, earth, air, fire, and water. We are in truth not separate from the environment—instead we are the environment. Whatever we do to the environment, we do to ourselves.[261] We are all parts of the same whole—the planet earth, and on a larger scale the cosmos.

We can't keep seeking to dominate, control and selfishly take from nature without any concern for the negative consequences of this patriarchal approach for us and our environment. Planet Earth does not have infinite resources and so we need to acknowledge her limits and work collaboratively with her. But how do we do this?

Changes in our thinking and values are very much required. Marie Byles said a few decades ago that the destruction of nature has its cause in the mind and so instead of asking *whether we want* something we should instead be asking *whether we need it* so that we do not destroy anything unless we really have to. We need to be aware of the unity of all life and consider that greater happiness comes from giving rather than taking.[262] And when we give, we are also giving to ourselves. This is a very different way of thinking to the patriarchal approach that says not only *'I want'* but also *'I do it because I can.'*

d. The power of love and natural beauty

The power of love gives our lives meaning and the motivation to be kind and gentle. We need to re-connect with our love and passion for nature and our love and concern for each other. Suzuki says that scientists have been guilty of removing emotions and passion from science which has led to a lack of reverence, awe, wonder for and connection to nature.[263] Feminists exposed the dangerous, patriarchal pursuit of what is considered 'objectivity' in the science and technology sectors just as they exposed it in law. It is this pursuit of 'objectivity' that has allowed for the removal of emotions, making it easier to be exploitive and to seek to dominate and control our environment.[264] Only love can help us appreciate and connect deeply with nature. But this is something that is not innate in a white, patriarchal society.

When Dr Carl Jung met with the chief of the Taos Pueblos in New Mexico in 1925, he was struck by the wisdom of the chief's observations of white man, whom he said was always restless and looking uneasy, always wanting something. He said that they regarded white people as mad because they only thought with their heads, whereas he and his people thought with their hearts.[265]

We must recognise that we need each other; we are truly interdependent with other humans and nature, and love recognizes this truth which we often suppress. Love sees unity, whereas hatred, greed, and selfishness see separation.

Changing our perception through the lens of love will bring about the outward change in how we relate to each other and nature. Suzuki explains that other species won't be seen as simply resources then but instead companions who generously provide us our most fundamental needs and enrich our lives with mystery and beauty.[266]

Suzuki adds that the need to be with other species is built into our genome. For example, people in hospitals and nursing homes experience more happiness when animals and plants are brought into their environment. People on their own as well as families have their lives enriched by pets, whom they love as family. I know that I enjoy waking up to the beautiful song of birds in the canopy of trees and welcoming people's dogs in nearby parks.

I've also known people with mental health issues who felt a greater sense of calm and ease amongst nature, just as those of us experiencing any sense of stress or alienation do as well. Parks and gardens bring us joy and relaxation and add beauty to the world.

But as our cities grow and green belts and forests shrink in the name of development, we have, as Jung said, created a firm boundary between ourselves and nature which Indigenous peoples did not do; consequently, they did not experience such anxiety, depression, emptiness, and isolation (before colonisation) that we experience and importantly I add the lack of love.[267]

Psychologist Dr Abraham Maslow also highlighted the fact that we are in effect social animals and our most fundamental social need is love. Suzuki refers to Maslow's psychological theories on what it means to be fully human and to realise our full potential; here, love is critical.[268] When children are not brought up with the experience of love, the consequences can be devastating—such as the mental health and behavioural problems discussed earlier in this book.

Patriarchy does not know what is truly valuable and what is of no value. It places no importance on love and kindness because they have no material worth. This is the danger of allowing patriarchy and the free market to guide us. They lead us into a very dark and destructive space with short term profit as their god and so we must make sure that we instead allow our highest values, such as love, to lead the way.

In becoming more loving to each other and other species in our family, our policies and laws would reflect this higher path. Not only would there be greater investment in mental health and social justice initiatives by governments but there would be stronger protections for the environment. Such is this need that in Australia in 2018, a coalition of environmental, legal, and medical NGOs called for a national independent agency to safeguard the environment and deliver climate change policy that is effective. It would have powers to co-ordinate environmental data collection, auditing and monitoring, and provide advice to governments.[269]

Secondly, there would also be far greater protections for animal welfare and to ensure abundance of species. For example, battery hens, sow stalls, tail docking and teeth clipping of pigs without anaesthetic, live cattle and sheep trades, would all be practices of a distant cruel past rather than still happening in the world today. Stocking density of hens to be considered free range would not exceed 1500 hens per hectare as recommended by animal welfare groups such as the RSPCA.

Cruel animal sports such as greyhound racing would be prohibited worldwide, and restrictions on fishing would exist to ensure plentiful future fish. Governments would also invest more in animal welfare programs and ensure that animal welfare organisations were included in consultations and decision-making with all industries involving animals.

And so much more needs to be done to protect the wellbeing of animals and our natural world.

e. We are not merely bodies—we are spiritual beings

Suzuki, like Marie Byles and Indigenous women and men, says that we are spiritual beings needing spirit more than ever. We must nourish our spiritual nature and see the sacred in our environment. For example, he asks if rivers are veins of the land or only potential irrigation and energy? Are forests sacred groves where we can connect to our spiritual essence or simply timber and pulp for commercial purposes? Is a house a home or merely real estate—its worth determined only by the profit made on selling it?[270]

I remember hearing an Aboriginal women's musical group from Tasmania singing about their love and connection to Mother Nature in all her wondrous manifestations and how the sacred beauty of our environment reflects the deep inner sacred beauty within us as spiritual beings. It was a completely different way of seeing.

We need new values for a new way of living, and the inner change has to happen with each of us. A return to a spiritual and poetic way of life has an important part to play in our new direction. To live without this leaves us feeling the empty void that no amount of the ego strivings for material wealth, fame, prestige, status, and addictions can fill. A loving and soulful existence is much richer than a life based on the patriarchal values of worldly power, exploitation, separation, and putting maximum profit before people, our fellow species, and the environment.

Our denigration and destruction of nature merely reflects our own inner poverty and denigration—inwardly we are starving and completely off balance as we deny and suppress a rich deep treasure within.

Dr Carl Jung was extremely concerned with modern humans' loss of connection to our environment, as he believed that nature was the soil that nourishes the soul.[271] He identified four elements that have undergone the most severe repression in the (patriarchal) Judeo-Christian world: 1. nature, 2. animals, 3. creative fantasy or enchantment, and 4. what he viewed as the instinctive, earthy or more natural side of humans, as well as the repression of indigenous cultures. To these elements of repression, I add a fifth category of women and what are commonly referred to as feminine qualities such as 'being', empathy, connectedness, unity, and intuition.

Jung saw our loss of connection to nature as a religious problem and one where nature has lost her divinity and so humans are lost and not centred.[272] He was concerned that we are suffering in our cities from a need for a more simple way of life and a connection to nature. He understood that modern humanity's pathological obsession with conquest, material wealth, speed, and technology was costing us our soul and happiness. Jung warned decades ago that in living an urban existence of what is essentially a manmade environment, civilised humans were in danger of losing all contact with our instincts. And so our contemporary culture is suffering from a pathological condition.[273]

We have over-developed our rationalization and intellectual processes, leading to us having an increasingly divided consciousness, rather than moving closer to wholeness and a balanced state of inner peace. Jung was of the view that we need to re-establish contact with our instinctive side and integrate this aspect with our modern 'civilized' self in order to survive and reach our full potential. This also means understanding our unity with Mother Nature, and to work co-operatively with her.

When a colleague was finding life difficult and needed guidance, Jung counselled him to listen to the symbolism of a dream that highlighted the need to return to the simple things and perhaps undertake a retreat amongst nature. Jung even wrote that a tree can say more than books.[274] This reminds me of the CEO I mentioned earlier who undertook a gap year living in a mountain hut in Wales, reconnecting with nature.

Practical measures to reconnect

Other solutions Jung gave for our loss of connection with our natural world and our spiritual essence was to live in small communities, to work a shorter day and week, to have a plot of land to ensure that our instincts and intuition are revived, and to make spare use of radio, television, newspapers and technological gadgetry wherever possible. This would allow nature to affect us and inform us, reversing patriarchy's approach of dominating nature. Energy, money, and time can then be dedicated to repairing our environment whilst also allowing nature to heal us.[275]

Jung saw that our evolutionary task was not to turn regressively to nature but rather to retain our level of consciousness developed over thousands of years and enrich it with the primordial foundations we have suppressed.[276]

Re-establishing contact with this part of ourselves and with nature in practical terms also means governments must pursue policies to help protect our environment and decrease alienation, such as the following:

i) Regional investment: Governments must invest more in regional areas to attract people to live there rather than simply expanding cities to become mega cities—increasing our sense of alienation as well as stress from congestion on our roads, public transport, nearby nature reserves, et cetera. Investing in smaller communities is also critical, with local jobs and necessary infrastructure.

ii) Sustainable population growth: Governments should employ measures to ensure there is sustainable population growth only—mindful as Suzuki and other environmentalists are of the ecological impact as well as the impact on our mental health and wellbeing.

iii) Careful use of technology: Thorough assessments of how much technology is too much technology are needed, ensuring a human rights framework for all technological advances including artificial intelligence. And from what feminists have taught us in law and science, it is dangerous to pursue advancements in AI with the patriarchal ideal of 'objectivity'. Emotions such as love and empathy must not be pushed aside.

With this in mind, we must ensure that AI advances don't increase our sense of alienation in our high tech cities that forever encroach on nature and distance us from our instincts. We don't want AI to take over meaningful employment as well, creating an underclass of humans.

Professor Toby Walsh and other experts in the field have also strongly warned against the creation of killer robots and virtual realities that involve illegal activity and the denigration of humans such as women. Meanwhile, Professor Kathleen Richardson has raised concerns about the dangers of sex robots being the same as those of pornography, as discussed earlier in this book.[277] We need love, empathy, connections to other people, and connections to our intuitive nature—sex robots really are an attack on all of these. If Jung was alive today, I think he might say that we have become insane or are teetering on the edge of insanity.

The benefits of AI, though, are also numerous. We should harness the benefits to increase the protection of nature and the wellbeing of humans in general, and in doing so remember that our connection with nature and each other is fundamental to our needs and technology can never replace this.

So how else can we reconnect to nature and our spiritual essence? It can quite simply involve having a media or technology-free day whenever we can, all of us taking the time (and having the time) to swim at the beach, walk in a park, go hiking, or rest beneath a tree, and to be still and go inwards without the distractions of the busyness of life. We can't delay this, though. Our happiness and survival depends on it.

Jung tried to shake us out of our complacency by saying that it seemed we had not learnt from the last war. By refusing to acknowledge and listen to our unconscious desire for quiet places, to reflect, and simply 'be' in our natural world, we may plunge ourselves into another catastrophe where we gas our lives out. And then there will be no one left to sit in the sun and dream.[278]

-11-

Patriarchy and Leadership

Patriarchy's influence on leadership across the political spectrum is both legendary and devastating. The purely commanding style where people are viewed as easily replaced, and without regard to relationships and compassion, is firmly embedded in our history and in leadership positions today.[279] So is a form of leadership that embraces patriarchy's values such as ambition, status, exclusiveness, material wealth, and dominating and triumphing over others—equating these with true power.

Such leadership is dangerous and fuels a toxic culture—including cruelty and corruption. At its most extreme, we can see how it has played out under dictators who thrive on eliciting only two emotions: fear and anger, serving to divide people rather than unite them with a high meaningful purpose.[280] We have also seen it play out in the exploitative policies of western governments that have propped up authoritarian regimes, as well as in the history of colonisation.

In addition, attempts to silence dissent (a tool of patriarchal leadership) do happen in democratic nations, including Australia. Examples are where governments engage in bullying or intimidation, public humiliation and denigration, and threats of withdrawal of funding against critics—including academics, researchers, public servants, not-for-profits, and journalists.[281] Governments intimidating or slandering those who raise legitimate human rights or environmental concerns about their policies on the world stage are also deeply troubling. Silencing dissent not only perpetuates bad government policy by shutting down much needed expert opinion and innovative ideas. It is also a slippery slope that isn't as far as people may think from creating an authoritarian state.

But now let's take an in-depth look at how patriarchal leadership plays out in various sectors of society.

The impact across sectors

Patriarchal leadership is unfortunately used in all areas of the public sphere including the corporate sector. Devoid of empathy, integrity, and wisdom, it is too focused on quick financial returns at any cost, harming people and the companies involved. In *The New Leaders*, Daniel Goleman and his associates Richard Boyatzis and Annie McKee write of how CEO Al Dunlap boasted in his autobiography *Mean Business* of his tough leadership style at Scott Paper that helped him fire thousands of staff. Later analysis found his cutbacks were excessive and damaged the company's ability to do business. Within two years after he was fired as CEO of Sunbeam, Dunlap and other executives were indicted by the Securities and Exchange Commission charged with fraud on the basis that they created the illusion of a successful restructuring of the company so that it could be sold at an inflated price.[282]

Journalist Jon Ronson says in his book, *The Psychopath Test*, that Dunlap also possessed many of the traits associated with a psychopath, according to the highly regarded twenty-point Hare PCL-R checklist by criminal psychologist Bob Hare. The traits on the list are:

1. Glibness and superficial charm
2. Grandiose sense of self-worth
3. Need for stimulation and proneness to boredom

4. Pathological lying
5. Cunning and manipulative
6. Lack of remorse or guilt
7. Shallow emotional responses/ways of relating: an individual who seems unable to experience the normal range and depth of emotions
8. Callousness and lack of empathy
9. Parasitic lifestyle
10. Poor behaviour controls
11. Failure to accept responsibility for own actions
12. Early behaviour problems
13. Lack of realistic long term goals (self-delusions)
14. Impulsivity
15. Irresponsibility
16. Sexual promiscuity
17. Criminal versatility
18. Juvenile delinquency
19. Revocation of conditional release
20. Many short-term marital relationships.[283]

When Dunlap became Sunbeam's CEO, it led to the shutdown not only of the company but made Shubuta, Mississippi, a depressed, dying town. Dunlap expressed no remorse. But this isn't surprising given that he was known to happily fire people, so much so that *Fast Company* business magazine included him in an article about potentially psychopathic CEOs alongside Walt Disney and Henry Ford.[284]

In reference to his behaviour as a child, his biographer John Byrne noted that Dunlap made some comments about how much he enjoyed beating people up, as he was a keen boxer as a child, and his sister said that he threw darts at her dolls. When Jon Ronson visited Dunlap's home, he observed the grounds of the mansion dotted with predator animals, as Dunlap spoke of a great belief in and respect for predators and claimed that everything he did *he had to make happen.* Inside his home, in a gold cabinet, he proudly displayed photographs that showed him with Donald Trump and Kerry Packer. After Ronson told Dunlap about the list of psychopathic traits, Dunlap redefined many of them as positive leadership qualities and gloated again how everything in his life, *he did his way.*[285]

Bob Hare's study of CEOs, directors, and supervisors found that 3.9 per cent had a high score for psychopathy, at least four or five times the prevalence in the general population. He told Ronson that the assumption is that psychopaths account for a little less than 1 per cent of the general population, but it showed that they are four or five times more likely to be in a position of power than someone just trying to earn a living for themselves or their family.[286]

Martha Stout from the Harvard Medical School and author of *The Sociopath Next Door*, told Ronson that sociopaths (who are extremely similar to psychopaths for example in lacking empathy) love power and winning, which is what happens when you take loving kindness out of the human brain. She noted that the higher you go up the career ladder, the greater the number of sociopaths you will find, which is why you find so much injustice and corruption in society.[287]

Even those people who aren't sociopaths or psychopaths but still rate high on psychopathic traits are a major cause for concern, not only as leaders but as co-workers, as later discussed.

Boards of all workplaces and political parties need to take action to be rid of a person in a position of power who exhibits such character traits and the purely commanding style of leadership that they and others use. The frightening fact is that our patriarchal society, by highly valuing worldly ambition, superficial charm, material wealth, status, and competitiveness whilst devaluing empathy, humility, and patience, enables sociopaths and psychopaths—and those people who, strictly speaking, are not these but lack sufficient empathy and compassion—to reach positions of power and stay there for too long.

In this light, it is not surprising that there has been a major failure in leadership both with the financial service industry and the regulators here in Australia. The 2018 interim report of the Australian royal commission into misconduct in the banking/finance/insurance sector found that dead people had been charged fees, documents had been forged, and there had been repeated failures to adequately check customers' living expenses before granting them a loan. But that's not all. Financial institutions were also lying to the regulator. Meanwhile, insurers were exploiting vulnerable people paying for insurance that wouldn't give them the full benefits they thought.

The Commission also said that the conduct in which the sector engaged was mostly unlawful. It had been consumed by greed—focussing on making short-term profits at the expense of honesty. And where misconduct was exposed, it either went unpunished or the consequences were not proportionate to its seriousness. The regulators ASIC and APRA also failed to identify the root causes for the misconduct.[288] The final report by the Commission outlined further cases of serious misconduct and made 76 recommendations for reform, with a backdrop of immense suffering and hardship in the community.

None of this came as a surprise to the general public, who already perceived a culture of greed and predatory conduct amongst the banks and the rest of the finance sector. Whilst the blame has been placed with greed, such greed needs to be seen as a result of a patriarchal system and its distorted view of power that opposes integrity and empathy.

All of the men and women in power in the industry who did not act to stop this behaviour need to go. The old proverb, *the fish rots from the head down,* is very true. And also importantly, all necessary criminal legal action should take its course. There also needs to be a complete overhaul of such organisations and a radical transformation of the patriarchal culture.

It's not just poor leadership and culture in the finance sector, either. At the time of writing, there are growing calls for a royal commission into the spate of suicides by veterans. Too many have not received the rehabilitation and support they deserved and needed upon returning from war-torn countries. It is also alarming that a royal commission back in 1924 found the same problem and its recommendations to overcome this were not heeded.[289] It's the patriarchal mentality at play. Compassion is devalued. Mental health problems are not taken seriously—viewed simply as signs of weakness. And there's the adversarial approach to claims for mental health support when such support should automatically be given to soldiers returning from any tour of duty. People are also too often viewed as 'machines' and easily replaceable: once they are used up—they are forgotten.

The royal commission into the aged care sector is also necessary due to stories of abuse, violence, and neglect of older people in nursing homes. The Commission aims to uncover how widespread this abuse is and what reforms should be implemented.

We know some residential aged care facilities provide high quality care. But there are those who don't and must be held to account for abuse and placing profits before people (just like the banks). And as we saw with the Oakden nursing home scandal in South Australia, there was chronic mismanagement by senior staff. They failed, along with state and federal authorities, to take necessary action when issues of abuse and neglect were raised. The overly commanding style of leadership that refuses to listen to others and lacks empathy and integrity is at the heart of this.

Such leadership has also failed to recognise that geriatric care must be seen as a highly specialised and complex area of healthcare requiring much greater government investment. This also means that we need a cultural change in our attitudes towards ageing and older people—to not denigrate our elders and not judge a person's value based on the patriarchal view of their economic worth and productivity. Our elders should be highly appreciated, respected, and cherished rather than treated like children, and it should be a privilege to work with them as they are making an important life transition.

Sexual misconduct in residential aged care facilities is also an extremely serious issue. This includes sexual misconduct by elderly male residents (even with dementia) against female residents. Male-only residential facilities for these men are needed not only to prevent further abuse but to prevent female victims from being further traumatised by seeing them where they live.

The sectors viewed as the 'caring sectors' (such as aged care, disability care, community mental health, and childcare) should also be elevated in importance and receive more government funding whilst ensuring a highly skilled workforce. Patriarchy's devaluation of them, due to a predominantly female workforce and the nature of the work, must end.

Finally, a royal commission into the abuse occurring in the disability sector is happening after a Senate inquiry recommended one back in 2015. Such royal commissions ideally shouldn't have to happen; they wouldn't if leaders in these sectors and governments didn't refuse to listen to and act on the calls for reform by staff, advocates, and key stakeholders for years until the problems reach crisis point. But we also need leaders to act on the findings and recommendations of these royal commissions rather than simply say 'we agree in principle' and then only implement a few if any of the suggested reforms.

Slaves to ambition and status

Meanwhile, across all workplaces and sectors, even whilst there are examples of good leadership, too many leaders are ego driven. They are slaves to ambition and status rather than focusing on what they have to give with a will to help others. This leads to the overuse of the commanding style and the need to feel powerful, rather than working in a collaborative, non-defensive way and relating to people with kindness.

This type of patriarchal leadership driven by ambition is not just employed by men but women too. So we cannot say that if more women were in power, just by virtue of our gender, that better leadership would prevail. This is because the ego is in all of us and we need to be vigilant against it. And worldly power is very addictive. The American political satire *Veep,* starring Julia Louis-Dreyfus as a self-absorbed, power-hungry Vice-President and later President, illustrates this well. We also just have to look at female leaders in history, such as Queen Mary I of England (who ordered the murders of hundreds of Protestants) and Jiang Qing (highly involved in China's notorious cultural revolution) to see this at its worst. But what is also helpful is looking at contemporary, less extreme but still harmful examples of leaders driven by ambition and lacking empathy.

If Denise Cosgrove was not so focused on her own ambition and status when she was CEO of WorkSafe in 2013, would she have sent an email to staff beginning with a description of her 'relaxing' weekend in Daylesford, eventually leading into an announcement of job losses? Where was the empathy and sensitivity? And where was the focus on the public interest and accountability when Worksafe under her leadership assured the government that what turned out to be contaminated water at the Country Fire Authority's Fiskville training centre was safe? It was also revealed that assurance couldn't even be given that the water had been tested.[290]

Would Facebook still have betrayed public trust over the Cambridge Analytica data scandal if the company executives were as focussed on the public interest and acting responsibly as they were on making profits and promoting ambition? This includes the female ambition that Facebook Chief Operating Officer Sheryl Sanders promotes in her 2015 book *Lean In.*

Would Amnesty International's London office have ended up a toxic workplace for staff in recent years if management weren't slaves to ambition? This led to them also embracing patriarchy's 'us and them mentality' and commanding style with widespread bullying, public humiliation, and other abuses of power that an independent review uncovered in 2019.

The focus on ambition and the overuse of the commanding style of leadership plays out in so many ways in the workplace. More examples to help us all make sure we don't go down this path include: managers/executives or politicians giving staff abrupt orders via email or face to face and not even addressing them by their names (I'm not talking about where they are dealing with an emergency or in the middle of a meeting or debate). And not saying thank you or even acknowledging receipt of the information or detailed briefings.

Being slaves to ambition and status has also meant that too many leaders have over-identified with their roles and their profession so that they haven't been able to step back and listen to constructive criticism from outside their inner circle and see their weaknesses, not just their strengths. It's this over-identification with the role/group/industry/party or political cause, and the arrogance that goes with it which is extremely dangerous for all of us, creating blind spots and causing us to shut down any criticism.

This hostility to criticism and use of the purely commanding style can also play out where leaders want to 'make their mark' in the organisation that they join. I know of a not-for profit where the new manager, Robert, entered a department eager to make changes. Instead of consulting staff and caring about their wellbeing, respecting their skill, knowledge, and commitment, he used the commanding style to make the changes he wanted. He also made it clear that if people didn't like what he was doing they could leave. A toxic culture ensued and some good staff did leave. Not surprisingly, the quality of work declined as did staff morale. I know of women leaders in workplaces using this type of leadership to this same effect.

Margaret Thatcher primarily used a commanding style of leadership, especially in her later years as Prime Minister of Britain. There was a lack of empathy as shown by Neoliberal policies that created a greater divide between the rich and the poor. During her tenure, unemployment reached record levels not seen since the Great Depression. Not only that, but she espoused the view that there was no such thing as society, only individuals.[291] The belief that we should allow people to act out of self-interest, adhering only to the 'invisible hand' that guides the market, and merely hope that this produces social benefits is both dangerous and naive. When a state fails to provide adequate regulations and laws to create a more level 'playing field', inequality thrives, as does corruption. But by saying that there is no such thing as society, Thatcher made the further error of failing to recognise that we are all interconnected and so what we do impacts on each other. Her attitude devalues the importance of being compassionate and encourages acting in self-interest at the expense of others.

The Roman Emperor and Stoic philosopher Marcus Aurelius also saw the inextricable connection between society and the individual, saying that what doesn't benefit the hive is also not of benefit to the bee.[292]

Moreover, Dr Carl Jung recognised the social quality inherent in human nature, saying the human psyche cannot function without a culture, and no individual is possible without a society.[293]

Women failing other women

In looking at patriarchy's impact on leadership, it is also useful to see how it has impacted on women leaders in terms of them helping other women. You might assume that because female leaders know of the disadvantages that women face they would be mindful to treat female staff well and assist them in pursuing their goals. But the truth is that it is not uncommon to hear of women in leadership doing the opposite; in fact, they may even place more obstacles in front of talented female staff.

This scenario has played out with other social groups. Sociologist E Franklin Frazier wrote in *Black Bourgeoisie*, published in 1957, of how successful black people did not return often enough to help less fortunate black people up the ladder, and were sometimes addicted to consumption of material goods and the display of material wealth. As Gloria Steinem says, this can be said of every group whose core self-esteem is low and who therefore crave situational esteem and approval from those higher up in the hierarchy than them. It can be analogised to the Queen Bee in relation to females: successful and educated women who separate themselves from other women as they feel the need to shine on their own and gain status from being one of the few women among men.[294]

Margaret Thatcher is a prime example, only promoting one woman to her cabinet during her 11 years as Prime Minister.[295] Sheryl Sandberg acknowledges that this Queen Bee attitude unfortunately lingers today and quotes Madeleine Albright, the former US Secretary of State, using powerful symbolic language to make the point, 'There's a special place in hell for women who don't help other women.'[296]

Psychologist Susan Jeffers shed further light on this issue back in 1987, saying that we can have a tendency to want others to have things as difficult as what we did. We should turn this around, seeking to help others as much as we can. She remembered the times when she felt professionally threatened by those around her and therefore thought about withholding information or refraining from helping them due to her fear. But instead she allowed herself to feel the fear and helped them anyway. And whilst it is important to give without expecting anything in return, she found that those whom she helped became valued friends and part of her support team. This may not always happen, and whilst I add it's important to be discerning with people, Susan Jeffers reminds us that when you give and people apply what you have taught them, your effect in this world is magnified greatly.[297]

Unfortunately, I am also aware of women in positions of power who covered up the misconduct and lack of competence of male staff and yet they expected higher standards from their female staff and bullied them. Even though these female leaders called themselves feminists, they were in fact patriarchal and sexist.

There have also been and still are women in leadership positions who have not sought to bring about the changes necessary to enhance the status and respect for women in our society because they have not advocated for women's issues. Of the women in parliament and other leadership roles over recent decades, not many have advocated for law reform needed against pornography, strip clubs, prostitution, the pay gap, stolen wages, family violence, sexual harassment, sexism, and misogyny wherever it has manifested and called for dismantling patriarchy.

And when some women leaders have raised these issues in recent years, for many they have merely been responding to the public outcry that 'enough is enough' and from the courageous leadership of campaigners against family violence like Rosie Batty. Activists have forced these matters to be high on the agenda whilst the impact of gender inequality and patriarchy has reached crisis point.

Margaret Thatcher was certainly no feminist, failing to advance the cause of women in many key areas. But even as Australia's Prime Minister Julia Gillard made her famous misogyny speech against Opposition leader Tony Abbott on 9 October 2012, sounding like a strong advocate for women, her government legislated that very day for what in effect further entrenched the feminisation of poverty. The new law by Gillard made parenting payments for children of single parents cease when a child reached eight years of age instead of sixteen. Most of these parents, who were largely women, would then be moved on to Newstart for jobseekers. Gillard's government did not consult with the women who would be affected by these changes beforehand.

What this meant for many vulnerable women who were single parents, was a loss of weekly income on average of $60 to $110 according to the Australian Council of Social Services. This was pushing more women and children into poverty and putting women at risk of taking dangerous and traumatic jobs such as prostitution. We also know that some of these women were single mothers because they had fled abusive relationships. Rather than giving them the support they needed, the Gillard government created further hardship for them.[298]

But the lack of care for single parents didn't end there. In 2019 the Coalition government's Minister for Women and Jobs, Kelly O'Dwyer, said that she would not overhaul the governments' ParentsNext program for single parents (as described in Chapter Three) even though a Senate Inquiry heard evidence that it was unethical and abused the human rights of women and children. Ms O'Dwyer defended the program as having the *right intention*.[299] But as we know, the path to hell can be paved with good intentions, so appropriate means to achieving a goal or purpose is essential. Whilst Ms O'Dwyer later decided to allow some administrative changes and a reduction in reporting requirements, this is seen to be by many as insufficient to protect women and children from further harm.[300] All of this could've been avoided if Ms O'Dwyer had ensured that single parents' contact with Centrelink and its programs was positive and empowering.

Meanwhile, the former Foreign Affairs Minister Julie Bishop declared in 2014 that she was not a feminist and that it was not a term that she found helpful 'these days.' She said this despite the known prevalence of violence against women and sex discrimination, the pay gap, stolen wages, and few women in positions of power. And she found feminism unhelpful despite too many women with insufficient superannuation due to lower wages, sexual harassment, and less full time employment whilst also doing the bulk of necessary unpaid work. Then there are the other disadvantages, including lack of access in rural areas to family planning services and lack of safe access to abortion.

Fast forward to 2018 and after being overlooked by her colleagues in the Liberal Party to replace Malcolm Turnbull as leader, Julie Bishop finally spoke of the need to increase the numbers of women for the Liberal Party in parliament and criticised the appalling behaviour towards women in the party including bullying and intimidation.[301]

The Victorian Greens party leader Samantha Ratnam supported a Greens candidate in the 2018 state election who had a history of gender vilification in his rap songs, including lyrics on date-raping women. Public criticism was widespread, given that we have a right to expect higher standards and integrity from people running for public office, just as we have a right to expect higher standards from people seeking judicial appointments.

At the same time, there are men in power who have had plenty of opportunities to recognise women's rights as human rights and do more to stop violence against women and achieve equality but didn't—until a few could no longer turn a blind eye to the crisis. Every male political leader in this country and overseas, needs to recognise that they could have and should have done much more to help women and young girls be respected, valued, and feel safe, and can still do more.

Women stepping up

Fortunately, there are times when women leaders, like their male counterparts, have listened to experts and people with wisdom from personal experience, as well as their own wisdom. In doing, so they have pursued policies and reforms of great benefit to society. For example, former Prime Minister Julia Gillard acted very much in the public interest by establishing the *Royal Commission into Institutional Responses to Child Sexual Abuse*, which uncovered systemic failings in handling widespread abuse and made several recommendations for reform.[302] And former Labor Senator and Minister for the Status of Women, Susan Ryan, introduced the *Sex Discrimination Act* in 1984 as part of the fight for women's equality and safety amid much controversy and opposition.

During her time as Australian Greens leader from 2012-2015, former Senator Christine Milne continued speaking out about the need for the economy to serve people and nature, and of the urgency for genuine action on climate change—elevating the importance of this issue and turning our attention to efficient, renewable energy. She also advocated strongly against Australia's mandatory detention of asylum seekers. And Samantha Ratnam in Victoria not only called on the state government to move away completely from coal-fired power stations, but also to act urgently on the recycling crisis by creating a world-leading recycling industry in Victoria. This would involve re-shaping and expanding our existing recycling industry and would create more sustainable jobs.

Dr Marlene Goldsmith, a NSW Liberal Member of Parliament whom I spoke of earlier, advocated strongly against violence against women and the harms of pornography back in the 1990s. And Kelly O'Dwyer introduced legislation in 2018 against 're-venge pornography'—protecting women from ex-partners and others sharing intimate images of them without their consent.

Prejudice against women in power

An examination of patriarchy's impact on leadership should also include how women in positions of power have also been unfairly ridiculed and attacked. I turn again to former Prime Minister Julia Gillard but this time to the *'ditch the witch'* and *'Ju—lia, Bob Brown's Bitch'* posters that then-Opposition leader Tony Abbott's supporters waved around him in March 2011. The blatant misogyny these posters conveyed, and Tony Abbott's failure to tell these supporters to ditch their posters and leave, shows not only just how patriarchal our society was even then, but also Tony Abbott's lack of leadership ability, which should have ended his political career. Julia Gillard also had to deal with radio presenter Alan Jones saying that her father had 'died of shame' because of 'lies she told in parliament'. This was after he previously said that she should be put into a *chaff bag and thrown into the sea*.[303] Such vitriol is misogyny and shows again why we need gender vilification laws: misogyny in this country is still not taken seriously.

US President Donald Trump, another politician who epitomises patriarchal leadership including lack of empathy, did not speak out against the misogyny perpetrated against Hilary Clinton during the lead-up to his election win. This included his supporters attaching images of her face to the decapitated head of Medusa and placing them on coffee mugs, T-shirts, and tote bags.[304] It was excused as just part and parcel of the rough and tumble nature of politics.

Greens Senator Sarah Hanson-Young was told to 'stop shagging men' by Liberal Democrat Senator David Leyonhjelm during a parliamentary debate on violence against women in the federal Australian parliament. This was in 2018, not 1950. Then-Prime Minister Malcolm Turnbull rightly condemned the comments, saying that they were damaging because they remind us that whilst not all disrespect of women leads to violence, such comments are often where it starts. He also said that Senator Leyhonhjelm should apologise, though Senator Hanson-Young went further and called on him to resign—a fair call.

Senator David Leyhonhjelm refused to resign, making the additional, absurd and condescending comment that he would not apologise to Senator Hanson-Young unless she said that she no longer believes that all men are collectively responsible for the actions of those men who commit violence, that she accepts that we are each individuals responsible for our own actions and cannot blame others, and that she accepts that women have the right to carry pepper spray or mace to protect themselves from violent people. He also told the Prime Minister to 'stop being a pussy' when Malcolm Turnbull called on him to withdraw his comments.[305]

When female politicians make mistakes, they are heavily criticised and held to account. But this doesn't always happen to male politicians. Mary Beard shows this discrepancy most clearly with the comparison of two disastrous radio interviews given by Tory MP Boris Johnson (later Britain's Prime Minister) and Labour MP Diane Abbott. Abbott provided woefully inaccurate figures on the cost of the party's police recruitment policy. Johnson was just as embarrassing, showing ignorance about the new government's major commitments on higher education and racial discrimination in the criminal justice system. Abbott was called 'boneheaded stupid', 'fat idiot', and worse, whilst Johnson was criticised not with the same viciousness, but instead a simple reminder to get a grip on things and be more focused.[306]

Women leaders are also unfairly criticised and judged for their appearance and style of clothing. I remember when Joan Kirner was Premier of Victoria and was ridiculed for wearing a polka dot dress. And whilst the media were criticising her appearance, she was not only busy running the state with her team of MPs, but involved in mentoring women to become future leaders and advocating for change to the (patriarchal) bullying environment of Australian politics, as she told me on an International Women's Day March in the early 1990s.

Patriarchy and work environments

To have more women in leadership roles and more men and women who are great leaders at all levels of workplaces, we need to ensure that men and women are respected, that they are encouraged to grow and increase their expertise, and that there isn't a toxic environment that they need to escape from.

We also need our leaders to move away from the patriarchal, highly hierarchical model for organisations, the excessively long hours expected of staff, and create workplaces with better work/life balance for everyone, including parliamentarians. This would produce healthier, happier, and more productive work environments where better decision-making is involved—such environments would also be more conducive to women taking on leadership positions. More power sharing through delegation and more consultation and collaboration would help, with input being valued from all staff based on their expertise, not just those at the top of the hierarchy. These ideas are not new. Feminists have long espoused them or similar ideas, including Eva Cox back in 1996. This provides a good segue into our discussion in the next chapter of what positive leadership looks like.

Note

It is not uncommon for patriarchal leaders to have backgrounds of child abuse including the emotional unavailability of parents mentioned in Chapter Three. And we know child abuse thrives in a patriarchal culture as well as not encouraging therapeutic treatment for distressed, traumatised, or disturbed children. At the same time we can also say these leaders chose as adults not to seek help that was available (particularly in the modern era) to address their past abuse nor engage in any self-examination to ensure they would not inflict harm onto others. Their narcissism including sense of entitlement and desire for worldly power took the lead instead.

-12-
What Makes Good Leadership?

Good leaders are so few and far between that it seems people are quick to praise anyone in politics who shows empathy and kindness. The situation is the same in the human rights and corporate worlds. Perhaps we have reached our rock bottom with patriarchal leadership and people are saying *enough is enough*? And we know that if we want patriarchy to fall, we need good leadership to be the rule, not the exception. Whilst good leaders will have faults and make mistakes like us all, they also possess several key qualities and approaches that make them stand out.

They are not only intelligent with the requisite knowledge for their position. But they also know how to inspire us to do our best, with powerful ideas, vision, and excellent strategies. Importantly, as psychologist Daniel Goleman and his associates suggest, they also embody emotionally intelligent leadership—a broad term that captures many different traits. Immediately, I think of an emotionally mature person who has cultivated both positive masculine and feminine qualities. So let's look at this more specifically with the assistance of experts like Goleman and his colleagues.

Resonate emotionally with people

Firstly, emotionally intelligent leaders speak and act in a way that resonates emotionally with the people working with them.

The best leaders understand the powerful role of emotions in the workplace in creating higher morale, motivation, and commitment. They know that how you make a person feel has a great impact.

Goleman says an example of such positive leadership is Monica Sharma at UNICEF. In 1989, when she became Chief of Health of UNICEF's Health Section Immunization project in India, she was concerned that most of the 400 office-bound employees felt disconnected from the value of their own work. They did not know how much it helped the health teams on the ground in treating children. So she found a solution by helping them connect emotionally to their specific roles.

Sharma lobbied UNICEF's senior management to allow her to send every one of the 400 office-bound employees to work in the village immunization clinics and see first-hand what their work was really about. Senior management agreed. Soon after, staff took children to clinics to observe how their roles were contributing to saving the life of a child. This provided them with the passion and sense of mission they needed for their work back at the office. No task became too small or unimportant anymore: they knew everything they did was critical and benefitted the whole.[307]

Self-awareness and authenticity

Goleman also says that great leaders are emotionally self-aware, recognising how their feelings affect their performance. In their self-awareness, they exercise self-control, not allowing negative feelings or thoughts to overwhelm them or lead them in their decision-making and how they treat others.

Good leaders have accurate self-assessment as part of their self-awareness by knowing their strengths and weaknesses. Goleman says this means that they know how to play to their strengths, what they need to develop in themselves, and when to seek expert advice.

They are also authentic and candid, which means they must be emotionally secure and honest with themselves and have good intentions rather than seeking to manipulate people to get their own way.[308] Being manipulative impedes a leader from making good decisions—it creates a block, preventing the leader from getting the information needed and narrows the mind, creating tunnel vision. And some people, including leaders, wear a mask in the workplace and so don't engage authentically with staff. This only builds mistrust—a recipe for disaster for any organisation.

When authentic leaders speak they are sincere and communicate with clarity and meaning, rather than simply using the latest catch phrases, buzz words, clichés, or formality that has more to do with putting on a performance than truly connecting with the people they are speaking to. This is also conveyed in how they oversee the communications of their organisation. As former speech writer Don Watson says, they ensure that language is plain and to the point but also embodies sentiment when needed. Sincerity and clarity would also be part of their organisation's language rather than the corporate convoluted and sterile language that says very little.[309]

Self-confidence and rising to the challenge

Good leaders have self-confidence and are not afraid of dealing with challenges. For example, as we have observed in earlier chapters, they don't turn a blind eye to bullying or sexual harassment or other allegations of misconduct or corruption. Nor will they 'shoot the messenger' but instead ensure that appropriate action is taken with transparency and accountability. Support is also provided for victims or whistle-blowers. Too many of us are familiar with the inaction or victim-blaming that happens in organisations, where managers and other leaders even make excuses for victimisers and can in fact enable such behaviour. This is particularly dangerous when a psychopath, a person with psychopathic traits, or a vindictive type is involved.

Other challenges include financial downturns, funding problems, or conflict with a stakeholder; a great leader will have the confidence to handle such situations skilfully and collaboratively.

Intuitive leadership

Intuition also plays an important part in leadership. Even Bill Gates acknowledged that gathering all the facts and using logic is not enough, that often you have to rely on intuition.[310] Goleman refers to a study of sixty entrepreneurs who built and led highly successful companies in California. Most of them said that in making business decisions, they weighed the relevant information in terms of their intuitive gut feelings. If a business plan looked good on the basis of the data but did not 'feel right', they would proceed either with caution or not at all.[311]

Dr Susan Jeffers wrote of the importance of listening to your intuition to make good decisions, and even UK Home Office researchers acknowledged what detectives always knew: that 'gut feelings' or intuition help solve crimes.[312]

Based on Goleman and his colleagues' insights, good leaders also exercise the following additional traits:

- They take initiative and can be decisive when needed.
- They are optimistic—optimism does not mean they are blind to problems but that they have a positive, level-headed approach to dealing with them.
- They show a genuine interest in staff and give praise where it is due. They also provide the opportunity for staff to increase their skills, and actively mentor and support those with talent and expertise to achieve the highest standards in their field.

- They read people and power relationships well—this requires wisdom.
- They know when to delegate and do not micro-manage.
- They are team players, working collaboratively as positive examples of friendliness, respect, and cooperation.[313] To this I add they have mastered the art of patience and also have zero tolerance for sexism, racism, and homophobia.

Empathy and compassion

Good leaders also care for others and have the imagination and depth of emotion to be able to 'walk in someone else's shoes.' They don't perceive themselves as the centre of the universe and so can reach out to others experiencing any type of difficulty, concerns or pain and seek to help them. They realise the importance of the wellbeing of all staff and customers or people they serve. Furthermore, they understand that staff wellbeing increases productivity and encourages high work standards as people know they are valued.

High personal standards

Whilst good leaders set high standards for staff and provide praise and constructive criticism, they also have high personal standards for themselves and are in effect excellent role models. These high personal standards mean that they are never complacent. They understand that it's a slippery slope as soon as they start letting go of wanting do their best and therefore keep improving their own performance and helping others do the same.

Question long term implications and focus on detail

The best leaders don't make short-term decisions but make decisions with consideration of the long-term implications and risk factors. Yvon Chouinard, the founder and owner of Patagonia, says that the best leaders have to lead an examined life. This also enables them to ask a lot of questions about their work, addressing the causes of problems rather than just focussing on the symptoms and fast 'solutions' which create more damage in the long term.[314]

Indeed, whilst the best leaders are visionaries and can see the big picture, they understand the *devil is in the detail*. Otherwise tragic consequences can happen. We witnessed this in Australia with the Rudd government's 'pink batts insulation scheme'. This scheme was seen as a worthy program to help stimulate the economy during a global financial crisis and to provide energy efficiency. But it was implemented too quickly. Careful consideration of all details of the scheme including risk factors was largely absent. And the profit motive was in charge of delivering the program in an unregulated industry. The Environment Department also lacked the resources to properly administer the program. A frenzy of unsafe work by unskilled workers ensued, four of whom tragically lost their lives in 2009-2010. Meanwhile, many homes were destroyed in fires.[315]

Asking a lot of questions and attention to detail is also critical while we embark on the era of artificial intelligence. As discussed in Chapter Ten, we must ensure that in all its aspects AI serves and benefits humanity rather than creates an underclass of humans, increases alienation, and further entrenches disrespect for and abuse of women. Dr Carl Jung warned that machines and technology could become the dragons of the modern era if we are not careful to ensure that they are only used in beneficial ways. Despite the fact that they are created by humans, within them dwell 'divine powers' that may destroy us.[316]

Value creativity and non-conformism

It's also through asking a lot of questions that we facilitate innovation as well as creativity. This means that leaders should turn their backs on the conformism that patriarchy promotes and be willing to take risks and make changes wherever necessary. Journalist Shelley Gare says that there are reports in Silicon Valley of an aversion to risk, originality, and boldness. This is in stark contrast to how Silicon Valley used to be when it was home to artists, anthropologists and people from diverse backgrounds, instead of the mainly law, business, and engineering graduates now living there. Business is essentially corporatized and focussed on profit to the extent that creativity is suppressed. Over-corporatisation and lack of creativity, clone-like executives, and unnecessary layers of management have even taken over Hollywood, and some argued Australia's own ABC under the leadership of Michelle Guthrie.[317] Sections of the not-for-profit sector have also been corporatized in this way.

Embrace diversity

For organisations to be truly effective, we need diversity in leadership as well as leaders embracing diversity within workplaces. Emotionally intelligent leaders that I have come across are secure enough in themselves to want different perspectives and life experiences to be brought to the table. Research has shown that organisations that have diverse workforces and executive boards are more innovative, creative, progressive, better at problem-solving, and have higher growth and higher returns.[318] Diversity in terms of age, gender, race, and socio-economic backgrounds, for example, coupled with merit-based appointments, is crucial.

Whilst diversity is important, we must remember that the person hired must also be a good fit for the organisation, a team player and have the right skill set. For example, at a female-dominated workplace, the executive team wanted to hire Tom from a short list of interviewees to create greater diversity. Tom also appeared to have slightly more knowledge in a specific area. But a short-listed female candidate interviewed better and was a better fit for the workplace in terms of her work ethos. And she could quickly acquire the additional knowledge that Tom seemed to have on a specific area. Executive management still believed though it was best to have a male in the office to create diversity, so Tom was hired. He ended up not only performing his tasks poorly, but was not a team player, refused to take direction, and bullied one of his colleagues.

We also can't say we value diversity if we don't listen to staff of diverse backgrounds. Jim Turley of Ernst & Young described a situation when he himself was called out. At a board meeting, three women made comments that were in the same direction, which he failed to respond to. Then when a man made similar comments, Turley told him *he was right*. The women then pulled Turley aside after the meeting and told him what had happened; pointing out that this is what occurs to women throughout their careers. It was an important learning experience for him.[319]

Embrace the holistic approach

Good leaders embrace a holistic approach to problem-solving to address all underlying causes, and have a holistic approach to the provision of goods and services. This ensures the highest standards are achieved and maintained. They recognise that everything is connected and forms part of the whole and therefore is important—even the administrative and record-keeping side of things.

To see just how the holistic approach is universally applicable, let's look at an example. We know that a holistic model with a person-centred or human rights framework is required for residential aged care facilities. So, similar to other areas such as prisons, childcare, and hospitals, there is a need for highly qualified, well-paid staff and ongoing professional education. Appropriate staffing levels are essential rather than having staff rushed off their feet trying to fully meet complex care needs within a short time frame, as well as ensuring zero tolerance for abuse of residents and staff.

And again, the design of the physical environment is important: older people thrive when they are in aged care facilities that resemble a home rather than a hospital or institution and are light filled. Holistic, high-quality care ranging from clinical care, allied health care (such as podiatry), personal care (such as assistance with clothing and hygiene), healthy nutritious meals, and meaningful leisure activities are also essential.

A good sense of humour

The best leaders also have a good sense of humour and do not take themselves too seriously. Former FBI Director James Comey writes of the importance of a sense of humour for leadership and notes how he struggled to find a time when President Trump ever laughed—not even during small talk, or before meetings, or even over dinner. He even searched on the internet for any images of Trump laughing and only found a mean one back in January 2016, when Trump asked a New Hampshire audience about what was causing the noise in the background to which someone shouted 'It's Hilary.'[320]

This is no surprise. Patriarchy and therefore patriarchal leadership is very heavy and serious, just as the environments they create, like the law faculty during my university years, the family home with the patriarchal head of the household, and the workplace with the female or male boss purely using the commanding style of leadership without empathy or collaboration.

Be aware of confirmation bias

Comey also writes of the importance of leaders being aware of confirmation bias: that it is human nature for us to seek out facts and arguments to support our beliefs and so leaders may not perceive facts that challenge those beliefs.[321] Here, open-mindedness is crucial, as is being a good listener and surrounding oneself with highly skilled advisors who are not 'yes' people.

Admitting mistakes and learning from them

As discussed earlier, good leaders, like all of us, make mistakes but importantly, as Comey says, they do not run from criticism but instead welcome it. They also take responsibility for their mistakes—a sure sign of strength of character, ethics, and authenticity. All people have flaws, and Comey admits that he has many, including at times being overconfident and driven by ego. There have been plenty of moments that he can look back on and wish he had done things differently, and a few that he is embarrassed by, but the most important thing is that we learn from such mistakes and hopefully do better.[322] Even if you disagree with his decision to make public the FBI's investigation of Hilary Clinton's private emails before the 2016 US election, his comments are insightful. They also give hope to all of us who want to be better, more ethical leaders in all aspects of our lives.

Integrity and transparency

Good leaders have integrity with a strong sense of fairness and loyalty towards good staff, customers or people whom they serve. And where they say they 'get things done' or are 'result-driven', integrity ensures that they bring people with them, and that how they get things done matters, rather than falling into the trap of thinking that the ends justify whatever means is used including unethical conduct.

Integrity is also at the heart of the way good leaders communicate so that they don't make false or deceptive statements. It also includes leaders not sexualising or dehumanising the language they use. For example, I recall in my politics studies learning that military strategists used sexual language in reference to weaponry and even described atomic bombs exploding with a giant 'orgasmic whump.'[323] They also referred to the killing of innocent civilians as simply 'collateral damage.' Such language enabled them to be too far removed from the human tragedy of war and take a cold, hard-line, brutal and even unethical approach to conflict and one that thrived on it. It also would have undermined any attempts to create a healthy respectful work environment—especially for women.

Integrity in leadership is also coupled with social responsibility. Dame Anita Roddick, founder of *The Body Shop*, showed how you can have a highly successful business/organisation that is socially responsible and ethical. For Roddick, integrity is about having a social purpose, being honest, and making business kinder. The evaluation of the success of any business or organisation shouldn't focus merely on measuring the financial bottom line. Instead it involves measuring a financial bottom line that does include human rights, social justice, environmental justice, and workers' justice.[324]

Leaders with integrity also welcome oversight for transparency and see it as essential to helping them and everyone else continue to act ethically. For example, as discussed in Chapter Seven, police forces would support independent handling of complaints against police. And politicians would endorse:

- the establishment of anti-corruption commissions with sufficient powers to tackle corruption,
- freedom of information laws that promote transparency and accountability along with a well-resourced system for the timely provision of information,
- strong whistle-blower protection laws, agencies to protect whistle-blowers, and strong laws to protect freedom of the press,
- an inquiry into laws to prevent false and misleading political advertising, and
- political donations reform that promotes governments acting in the public interest rather than in the special interest of donors.

Consistency

Good leaders are consistent in doing the right thing and this is where true honesty lies. They don't pick and choose when they will be ethical and compassionate. The staff and people around them, and the community they serve, can trust that they will consistently reflect the higher values they speak of as important and which drive the mission of the organisation.

Avoid creating cliques and 'special interests'

Good leaders treat everyone with the same respect and courtesy. They are inclusive rather than forming their own elite cliques that leave the rest of the staff effectively shut out. Importantly, as we see in workplaces, religious institutions, and political parties, good leaders don't succumb to the temptation of forming their own power bases that feed narcissism and prevent people with helpful insights from having a voice. They also value all aspects of the work of any organisation or party rather than being focussed only on their personal special interest area.

Don't try to please everyone

Good leaders don't try to please everyone and so check the reasonableness of all requests made by staff and assess the consequences of saying 'yes' or 'no' to the request. Examples include where staff have requested to attend a conference for a few days or take leave at a time that is exceptionally busy and would place too much of a burden on other staff. Meanwhile, political leaders have to pursue policies that are in the public interest knowing they can't please every stakeholder, lobby group, or member of the community.

Humble, ethical leadership for us all

Leadership isn't just about those in CEO or management roles, judges, and politicians, and activists; it's for all of us to be better leaders in our families and communities and in all that we do. The renowned scholar of comparative mythology, Joseph Campbell, would call it being the hero of our life journey, heeding the call to adventure and embarking on it with integrity and compassion, seeking to find our own authentic way of living whilst realising that we are all in this together, and being mindful of the wisdom of the leaders and teachers who have gone before us.

It also means remembering the importance of humility and that everything we do matters, great or small. It is the humility that allows us to come from a higher place within ourselves rather than the ego, to heed the wisdom of others, and to be kinder. Spiritual philosophies also emphasise the importance of not projecting into our work the selfishness of 'mine' and 'I'.[325]

Marcus Aurelius supports this view in *Meditations*—a private journal of his reflections on leadership and self-improvement. Marcus Aurelius wrote of the importance of humility, and having a clear and sane mind. This is achieved through being kind, decent, and simple. In this way, the mind will be like an everlasting spring.[326]

This decent and humble way Aurelius learnt from his various teachers. It includes not succumbing to a desire for rhetoric or giving one's own moral sermons, keeping clear of pretentious language, and not taking notice of our own superficial thoughts. He also warned not to focus on or become attached to expensive clothing/living—in other words, patriarchy's values of materialism.

Leaders must also be ready to conciliate with those who have taken or given offence as soon as they are ready to turn back. In doing so, they don't hold grudges nor live in the past. They also have a gentle and dignified character complementing a love of family, justice, and truth—and so are open to being proved wrong.[327] Aurelius also knew strength lies in the calm mind not in anger. But that's not all.

He also emphasised that leaders should be generous in doing good works, have no vain taste for so-called honours or awards, be beyond flattery, have a ready ear for anyone with good advice, and reward impartially.[328]

Marcus Aurelius also warned against having any pre-occupation with fame. He wrote of the speed of universal oblivion, the vacuity of applause from supporters, that people are fickle, of our tiny place in space and time, and how quickly life is over. He knew that the preoccupation for fame was a sure killer for living the decent, kind, and simple life—secrets to having a clear, peaceful mind and good leadership.[329]

In the spirit of his teachers, such as the Greek Stoic Philosopher Epictetus (a former slave), Marcus Aurelius reminds us all to reassess our values and dig deeper into the process of self-examination for self-empowerment, a process that leads into the next chapter on what true power really is.

Note

According to the historian Edward Gibbon, the reign of Marcus Aurelius was part of a golden age for humanity. Indeed he was revered by many for being a more humane leader and doing good works (as far as what was possible under a patriarchal empire). But there are other important aspects of his rule that are often overlooked. Marcus Aurelius not only failed to advocate for women's equality in all areas of life, but Christian persecution occurred during his reign. This is ironic given not only his desire to do what is good or virtuous, but also because much of the content of Meditations is extremely compatible with the teachings of Jesus. I have included insights from Meditations because they are wise, and importantly Marcus Aurelius did not preach his Meditations, but used them privately as encouragement to try to live up to his ideals, which he at times struggled with.

-13-

True Power

When we look closely at what patriarchy's notion of power means, we can see that it offers a wasteland as a kingdom. Patriarchy's distorted values and perception lead us in a dark dance of personal and global destruction. For our own happiness and survival, we need to remember that we are all connected and part of a whole, as well as the importance of love—true power.

Dr Carl Jung warned that where love stops, (patriarchal) power begins along with violence and terror. To counter this danger, society needs a love for one's fellow human being, and this suffers when there is no self-knowledge or process of self-examination.[330]

Jung wants us to remember that love, and I add inner peace, embody what true power really is. This contradicts patriarchy's view that power lies only in the externals of competition and winning, worldly ambition, prestige and status, conquering and humiliating others et cetera. Instead we must undergo an inward journey through self-examination to remove the blocks to accessing true power that lies within us all.

And so this chapter differs to the preceding ones. It focuses on an inner process of transformation rather than relying solely on changing our laws, organisational structures and culture for our happiness and future survival. By examining our minds and changing our way of thinking we will naturally bring about the radical positive change needed in the world. We could then create a society where love and kindness bind us together rather than relying so heavily on laws to do this. Instead of coming from a place of scarcity, fear, selfishness, and not feeling 'good enough' under patriarchy, we could feel more whole and care for eachother. Whilst I don't think a perfect society is possible, a more compassionate and just one is.

Each of us is being asked to be a leader on this. Jung knew that we cannot leave it to politicians and their political parties and activists, though they must also undergo self-examination to experience the self-awareness and true power we all must have for positive leadership. Unfortunately, many of them speak of ideals and promote worthy causes but do not embody those ideals themselves nor have the humility to acknowledge this. Mystical scholar and writer Andrew Harvey relates in his book on sacred activism, *The Hope*, that he has even seen the messiah complex in activists—a dark egoistic delight in humiliating and destroying one's opponents and not valuing every-day life whilst 'sacrificing for the cause' or playing the 'saviour'. (I've even thought that it can be easier to try to 'save' humanity than to try to 'save' oneself.) Harvey says there is also an addiction amongst activists for doing things just for the sake of busyness and an inability to simply 'be'.[331] And then there is the narcissism that can arise from 'fighting the good fight'. But that applies to both sides of the political spectrum. Everyone thinks they are fighting the good fight.

And so many times we discover that a public person or organisation advocating for social justice and human rights, or a highly regarded and eloquent spiritual teacher, are engaged in bullying, corruption, sexism, womanising, sexual abuse, homophobia, and more.

People often asked Jung if we would make it through the cataclysm of our time and he always replied it depended on us doing our inner work.[332] I don't think Jung said this lightly given that, like Freud, he knew how dark our psyches are, and that he had his own faults to work on, including sexist attitudes.[333]

The self-examination process must happen daily and this can involve using the methods offered to us by psychology, philosophy, and/or the world's various spiritual paths. We are particularly tested when under pressure or when given even a small amount of worldly power. And no matter how advanced or evolved a person may seem, they, like all of us, have to remain vigilant knowing that every moment we are choosing between the ego or love and kindness.

For example, Aung San Suu Kyi was awarded the Nobel Peace prize in 1991 for her non-violent struggle for human rights and democracy in Myanmar (Burma), and spoke of how Buddhism influenced her worldview. And yet once she obtained power with her National League for Democracy Party in 2015, she failed to speak out against the atrocities committed by the military against the minority Muslim Rohingya population—atrocities that include genocide, rape and other forms of torture.[334] And how many times do we hear of politicians in opposition speaking out on ethics and transparency based on their philosophical or spiritual values and then as soon as they are in government, they are less transparent and less accountable to the people.

Jung wrote of an ancient Chinese saying, *If the wrong man uses the right means, the right means work in the wrong way.* This is so true, highlighting that no matter how 'right' the method may be, so much depends on the integrity and development of the person who applies it.[335]

The self-examination process occurs in every aspect of our lives including the personal. Without it we too easily take advantage of another person and can even use a philosophical, spiritual, or psychological theory or practice to justify it. An example of how this plays out is where people say they don't have time to help their partner with the housework as they need time for prayer or meditation. They complain that their partner does not understand the importance of their spiritual practice. What these people (and it's mainly men) do not understand is that the spiritual practice is to help their partner do the housework and that prioritising the 'prayer and meditation' over helping their partner is in fact selfish. They are still embracing patriarchal values rather than true power.

And then there are those men or women who want to have a partner but don't want to have to commit to him or her, confront their own fears of intimacy and responsibility, and their own sense of entitlement. Instead they use the excuse of not wanting to get 'too attached' to justify not being emotionally available for their partners and so they cannot be fully present and giving.

But how do we undertake self-examination to remove the blocks to accessing the inner power that patriarchy opposes? There are many ways to do this to suit every individual. I will explore a few methods that hopefully you may find helpful.

1. Integrating our shadow side

As part of the process of self-examination it is important to confront the problem of hero worshipping which can stem from our own difficulty to show noble qualities. According to Jungian analysts such as Robert Johnson, we push such qualities into our shadow side (our unconscious) and then project them onto others who we then worship as heroes.[336] This means that we refuse to take responsibility for our lives and our decision-making, wanting someone else to take over due to our fears and feelings of unworthiness, and/or we may seek to be seen as 'special' by aligning ourselves with those who we or others worship. Either way, it means that we keep ourselves small and undeveloped. Our hero worshipping is also dangerous since history is full of examples of charismatic figures who led their followers down paths of self-destruction and barbaric cruelty to fellow humans.

Our shadow side also has darker qualities which we disguise beneath the veneer of our public persona such as our hidden hates, rage, guilt, jealousies, and vulnerabilities (which may stem from low self-worth). These we also project onto others rather than face up to and heal, blocking our ability to experience love and inner peace, and at times leading to us attacking others outright. This is seen in the social context where men project their shadows onto women, white people project their shadows onto black people, et cetera.[337]

Jungian analysts add that we must integrate both the masculine and feminine to produce a more positive and vibrant age. Masculine or feminine qualities will be pushed into our shadow side if we are trying to live up to the patriarchal ideal of gender stereotyping—which the feminist philosopher Mary Wollstonecraft challenged back in the eighteenth century. We must restore the wholeness of the personality that was lost in the cultural ideals of patriarchy as well as in the particular circumstances of our lives. If we don't do this, we will live in a state of dividedness that grows more and more painful[338] and may even lead to our own extinction.

2. Intellectual self-inquiry and self-knowledge

Xenophon described one of the greatest advocates of self-inquiry, Socrates, as the one who is most happy,[339] and I would add that he maintained his happiness and serenity right up to his execution— a very powerful teaching. Socrates's happiness was achieved by ensuring love was his most important goal through intellectual self-inquiry. He emphasised that it is through probing and questioning our beliefs, values, and actions until we see our errors, that brings truth, self-knowledge and love. What is justice? How do we live the good life? What is 'good'? What's my true motivation for doing this action—is it really to help or to control others, win praise and/or avoid criticism? The unexamined life is not worth living. Why? Because we are operating from values and beliefs, (some of which we are unaware of), that often lead to decisions and actions that are unkind and make us unhappy.

Living the ethical life through self-examination, means leaving no stone left unturned in our minds. Every time we point the finger out there we need to bring it back to ourselves and focus on our own conduct and thoughts—a task patriarchy doesn't encourage. Patriarchal leaders like Donald Trump are all about finger-pointing and blaming others. But they not only show us the path not to follow. They are a mirror of what we need to work on in ourselves—of where we are selfish and uncaring, impulsive, materialistic, seeking attention and status, led by cravings, sexually objectifying others, prejudiced, betray trust, vengeful, et cetera.

The process of self-examination doesn't mean we stop being discerning about people or situations or that we don't hold others to account for their misconduct. But it does mean that by looking inwards at where we may have committed the same wrongdoing, or something similar even to a much lesser degree, we see our errors and commit to doing better, removing any blind spots. This process also helps us to have compassion for others and ourselves—we are all in this together.

Self-examination involves looking at the grievances we need to let go of as well—moving towards feeling lighter, more joyful, healthy, and at peace. I've heard it said that forgiveness is a lifetime's work and whilst it can be very hard (especially when our ego's resistance is strong) the goal is very much worth it. Not holding on to our anger and resentment is such an important part of our life journey that gardens of forgiveness have been made throughout the world as reminders of this, such as the Beirut Garden of Forgiveness. They are quiet sacred places for calm reflection on understanding, unity, and releasing past hurts.

And finally it is helpful to look at our shame and guilt, our fears around these and how the defences we use to overcome them actually make things worse for us and others. In *Above the Battleground*, my sister Stephanie Panayi explores how shame and guilt play out in our lives, often in ways we may not realise. Whilst we have a mixture of them both, we have a tendency towards one or the other based on significant life events, our upbringing, and our socialisation (which is influenced by patriarchy). As we saw in Chapter Two, a shame-prone person is ashamed of helplessness and vulnerability—so much so that they fear these as well as intimacy and abandonment. They then use the defence of seeking power through externals such as status, admiration, wealth, and may even use control, aggression and attack to overcome these fears. This contrasts with a guilt-prone person fearing punishment, personal power and taking initiative. Their defences to such fears include keeping people close and focusing on making them happy even at a cost to themselves, and being compliant or submissive. Moving beyond shame and guilt, we become more whole, authentic, and self-aware.[340] We also experience more love and peace—keys to better decision-making and happiness.

3. Living our values

Even politicians are now using the catchcry of 'living our values' but what does this really mean? We could argue if they truly lived the values of serving humanity and being ethical, we would be living in a fairer and more compassionate society. But as mental health experts say, it is also our responsibility to step up and define and live our values regardless of what governments say or do. This only serves to empower us and helps us shape our hopes for our future and navigate the difficult times in life as well.

Reflecting upon and living values such as truth, integrity, love, and friendship, helps us to be more consistent, honest, and at peace. It's also useful to examine what living a life of integrity and one that values friendship looks like. Integrity helps to guard against misguided loyalty and other harmful friendships. An example of these in our patriarchal culture is the 'mateship' many men have enjoyed that has been very harmful for women and children. This is not only because they have been excluded, but also because the mateship culture has covered over, enabled, and even encouraged abuse of women and children.

I know of one family where the husband, Frank, was a perpetrator of violence against his wife and children on a daily basis. Yet the neighbour next door, Simon, who knew about the violence, not only failed to call the police, but considered Frank a 'mate'. He continued their friendship, playing tennis together and drinking at the local pub, never calling out Frank's abusive behaviour towards his family. Several years later, Frank suddenly ended their friendship, falsely accusing Simon of trying to have an affair with his wife. This was no surprise given that perpetrators of family violence are known to be possessive of their partners and prone to irrational jealousy. But Simon was surprised nevertheless and couldn't understand how Frank could turn on him.

Friendship or mateship can also lead to misguided loyalty in workplaces, where people are loathe to report a superior or colleague for corruption or misconduct when this person has gone out of the way to be friends with them or help them in some way. This has been highlighted for example in reports into police misconduct and corruption. Integrity and honesty help us to know what true friendship is and isn't, and realise that not all friendships are meant to last forever. People can also change at any time and we need to be ready for that.

Meanwhile, the value of creativity helps us live with vitality, think outside the box, and express ourselves with our own aesthetic in every aspect of our lives. The value of integrity also informs how we express ourselves creatively, helping us reach our full potential rather than using our creativity in harmful ways such as songs or other media that convey hate speech. Integrity also informs what creativity inspires us and nourishes us such as beautiful music, artwork, or craftwork. Such artistic beauty helps us connect to our own inner beauty just as nature does. Alternatively, an artistic creation, that we view or listen to, can help us have a greater understanding and compassion for someone's sorrow or other form of suffering. Or it can help us see the lighter side of life, even the absurdity of it, and maintain our sense of humour.

4. Self-empowerment

More and more people are seeking ways to feel empowered when things don't seem to go their way or when dealing with others who are rude or unthoughtful. Stoic philosophy is one approach becoming increasingly popular to help achieve this.

For the Stoics, true power rests in the love and divinity within us and accessing this power depends a great deal on our thoughts and judgments. Whilst so much in life is outside of our control, we can instead control our reactions to externals by engaging in mind training. For example, if we remove the judgment that a person's rudeness 'hurt us' we can experience more peace and maintain our emotional freedom.[341] Epictetus further emphasised our freedom by saying our will cannot be stolen by a thief.[342] He also advised not to take anyone's rudeness personally nor be surprised by it. Instead we should prepare ourselves for it by acknowledging before we engage in any activity that we may encounter people who are rude et cetera but we must remember to maintain our goal of harmony with nature (or peace)—a goal we should establish at the outset.[343] (It may also be helpful to remember that we never know what is going on for someone else.) This is unlike the patriarchal view of striking back and seeking revenge with the 'us and them' mentality.

And as for being quick to judge incidents as being negative if they seemingly don't go our way, Marcus Aurelius wrote that it is good fortune if we bear it true to ourselves and our highest nature[344] and so maintain our peace. Besides the Stoic approach, it may be helpful to recognise as well that we can't see the big picture. Sometimes, we even later discover that the 'negative incident' was actually in our favour. Either way, as hard as it may be, we can remember our higher goal (and have compassion for ourselves when we don't).

Such vigilance with one's thoughts and judgements is beneficial. However, a common sense approach is needed with this. It's important to keep checking where we are at and also with what we are dealing with. This is no substitute for therapy in working through trauma, or leaving a toxic relationship or toxic workplace, and psychological processes must be respected. It is harmful to repress emotions or go into denial.

Buddhist monk and peace activist Thich Nhat Hanh writes in *The Art of Power* of various mind training tools, such as meditation and mindfulness, to assist with accessing the true power of inner peace and love. He says it is the present moment that is our true home and where this inner power resides, bringing us happiness. Meditation and mindfulness techniques also exist in other spiritual paths and are popular with secular communities. They are now even being used in workplaces to help alleviate stress and increase self-empowerment.

Thich Nhat Hanh also says the silence of simply 'being' is essential for our wellbeing as opposed to patriarchy's view of keeping busy and pursuing distractions. The 'being' makes your doing, your action, much deeper and more effective.[345] This is particularly relevant in Australia where former Prime Ministers are highly esteemed by former colleagues and political commentators for having been workaholics. It isn't highlighted that they could have achieved more good if they had taken the time to simply 'be' as well as spending quality time with their families.

Thich Nhat Hanh adds it's important not to get too invested or attached to anything in this world whether it be our work, relationships, a particular worldly goal, or just having things go 'our way'. We can still enjoy them and feel passionate about them but by not being too invested (or believing they are the only way to feel 'good enough' or happy) we won't lose our peace if things don't seem to work out.

An example of non-attachment at work was when I had a placement with the Sexual Offences Section of the Office of Public Prosecutions nearly twenty years ago. They were dealing with a high number of non-convictions for sex crimes due in part to the need for law reform in this area. When I asked the Manager of the section how he dealt with the high non-conviction rate, he said that he practiced non-attachment. He and his staff did their absolute best with every case without having an investment in the outcome. If there were no grounds to appeal, they simply moved on to the next case knowing that they had done all they could and were then able to focus on whatever matter they were dealing with and without loss of motivation.

In wanting to access true power for ourselves it can also be helpful to look at the lives of those who managed to access it in part or fully for inspiration. And so now we turn to the remarkable life of Marie Byles, as she can encourage so many of us, regardless of our backgrounds, to find our own way towards true power.

Marie Byles: the pioneer

We cannot be true to ourselves if we worry what others say or think about us. Dare to be a Daniel, dare to stand alone. We could easily think that such philosophies would be taught by a mother to her daughter in the modern era only. But in truth, these philosophies were taught by Ida Byles, a feminist and progressive thinker in the early twentieth century, and they had a profound impact on her daughter Marie.[346]

They helped shape Marie's enjoyment of not following the crowd and being the 'heretic'. But that's not all. Her biographer, Anne McLeod, says in *The Summit of Her Ambition—The spirited life of Marie Byles*, that these philosophies also helped Marie triumph over the patriarchal legal profession. Despite contemporary lawyers' vehement opposition to women being admitted to their ranks, Marie achieved this by becoming the first female solicitor to practise law in New South Wales in 1924. McLeod writes that at the time, married women were denied the right to own property or have custody of their children, and did not even own their own clothes. Marie saw how men who made and applied the laws had no concern for the suffering of women and this made her determined to fight the struggle for equal rights. It's also not surprising that given Australian society was even more patriarchal back then, the judiciary and police were notoriously corrupt.[347]

Whilst Marie was deeply concerned by the dishonesty, inequality and suffering she saw around her, she also sought very early in life to understand true power. McLeod tells us that whilst still a university student, Marie joined a society that studied the meditations of Marcus Aurelius. It was his Stoic philosophy of self-discipline and inner peace gained from the ability to step aside from mental judgments which had a natural appeal to her.[348] Such study was grounding Marie to not be overcome by despair with the oppression of women, whilst also devoting herself to the values of simplicity, truth, and justice.

The writings of Marcus Aurelius would have also assisted Marie whilst she was being mocked and taunted by male students and lecturers in the almost all white, male law faculty. She refused to allow the sexism to stop her from pursuing her goals and sought support among leading feminists at university.

After she was admitted to practice, throughout the 1920s and 1930s Marie displayed her commitment to justice and helping others by writing articles telling women how to subvert the law and assert their rights.[349] She also promoted and supported other women attempting to become professionals in other fields,[350] and later mentored young women needing support rather than being competitive towards them.

Marie, alongside other feminists, fought for equal pay, divorce law reform, family planning services, and for women to have custody of their children—a reform which was achieved in 1934.[351] Marie was also Australia's first environmental lawyer. Influenced by her father Cyril's conservation principles, she conserved vast tracts of land for national parks and pursued her own love of nature through mountaineering and bushwalking.[352] At the same time, Marie established her own law practice and rejected the patriarchal overly hierarchical approach. Instead she treated her female employees with respect, making it clear that each of them were very much needed and valued.

But whilst Marie experienced worldly success and was living the values of justice and non-conformity—especially as a female lawyer—she still had tensions in her own personality that she needed to address. Even though she possessed sufficient empathy to advocate for women's rights, she often lacked enough empathy on an interpersonal level, being quite abrupt with people and upsetting their feelings without realising it.[353] This was a major block to her accessing true power.

The inner tension increased after a failed expedition that she led to climb an unconquered peak in China. She became disenchanted with worldly success, but this external 'failure' was also her 'saviour'. It led to Marie realising to a greater degree the importance of undertaking the inner work needed to experience a sense of wholeness and inner peace, rather than be left at the mercy of life's tribulations and the emptiness of patriarchy's values. Marie began exploring different tools or methods to help her achieve this that were suited to her own temperament and individual needs. She soon began combining her law practice with her study of Jungian psychology but also spiritual philosophies.

Along the way Marie was influenced by Gandhi and his disciples practicing ahimsa, a quality of love in its purest, all-embracing form, which aids forgiveness.[354] Marie then decided to focus more on ethical service in line with Gandhi's teachings where money is only a sideline. Ironically, the less interested she became in making a high income, the more her law firm thrived financially. McLeod says Marie's honesty was known throughout the community and it attracted more and more clients. She also followed Gandhi's example by becoming a conciliator, encouraging parties to negotiate a settlement rather than take legal action in the courts.[355]

In the 1940s Marie corresponded with Gandhi, admiring his approach of non-violent protest and his belief that dissolution of his ego (which he was struggling with) was an essential part of being an instrument of peace.

As Marie travelled inward, it was through her poetry that she found a way to connect with her emotional side that had not previously been acknowledged or expressed, as she was a person not comfortable with emotions and intimacy. The poetry was also a good contrast to the intellectual pursuit of the law.

Through her poetry, Marie was connecting to a yearning for an inner peace and love that was inspired in part by Saint Teresa of Avila—a Christian mystic, feminist, and reformer who had attained this inner power. Marie later adopted meditation and mindfulness techniques from Buddhism and engaged in self-examination to access this power herself.[356] Marie also experienced a greater reverence for the natural world during this period that provided much peace and respite from her feelings of discontent.[357]

However, people who are new on any path can misconstrue philosophies or teachings to suit their own weaknesses as discussed earlier. Comfortable with the intellect rather than the heart, Anne McLeod writes that Marie believed that the heart did not come into her practice towards inner peace. She followed a common trap for people interpreting the concept of non-attachment to mean being non-emotional and so reinforced her tendency for repressing her emotions.[358]

Marie then embarked on a pilgrimage in India for inspiration for the book that she was writing, *Footprints of Gautama Buddha*. She also spent time during this twelve-month sabbatical in retreat surrounded by the majestic Himalayas. The greatest lessons for her, though, were what she learnt from Uttam Singh, a local man who assisted her on retreat with firewood and all practical matters. She said that Uttam taught her by example the meaning of selfless and kind service and she was struck by his humility.[359] Prior to leaving India, Marie also experienced a deep connection to the Hindu Goddess Kali, which McLeod says spoke to her own need to integrate the feminine qualities that she had rejected in her character.[360]

On her return to Australia, Marie came to the conclusion that training in loving-kindness (a heart practice, no less) was essential before attempting to reform the outer world. Even Gandhi realised after witnessing the carnage of the Hindu-Muslim riots that it was hopeless expecting non-violence unless there was peace within the heart of the individual; this inner work is essential[361] and thus it is where real power lies.

It is helpful for us to know that Marie had periods of depression. But rather than seek refuge in outward distractions, which she knew could only bring temporary relief if any, she engaged in her own mind training practice more and allowed herself time to simply 'be', welcoming inner guidance to emerge from the quiet. Marie also taught meditation whilst continuing her law firm. One of the participants, Bart, was on the edge of suicide and found that these sessions with Marie provided him with a mental calm that he had never before experienced in his life.[362]

Ironically, Marie still felt frustrated about her own progress towards true power. But she later reflected that what constitutes success and failure cannot be judged at the time. It is only looking back over the many years that one can see increasing kindness and serenity.[363]

Indeed, when her trusted only male employee, Robert Moin, left her practice to set up his own law firm, taking his own clients as well as one of Marie's, she was resigned to the situation to the disgust of her staff. But he wasn't doing anything illegal, and there was nothing that Marie could do to stop him, so there was no point getting angry about it. She could still be calm regardless. This allowed her to remain focussed and clear-minded in managing her law practice and getting on with her life. For Marie, everyday problems were themselves the training course for developing kindness and equanimity[364]—the power of not being at the mercy of external forces.

Marie was also learning to focus on gratitude and dealing with the realisation that a big part of her struggle was letting go of her ego and her ideas about how the world should be.[365] Like so many of us, she had a vested interest in wanting things to be done her way. This didn't mean she didn't speak up anymore, though, about inequality. She knew the aim was to do so without her ego getting in the way. In her book *Journey into Burmese Silence*, Marie was critical of the autocracy of male monastics and the patriarchal hierarchy in their Theravada tradition,[366] similar to feminists criticising the patriarchy in Tibetan Buddhism, Christianity, Islam, Judaism, and other religions.

Marie also continued working on herself to remove obstacles to love and inner peace. But the rest of her path was not without intense struggle. She was confronted with health problems and a violent sexual assault that left her with serious injuries. Fortunately, Marie had much support and love around her. McLeod writes that her friends believed she was indeed her sweetest self at this time and they did not come across the usual prickliness when they gave her love.

Marie did, understandably, experience depression and fears arising from the trauma though, and repeated inspiring affirmations to prevent her spirit from being crushed. She refused to give up. Instead as best she could, she continued her inner 'work' to feel compassion for herself and everyone else, and still engaged in her process of self-inquiry. When a friend treated her with condescension, it was as if a mirror was held up to her. Marie realised amongst her faults how at times she had imposed her opinions on others without regard for their feelings.[367]

Her neighbours helped nurse her for three years, a period when she reflected that life brings lessons to take us further along and if we accept them and work through them, we move away from the bondage of worldly (patriarchal) values to experience more peace and joy.[368] She later progressed deeper into the depths of compassion and humility and developed a deeper wisdom that, as McLeod says, was spiritually the summit of her ambition. It may seem humble compared to her worldly achievements but it is extremely difficult to accomplish[369] and is truly the most important goal.

Marie recovered and maintained her love of being amongst nature, her meditation and writing pursuits. Her desire to be of service to others was as strong as ever whilst she lived in the company of like-minded companions.

In her 70th year, she ceased her legal work and instead enjoyed a more quiet life but still one of service, which included gifting her beautiful home Ahimsa to the State Branch of the National Trust of Australia so there could be no development of this semi-natural bushland.[370]

When reflecting on her life achievements, Marie wisely said that what was important in one's life were not the external events but rather what occurs inwardly.[371]

When death eventually drew closer, she had no fear, only interest, and simply wanted to experience more of the force of light and love that was growing within her, along with a strength that was far beyond anything of this world that ordinary people desire or regard as power.[372]

Marie passed away on 21 November 1979, experiencing a state of harmony she had long sought. Her many friends and admirers gathered to celebrate her wonderful and remarkable life with her commitment to serve humanity. She also showed us the importance of not over-identifying with our roles and that the most important work is the inner work towards peace and love which we express outwardly.

Marie Byles had, in the words of Joseph Campbell, followed her bliss, choosing as her life classrooms the roles of a lawyer, activist, writer, and teacher as she pursued living her values. Her legacy encourages us to follow our own 'bliss', wherever that may be, and to learn our lessons through self-inquiry, forgiveness (including self-forgiveness), humour, and humility. To do so will lead to inner peace and love—true power. It is through undertaking such a journey we can then be a true friend to ourselves, each-other, and our planet.

Notes

Introduction

1   Beard, Mary, Women and Power, A Manifesto, Profile Books Ltd, 2017, pp. 3, 4
2   Gilligan, Carol, Resisting Injustice: A Feminist Ethics of Care, lecture given as guest speaker at Josep Egozcue Lectures, invited by the Victor Grifols Foundation for Bioethics, published on 6 May 2013
3   Plato, Apology, cited in Hughes, Bettany, The Hemlock Cup, Socrates, Athens and the Search for the Good Life, Vintage, 2011, p. 78
4   Doidge, Norman, The Brain's Way of Healing, Scribe, 2015, p. xxi

Chapter One: There Must Be a Better Way

5   Wright, Richard, Black Boy, Longman Group, 1970, p. 172
6   Steinem, Gloria, Revolution From Within, A Book on Self-Esteem, Corgi, 1993, p. 146
7   Graycar Regina, and Morgan Jenny, The Hidden Gender of Law, The Federation Press, 1992, pp. 25-26
8   Australian Law Reform Commission Equality before the law Report 67, 1994.
9   Graycar and Morgan, The Hidden Gender of Law, p. 69
10 Woodson, Carter G, The Miseducation of the Negro, Washington DC: Associated Publishers, 1933 pp.xiii, 5, cited in Steinem, Gloria, Revolution From Within, p. 147
11 See for more information: http://consciouscontracts.com/conscious-contracts-in-the-media/

[12] Walsh, Katie, Women Barely Speak in Victoria's Top Court, Australian Financial Review, 17 September 2017

[13] Andrews, Penelope, Despair and Depression in Law School Are Real and Need Attention, The Conversation, 15 August 2017

[14] 2014 Survey: Suffering in Silence: The Survey of Law Student Well-Being and the Reluctance of Law Students to Seek Help for Substance Use and Mental Health Concerns, Jerome M. Organ, David B. Jaffe, and Katherine M. Bender, Ph.D.

[15] Flores, Rosa, and Arce, Marie, Rose, Why Are Lawyers Killing Themselves? CNN January 20, 2014

[16] Harding, Polly, Lawyers' Working Hours—Who Cares?, Lawyers Weekly, 4 February 2019

Chapter Two: Simply Locking Them Up Won't Work

[17] Hughes, Bettany, The Hemlock Cup, p. 331

[18] Hawthorn Roger, and Champion John, Problems of the Criminal Justice System, Edward Arnold (Australia) 1988, p. 122

[19] Australian Productivity Commission, Steering Committee for the Review of Government Service Provision (2018), Report on Government Services 2018, Part C, Table CA.4 (external link opens in a new window). Showed 43.6 per cent of prisoners re-offend within two years of leaving prison in Victoria

[20] Australian Bureau of Statistics, Prisoners in Australia 2013, cat. no. 4517.0 (2013), 13, Table 1

[21] Smart Justice fact sheet, More Prisons Are Not The Answer To Reducing Crime, 2014

[22] Ibid

[23] Harper, David; Mullen, Paul; McSherry, Bernadette, Complex Adult Victim Sex Offender Management Review Panel, Advice on the Legislative Governance Models under the Serious Sex Offenders (Detention and Supervision) Act 2009, Victoria, November 2015, p. 46

[24] Salter, Anne C, Phd, Predators, Basic Books, 2004 p. 73

25 Ogloff, James, et al., Child Sexual Abuse and Subsequent Offending and Victimisation: A 45 Year Follow Up Study, Trends and Issues in Crime and Criminal Justice no. 440 (Australian Institute of Criminology, June 2012), 1-2, cited in Harper, David, et al., Advice on the Legislative Governance Models under the Serious Sex Offenders (Detention and Supervision) Act 2009, p. 46
26 https://changetherecord.org.au/
27 https://www.creativespirits.info/aboriginalculture/law/royal-commission-into-aboriginal-deaths-in-custody#toc2
28 Grant, Stan, Talking to My Country, HarperCollins, 2016 p. 106
29 Ibid, p. 106
30 Wahlquist, Calla, Indigenous Youth Incarceration Rate is a National Crisis and Needs Action, PM Told, The Guardian, 31 March 2017
31 Victorian Ombudsman, Investigation into the Rehabilitation and Reintegration of Prisoners in Victoria, 2015, p. 97
32 Senate Select Committee on Mental Health, Parliament of Australia, A national approach to Mental Health – From Crisis to Community (2006) 334.
33 Moorehead, Joanna, Why Prison Isn't Working for Women, The Guardian, 22 April 2014
34 Harper, David, et. al, Advice on the Legislative Governance Models under the Serious Sex Offenders (Detention and Supervision) Act 2009 p. 48
35 Nussbaum, Martha, Upheavals of Thought: The Intelligence of Emotions (2003) cited by Callinan, Ian, AC, Review of the Parole System in Victoria, July 2013, p. 21
36 Mandatory Sentencing: Does it Reduce Crime? ABC News Fact Check: 5 February 2014
37 'UN Calls for End to Mandatory Sentencing to Cut Indigenous Jail Numbers', The Guardian 9/12/2014 cited in https://www.creativespirits.info/aboriginalculture/law/mandatory-sentencing#ixzz5XYr6VffR

[38] 'Many Fear Barry O'Farrell's Mandatory Sentencing Reforms a Bridge Too Far', SMH 1/3/2014 cited in https://www.creativespirits.info/aboriginalculture/law/mandatory-sentencing #ixzz5XYr6VffR
Note: The debate on mandatory sentencing intensified in Victoria in 2018. At the time the government restricted the special circumstances exceptions for a mandatory custodial sentence for assaulting an emergency worker.

[39] Law Council of Australia, Mandatory Sentencing Discussion Paper, May 2014, p. 14.

[40] Law Oration 2018, The Law Foundation of Victoria, Are Courts Soft on Crime? Lessons from the Victorian Jury Sentencing Study, Presented by Her Excellency Professor the Honourable Kate Warner AC, Governor of Tasmania.

[41] Drugs and Crime Prevention Committee's report, Inquiry into Violence and Security Arrangements in Victorian Hospitals, Parliament of Victoria, 2011

Chapter Three: Tackling The Root Of Crime

[42] Harper, David, et. al., Advice on the Legislative Governance Models under the Serious Sex Offenders (Detention and Supervision) Act 2009, p. 48

[43] Morgan David, and Ruszczynski Stanley, Lectures on Violence, Perversion, and Delinquency, The Portman Papers, Karnac, 2007 p. 7

[44] Scott, Andrew, Northern Lights, The Positive Policy Example of Sweden, Finland, Denmark, and Norway, Monash University Publishing, 2014 pp. 70, 71

[45] Manne, Anne, The Life of I, The New Culture of Narcissism, Melbourne University Press, 2014 pp. 85-98

[46] Morgan, David, et. al., Lectures on Violence, Perversion, and Delinquency, p. 6

[47] Salter, Anne, Predators, p. 9

48 See Women and Mentoring website for details: *womenandmentoring.org.au/*
49 Jetta, Neville, It's a Privilege to Meet and Work with Kids, Opinion, Herald Sun, 27 September 2018
50 Walhquist, Calla, Indigenous Incarceration: Turning the Tide on Colonisation's Cruel Third Act, The Guardian, 20 February 2017
51 Twentyman, Les, Respect Grows If Kids Get to Know Police As People, Herald Sun, 18 June 2019
52 Sansom, Marie, 'Prisoner Reoffending Hits Record High in Victoria', Government News, 29 September 2015
53 Harper, David, et. al., Advice on the Legislative Governance Models under the Serious Sex Offenders (Detention and Supervision) Act 2009, p. 12
54 Doyle, William, This is Why Finland Has the Best Schools, Sydney Morning Herald, 26 March 2016
55 Scott, Andrew, Northern Lights, The Positive Policy Example of Sweden, Finland, Denmark, and Norway, Monash University Publishing, 2014, p. 92
56 Ibid, p. 88
57 Tuffield, Rhiannon, ParentsNext Program Draws Condemnation from Senators, Support Servicers, As Unethical, Distressing,' ABC Goulbourn Murray 4 April 2019, and Hermant, Norman, ParentsNext Program Comes Under Fire From Single Mothers Who Say 'It Makes Life Harder', ABC 1 February 2019
58 Australian Services Union submission to the Productivity Commission Inquiry on The Social and Economic Benefits of Improving Mental Health, 4 April 2019 p. 4
59 Scott, Andrew, Northern Lights, p. 94
60 Yogachandra, Natascha, Teaching Positive Masculinity, The Atlantic, 14 May 2014
61 Alexander, Jessica, America's Insensitive Children? Perhaps Unlike Their U.S. Peers, Kids in Denmark—Where Happiness Levels Are The Highest on Earth—Are Taught in School to

Care For One Another From A Young Age, The Atlantic, 9 August 2016

[62] Waters, Lea, Why Meditation Should be Taught in Schools: The Conversation, 30 June 2015

[63] Jung, Carl, Man and His Symbols, Picador, 1964, p. 191

[64] Heckel, N.M, Sex Society and Medieval Women, Rochester New York, 2004

[65] Manne, Anne, The Life of I, The New Culture of Narcissism, Melbourne University Press Ltd, 2015 pp. 124-130

[66] Doring, Mia, We Need to Talk About Porn, blog post: Collective Shout, 8 May 2017

[67] Kimmel, Michael, Guyland, The Perilous World Where Boys Become Men, HarperCollins New York, 2008, p. 186, cited in Manne, Anne, The Life of I, p. 123

[68] Goldsmith, Marlene, Pornography and the Press Council, Australian Press Council News February 1993.

[69] Reist, Tankard, Melinda, Never Again: Addressing Sexual Violence Must Include Pornography, Collective Shout, 3 July 2018

[70] Shropshire Star: Extreme Online Porn Fueled Murder of Georgia Williams, Says Britain's Top Judge, 28 January 2015

[71] American Booksellers Association, Inc et al v William Hudnut III, Mayor, City of Indianapolis, et al, United States Court of Appeals, Seventh Circuit, 1985, cited by Graycar and Morgan, The Hidden Gender of Law, p. 379

[72] Doring, Mia, We Need to Talk About Porn

[73] Miller, Max, Is Your Brain Addicted to Porn? Bigthink.com 14 September 2010

[74] Doring, Mia, We Need to Talk About Porn

[75] Cline, V: Pornography's Effects on Adults and Children, article, 2001, Pornography and Science: A Collection of Scientific Articles On the Impact of Pornography

[76] Fight the New Drug, The Concerning Connection Between Sex Crimes and Pornography, 2 April 2018, https://fightthe newdrug.org/the-disturbing-link-between-porn-and-sex-crimes,

77 Collective Shout, Submission on enhancing the Online Safety Act 2015 and Online Content Scheme reviews.

78 Haney, John Mark, Teenagers and Pornography Addiction: Treating the Silent Epidemic, Vistas Online, ACA Knowledge Centre, Article 10, 2006

79 See eChildhood submission for the Queensland Anti-Cyberbullying Taskforce, 8 June 2018, p.5, and also eChildhood submission: Review of the Enhancing of the Online Safety Act 2015 and the Online Content Scheme, 1 August 2018. See echildhood website for more information: www.echildhood.org

80 See Lifestar Intensive Outpatient blog https://www.lifestar-therapy.com/which-states-have-declared-pornography-a-public-health-crisis/ 4 April 2017

81 Pulldo, Mary, Exploring Why Offenders Use Internet Child Pornography, Huffington Post, 29 February 2016

82 See post of this letter under: http://melindatankardreist.com/tag/equality/page/2/

83 NSW Law Reform Commission, Review of the Anti-Discrimination Act 1977 (NSW) No. 92 (1999) at 7.87

84 Hooper, Ryan, Police Forces Across the Country are Being Asked to Record Abuse and Harassment of Women as a Hate Crime, The Independent UK, 9 July 2018

85 Wood, Heather, article: Compulsive Use of Virtual Sex: Addiction or Perversion? In Lectures on Violence, Perversion and Delinquency, The Portman Papers, Edited by David Morgan, and Stanley Ruszczynski, Karnac Books 2007 at pp. 160-161

86 Ibid, p. 167

87 Morgan, David, Psychoanalysis and Perversion—How Pornography and Other Distractions Lead to a Disturbance in Real Relationships, Freud Conference, Melbourne 2016

88 Anderson, Raffaela, Hard, Grasset, 2001, cited below: https://antipornfeminists.wordpress.com/2018/05/18/raffaela-anderson-and-the-french-porno-industry/

See also Somarriba, Marie Rose, The Porn Industry is Abusive and These Women are Telling it Like it is, Verily Mag, 5 August 2015

[89] See Matt Fradd's interview with Dr Gail Dines "Why Feminist Pornography is an Oxymoron", on Love People Use Things, 23 April 2018

[90] Kalms, Nicole, No Harm Done? Sexual Entertainment Districts Make the City a More Threatening Place for Women, The Conversation, 10 August 2017

[91] Farley Melissa, Schuckman Emily, M. Golding Jacqueline, Houser Kristen, Jarrett Laura, Qualliotine Peter, and Decker Michele, Comparing Sex Buyers with Men Who Don't Buy Sex, Psychologists for Social Responsibility Annual Conference Boston, Massachusetts July 15, 2011 Research by Prostitution Research & Education Research Supported by Hunt Alternatives Fund, p. 4

[92] Ibid p. 30

[93] Coalition Against the Trafficking of Women (CATWA), Demand Change: Understanding the Nordic Approach to Prostitution 2017, pp. 5-7

[94] Chapman, Clare, If You Don't Take A Job As a Prostitute We Can Stop Your Benefits, The Telegraph, 30 January 2005

[95] See CATWA website: https://www.catwa.org.au/faqs/

[96] News of European Parliament: Press Release: Punish the Client Not the Prostitute, 26 February 2014, and see also: Coalition Against the Trafficking of Women in Australia (CATWA), Demand Change: Understanding the Nordic Approach to Prostitution 2017, and CATWA submission for the Inquiry into Establishing a Modern Slavery Act for Australia, April 2017 See also the CATWA website for debunking myths on prostitution including the myth that men with disabilities have a right to prostituted women: https://www.catwa.org.au/faqs/

[97] Media Release: Women's Health Victoria 2017, Community Calls for Ban on Sexist Ads, 5 December 2017

[98] Valentine, Rebekah, One-third of UK Women Gamers Report Abuse or Discrimination from Male Gamers, gamesindustry. biz 5th June 2018

[99] O'Halloran, Kate, 'Hey Dude, Do This: the Last Resort for Female Gamers Escaping Online Abuse,' The Guardian Australia, 24 October 2017

Chapter Four: The Law As Therapy

[100] Backhouse, Constance, An Introduction to David Wexler, the Person Behind Therapeutic Jurisprudence, (March 1, 2016) International Journal of Therapeutic Jurisprudence, Vol. 1, No. 1, pp1-21 Spring; Ottawa Faculty of Law Working Paper No. 206-13, p. 9

[101] Ibid p. 13

[102] Magistrates Court of Victoria Annual Report 2015, p. 62

[103] KPMG, Evaluation of the Drug Court of Victoria, Final Report, Magistrates Court of Victoria, 18 December 2014, p. 4

[104] Supervising Magistrate of ARC list John Lesser on Radio National 16 April 2011 with Natasha Mitchell: Mental Health Courts and the Challenge of Therapeutic Jurisprudence

[105] Ibid, Interview with Chief Magistrate Michael Hill

[106] Chesser, B. J & Smith, KH. (2016). The Assessment and Referral Court List program in the Magistrates Court of Victoria: An Australian study of recidivism. International Journal of Law, Crime and Justice, J. Carrier, S. Charman, S. Savage. See also https://www.mcv.vic.gov.au/about-us/assessment-and-referral-court-arc, for more information.

[107] Topsfield, Jewel, A Question of Koori Justice, Sydney Morning Herald, 6 December 2008

[108] Anderson Ian, Baum Fran, & Bentley Michael, (eds) 2007, *Beyond Bandaids: Exploring the Underlying Social Determinants of Aboriginal Health. Papers from the Social Determinants of Aboriginal Health Workshop, Adelaide, July 2004, CRC for*

Aboriginal Health, Darwin. See Chapter 13 Healthy Change at the Micro Level Victoria's koori courts: by Rosie Smith, Victorian Department of Justice in Courts and Program Development p. 225

[109] Ombudsman of Victoria Review into the Rehabilitation and Reintegration of Prisoners 2015 p. 8

[110] Centre for Innovative Justice, Gambling Harm: Compulsion, Conversion or Crime? Criminal Justice System Contact as a Form of Gambling Harm, 2017, p. 69

[111] Guenaga, Amaia, Improving the Odds, Changing the Perception of Problem Gambling and Supporting the Growth of Gambling Courts, UNVL Gaming Law Journal, Vol 2:133, 13 June 2011 p. 144 citing Ken Belson, Stressing Help, Not Penalties, In Gambling Treatment Court, N.Y. TIMES, May 1, 2007, at B4, available at http://www.nytimes.com/2007/05/01/nyregion/01gamble.html?_r=1.

[112] Centre for Innovative Justice, Gambling Harm, p. 70

[113] Livingston, Charles, Pokies in Victoria: Joan Kirner's Difficult Legacy, The Conversation, 4 June 2015

[114] KPMG Review of Youth Justice Group Conferencing Program Final Report Department of Human Services 2010, p. 1

[115] Weatherburn, Don, The Effect of Youth Justice Conferencing on Sentencing, NSW Bureau of Crime Statistics and Research, 15 March 2012

[116] Backhouse, Constance, An Introduction to David Wexler, p. 15

Chapter Five: Once Inside—Prisoner Rehabilitation

[117] Hughes, Bettany, The Hemlock Cup, p. 343

[118] Davidson, Helen, Shocking Failures: NT Royal Commission Calls for Closure of Don Dale, The Guardian, 17 November 2017

[119] Ombudsman Victoria, Review into the Rehabilitation and Reintegration of Prisoners, 2015, pp. 3, 4

[120] Ibid p. 55

[121] Looser, Devoney, Teaching Jane Austen to Sex Offenders, Salon, 2 March 2019

[122] Burton, Lydia, Don Dale Youth Detention Centre Prepares Detainees for Life Outside Through Horse Program, ABC Rural News, 22 April 2019

[123] Ross, Monique, Somebody's Daughter Theatre Helps Transform Lives of Women in Prison, Marginalised Rural Youth, ABC News 16 September 2013

[124] Doidge, Norman, The Brain's Way of Healing, Scribe 2015, pp. 343-345

[125] Goodman, Amelia, Inside Halden, the Most Humane Prison in the World, The Guardian, 19 May 2012

[126] Howe, Carol. M, Never Forget to Laugh, Published by Carole M. Howe, 2009, p. 212

[127] Moorhead, Joanna, Why Prison Doesn't Work for Women

[128] Williams, Evan, Prison with No locks, Dateline SBS Tuesday 16 October 2018

[129] Jewkes, Yvonne, How to Build Better Prisons, The Conversation, 26 February 2016, see also https://wakeup-world.com/2016/08/04/the-most-successful-prison-system-in-the-world-is-also-the-most-radically-humane/ by Carolanne Wright

[130] Sansom, Marie, Prisoner Reoffending Hits Record High in Victoria, Government News 29 September 2015

[131] VAGO—The Safety and Cost Effectiveness of Private Prisons, An Overview, 29 March 2018.

[132] Owens, Leigh, Private Prison in Violation of Ohio State Law, The Huffington Post, 10 October 2012

[133] Wing, Donna Red, Say No to Private Prisons in Florida, The Huffington Post, 2 April 2012

[134] Callinan, Ian, Review of the Parole System in Victoria, p. 59

[135] Victorian Ombudsman, Investigation into the Rehabilitation and Reintegration of Prisoners in Victoria, 2015, p. 2

[136] Australian Institute of Health and Welfare, The Health of Australia's Prisoners 2018, p. viii

Chapter Six: Kicking Them While They're Down

[137] Webster K (2016) A Preventable Burden: Measuring and Addressing the Prevalence and Health Impacts of Intimate Partner Violence in Australian Women, ANROWS, Sydney

[138] Cussen T & Bryant W (2015) Domestic/Family Homicide in Australia, Research in Practice No.38, Australian Institute of Criminology, Australian Government, Canberra.

[139] Cox P (2016) Violence Against Women: Additional analysis of the Australian Bureau of Statistics' Personal Safety Survey 2012, ANROWS, Sydney

[140] Finkelhor, D., Hotaling, G., Lewis, I. A., & Smith, C. (1990). Sexual Abuse in a National Survey of Adult Men and Women: Prevalence, Characteristics and Risk Factors. Child Abuse & Neglect 14, 19-28. doi:10.1016/0145-2134(90)90077-7 cited by National Sexual Violence Resource Centre, Child Sexual Abuse

[141] Kaspiew, Rae, Rape Lore: Legal Narrative and Sexual Violence: 1995 Melbourne University Law Review Vol. 20, 356

[142] Channel 4 Fact check: https://www.channel4.com/news/factcheck/factcheck-men-are-more-likely-to-be-raped-than-be-falsely-accused-of-rape

[143] Australian Law Reform Commission report 114: Family Violence, a National Legal Response: Chapter 24 Sexual Assault and Family Violence.

[144] Hughes, Bettany, The Hemlock Cup, p. 50

[145] Change Legal System to Give Rape Victims Justice: The Age editorial, 21 March 2017

[146] Milliken Robert, Judge's Rape Tales Infuriate Australian women, The Independent UK 14 January 1993

[147] Milliken, Robert, Judges Accused of Anti-female Bias: Anger in Australia as Victims Blamed for Rapes, The Independent, 20 May 1993

[148] Silvester, John, 'Rape Victim Attacks Judges', Sunday Age (Melbourne), 18 September 1994.

149 Lee Jane, Court of Appeal Chief Justice Rebukes Judge for Inappropriate Comments over Nubile Girl, 14. The Age 22 November 2016

150 Director of Public Prosecutions v Dalgliesh (a pseudonym) [2017] HCA 41 (11 October 2017)

151 Milligan, Louise, The Kings Cross Case that put Consent on Trial, I am that Girl, ABC news, 11 May 2018.

152 See Dr Carolyn McKay, Dr Tanya Mitchell, Associate Professor Rita Shackel, Submission to the NSW Law Reform Commission Review Concerning Consent and Sexual Abuse Law 28 Jun 2018 p. 6

153 Milligan, Louise, The Kings Cross Case that put Consent on Trial, I am that Girl, ABC news, 11 May 2018 And See Four Corners Episode: https://www.abc.net.au/4corners/i-am-that-girl/9736126

154 Rape Crisis Scotland/Police Scotland

155 Easteal, Patricia, Submission to the NSW Law Reform Commission's Inquiry Concerning Consent in Relation to Sexual Offences Law, 2018 pp. 22-23

156 Victorian Health and Human Services website: https://services.dhhs.vic.gov.au/what-family-violence

157 Farnsworth, Sarah, Focus on Alcohol in Shannon Grant case Sparks Anger from Family Violence Groups ABC news 14 August 2018

158 The Queen v Kilic [2016] HCA 48 (7 December 2016)

159 Doran, Matthew, Domestic Violence Offenders No Longer Allowed to Question Abuse Victims in Family Court, 28 June 2018 ABC News

160 Worth, Caroline, SECASA Monash Health, Restorative Justice, Sexual Assault & Family Violence, 2016

161 Gakawe, Sam, Restorative Justice from the Perspective of Crime Victims, QUTLJ 1999, p. 14

162 Restorative Justice for Victim Survivors of Family Violence

Framework Victoria Department of Justice and Regulation, Victorian Government, August 2017, p. 3

[163] Ibid p. 4

[164] Dickson Wright, Clarissa, Spilling the Beans, Hodder, 2007, p. 186

Chapter Seven: Policing The Police

[165] Equal Opportunity and Human Rights Commission Independent Review into Sex Discrimination and Sexual Harassment Including Predatory Behaviour in Victoria Police. Phase One report 2015 p.12

[166] Ibid p. 11

[167] Ibid p. 64

[168] Ibid p. 11

[169] Ibid p. 97

[170] Ibid p. 96

[171] Ibid p. 71

[172] Ibid p. 78

[173] Ibid p. 85

[174] Ibid p. 18

[175] Wahlquist, Calla, Victoria Police Has Unacceptably High Levels of Sexual Harassment—Report, The Guardian, 27 August 2019

[176] Hughes, Gary, Inquiry Finds Fault with Sex Crime Squad, The Age 8 July 2004

[177] Farouque, Farah, Files Reveal Failed Sexual Assault Cases, Sydney Morning Herald, 28 September 2011

[178] Farnsworth, Sarah, Woman Sues Victoria Police for Failing to Protect Her from Her Violent Ex-Partner, ABC News Updated 28 August 2018

[179] McKenzie Nick, Miletic Daniella, Cowie Tom, Six Victoria Police Members Accused of Brutality Could Face Suspension, The Age 3 April 2018, and also updated with report by: King, Charlotte,

Ballarat Police Officer Found Guilty of Assaulting Woman In Custody Escapes Conviction, ABC news 22 February 2019

[180] McKenzie Nick, Miletic Daniella, Cowie Tom, Six Victoria Police Members Accused of Brutality Could Face Suspension, The Age 3 April 2018

[181] Cooper Adam, Cowrie Tom, Police to Fight Charges They Used Excessive Force on Disability Pensioner, The Age 6 December 2016

[182] Milligan, Louise, United Nations Says Victoria Breached International Covenant on Civil and Political Rights by Not Compensating Police Bashing Victim 7.30 ABC 6 May 2014

[183] Bucci, Nino, IBAC Charges Officer Over Alleged 1996 Bashing of 21-year-old Corinna Horvath, The Age, 29 November 2016

[184] Comey, James, A Higher Loyalty, Truth, Lies and Leadership, Macmillan 2018, p. 136

[185] Ibid p. 104

[186] Wahlquist, Calla, One in Five Victoria Police Say Reporting Corruption Could Cost Their Job, The Guardian, 5 December 2017

[187] Vedelago, Chris; Houston, Cameron; Mills, Tammy, High Court Blasts Police for 'Reprehensible' Conduct Over Informer 3838, The Age, 3 December 2018

[188] Oaten, James, Victoria Police Has 'Conflict of Interest' When Investigating Misconduct, Police Assaults, Inquiry told, ABC News, 19 February 2018.

[189] Rizmal, Zalika, Victoria's 'Broken' Police Complaints System Needs Major Overhaul, Committee says, ABC News 4 September 2018

[190] Corsetti, Stephanie, Victoria Police tackles Mental Health Stigma following Officer Suicides, ABC News, 7 October 2017

Chapter Eight: Turning A Blind Eye

[191] McLeod, Anne, The Summit of Her Ambition—The spirited life of Marie Byles, Published by Anne McLeod, p. 128

192 Australian Discrimination Law Experts Group to the AHRC National Inquiry into Sexual Harassment, 4 March 2019, p. 20

193 Everyone's Business 2018: Australian Human Rights Commission Survey

194 Everyone's Business 2018 Australian Human Rights Commission Consultation with Vulnerable Workers in Melbourne November 2018.

195 United Nations, Towards an End to Sexual Harassment: the Urgency and Nature of Change in the Era of #Metoo, 2018, p. 19

196 Hollaback, DLA Piper, Thomson Reuters Foundation, Street Harassment: Know Your Rights, September 2014, p. 5

197 Trioli, Virginia, Generation F—Sex, Power and the Young Feminist, Minerva, 1996, pp. 23-24

198 Sperino, Sandra and Thomas, Suja A, Unequal: How America's Courts Undermine Discrimination Law, Published to Oxford Scholarship Online: May 2017

199 Hall v Sheiban (1988) EOC at 77, 144

200 Hall, S. & Ors v A & A Sheiban Pty Ltd & Ors [1989] FCA 65; 20 FCR 217 See also Trioli, Virginia, Generation F—Sex, Power, and the Young Feminist, p.74

201 Pelly Michael, Nothing Wrong With Rush Calling Co-Star Yummy, Says Judge, Financial Review 7 November 2018

202 Rush v Nationwide News Pty Ltd (No 7) [2019] FCA 496 (11 April 2019)

203 Jenkins, Kate, AFL's Handling of Sexual Harassment is Broader than Hush Money, The Age, 2 May 2018

204 2008 Gender Equality, HREOC Report 16, 14

205 In Lee v Smith (Lee v Smith & ORS [2007] FMCA 59

Chapter Nine: Patriarchy, Race, and Culture

206 https://www.sbs.com.au/news/paul-keating-s-redfern-speech-still-powerful-after-25-years

207 Grant, Stan, Talking To My Country, p. 22

208 Perche, Diana, Ten Years On, It's Time We Learned the Lessons from the Failed Northern Territory Intervention, The Conversation, 26 June 2017

209 Greer, Germaine, On Rage, Melbourne University Press, 2008, p. 51

210 Ibid p. 52

211 Ibid p. 53

212 NITV 9 March 2018, Victorian Government to Expunge Criminal Records Wrongly Given to Stolen Generation Survivors: by Robert Burton-Bradley:https://www.sbs.com.au/nitv/nitv-news/article/2018/03/08/victorian-government-expunge-criminal-records-wrongly-given-stolen-generations

213 Tran, Danny, Victorians will Address Historical Injustice for Wards of the State, ABC News 24 July 2018 http://www.abc.net.au/news/2018-07-24/victorians-with-criminal-history-over-welfare-get-record-wiped/10026194

214 https://www.sbs.com.au/news/paul-keating-s-redfern-speech-still-powerful-after-25-years

215 Liddle, Celeste, Police Still Failing Aboriginal Women, Eureka Street, 25 June 2018

216 Change the Record, Blueprint for Change, Changing the Record on the Disproportionate Imprisonment Rates, and Rates of Violence Experienced by Aboriginal and Torres Strait Islander people, November 2015

217 McGlade, Hannah, It's Time for Change: Aboriginal Women Will Stand Strong Against Sexual Violence, 12 February 2019 SBS NITV

218 McGlade, Hannah, Cashless Welfare Card is Not the Answer to Social Problems in Remote Communities, 11 August 2017 SBS NITV

219 Scott, Andrew, Northern Lights, pp. 68-69

220 Source: https://www.creativespirits.info/aboriginalculture/people/admired-overseas-shunned-at-home#ixzz5W9J5UoQW

221 These fees were abolished under the Migration Amendment (Abolishing Detention Debt) Bill 2009 (Cth)

222 Doherty, Ben, UN Body Condemns Australia for illegal Detention of Asylum Seekers and Refugees, The Guardian, 8 July 2018

223 Doherty Ben, Evershed Nick, Boochani Behrouz, Self-harm, Suicide and Assaults: Brutality on Manus Revealed, The Guardian, in Sydney, 18 May 2017

224 Between 70-100 per cent of asylum seekers arriving by boat to Australia at different times have been found to be genuine refugees, see this link below:https://www.aph.gov.au/About_Parliament/Parliamentary_Departments/Parliamentary_Library/pubs/rp/rp1415/AsylumFacts#_Toc413067445

225 https://www.refugeecouncil.org.au/getfacts/statistics/aust/asylum-stats/detention-australia-statistics/

226 Razak, Iskhandar, Victoria Apologises to Chinese Community for Racist Policies During Gold Rush Era, ABC News, 25 May 2017

227 Barrowclough, Nikki, The Shameful Story of Australia's Serial Husbands, The Age Good Weekend, Updated 17 September 2014

228 Acharya, Mosiqi, Is Australia Racist? Here Are the Ten Stunning Stats, SBS News, 27 February 2017

Chapter Ten: Nature, the Economy, and Technology

229 Stafford, Fiona, The Long Long Life of Trees, Yale University Press, 2016, pp. 4-6

230 Ibid, p. 6

231 Source of John Fowles comment: Patrick Curry. Defending Middle Earth: Tolkien, Myth and Modernity, New York: Houghton Mifflin, 2004

232 Suzuki, David, The Legacy, Allen and Unwin 2010, p. 9

233 Gammage, Bill, The Biggest Estate on Earth, How Aborigines Made Australia, Allen and Unwin, 2011, p. 2

234 Ibid 3, 4,

235 Suzuki, The Legacy, pp. 18-19

236 Ibid p.26

237 SBS News, One Million Species At Risk of Extinction, 7 May 2019: See the Intergovernmental Science-Policy Platform on Biodiversity and Ecosystem Services assessment report. Platform on Biodiversity and ceassessment

238 Suzuki, The Legacy, p. 29

239 Ibid p. 31

240 Strehlow, Professor T.G, in a piece he wrote titled *Professor T.G. Strehlow's Appreciation* for Australiandia Land of the Holy Spirit, A Booklet on the artist William Ricketts and William Ricketts Sanctuary, 1994, p. 10

241 Steffen Will, Vertessy Rob, Dean Annika, Hughes Lesley, Bambrick Hilary, Gergis Joelle, Rice Martin. The Climate Council of Australia report: Deluge and Drought: Water Security in a Changing Climate 2018

242 Suzuki, The Legacy, pp. 20-21

243 Ibid p. 21

244 Jung, Carl, The Earth Has A Soul: C.G Jung on Nature, Technology and Modern Life, Edited by Meredith Sabini Phd, North Atlantic Books, 2002, p. 121

245 Kelly, Lidia, Fiji PM Accuses Australia's Morrison of Insulting Pacific Island Nations, Reuters, 17 August 2019

246 Suzuki, The Legacy, p.70

247 Ibid p. 61

248 Ibid p. 39

249 Ibid p. 40

250 McLeod, Anne, The Summit of Her Ambition, p. 100

251 Suzuki, The Legacy, p. 41

252 Juniper Tony, Why the Economy Needs Nature, The Guardian UK, 9 January 2013

253 Suzuki, The Legacy, p. 50

254 Ibid p. 47

255 Ibid p. 47

256 Ibid p. 53

257 Cox, Eva, Leading Women, Random House Australia, 1996, p. 245

258 Suzuki, The Legacy, p. 55

259 Ibid p. 65

260 Ibid p. 65

261 Ibid p. 71

262 McLeod, Anne, The Summit of Her Ambition, p. 190

263 Suzuki, The Legacy, p. 57

264 See: http://www.wloe.org/what-is-ecofeminism.76.0.html

265 Jung CG, The Earth Has A Soul: C.G Jung on Nature, Technology and Modern Life, p. 42

266 Suzuki, The Legacy, p. 91

267 Jung CG, The Earth Has A Soul: C.G Jung on Nature, Technology and Modern Life, p. 13

268 Suzuki, The Legacy, p. 80

269 Shearman, David, Why Australians Need a National Environment Protection Agency to Safeguard Their Health, The Conversation, 27 March 2018

270 Suzuki, The Legacy, p. 91

271 Jung, CG, The Earth Has A Soul: C G Jung On Nature, Technology and Modern Life, p. 1

272 Ibid pp. 2-3

273 Ibid p. 15

274 C.G. Jung Letters I and II. Ed., G. Adler. Princeton, NJ: Princeton University Press, 1975. 2 Volumes. I, p. 479 cited in C.G.Jung, The Earth Has A Soul: C.G Jung on Nature, Technology and Modern Life, p. 6

275 C.G.Jung, The Earth Has A Soul: C.G Jung on Nature, Technology and Modern Life, p. 19

276 Ibid p. 195

277 Taylor, Andrew, There Are No Rules: The Unforeseen Consequences of Sex Robots, Sydney Morning Herald, 28 October 2018

[278] C.G. Jung Speaking: Interviews and Encounters. Ed., Wm.McGuire and R.F.C. Hull. Princeton, NJ: Princeton University Press, 1977 pp48-9 cited in Jung C.G, The Earth Has A Soul: C.G Jung on Nature, Technology and Modern Life, p. 151

Chapter Eleven: Patriarchy and Leadership

[279] Goleman, Daniel, Boyatzis, Richard, McKee, Anne, The New Leaders, Transforming the Art of Leadership into the Science of Results: Time Warner, 2002, p. 321

[280] Ibid. p. 29

[281] Hamilton, Clive, Maddison, Sarah, Silencing Dissent, How the Australian Government is Controlling Public Opinion and Stifling Debate, Allen & Unwin, 2007

[282] Ibid. p. 102

[283] Ronson, Jon, The Psychopath Test, Picador 2011, p. 102

[284] Ibid, pp. 146-152

[285] Ibid, pp. 155-165

[286] Ibid. p. 170

[287] Ibid. p. 119

[288] Commissioner Kenneth Hayne's Interim Report, The Royal Commission into Misconduct in the Banking, Superannuation and Financial Services Industry, 28 September 2018

[289] Bird, Karen, A Lesson From the Past May Have Helped Veterans Like My Son, ABC news 2 May 2019

[290] Donaldson, David, Victoria's Worksafe Management Sacked over Contamination, The Mandarin, 3/3/2015

[291] Rogers, Simon, Datablog, How Britain Changed under Margaret Thatcher in 15 Charts, The Guardian, 8 April 2013

[292] Aurelius, Marcus, Meditations, Penguin, 2006, p. 57

[293] Progoff, Ira, Jung's Social Concepts and Their Significance, Dialogue House Library, 1981 pp. 160-161

[294] E. Franklin Frazier, Black Bourgeoisie, New York: Collier

Books, 1962, p112, cited in Steinem, Gloria, Revolution From Within, pp. 147-148

295 Freeman, Hadley, Margaret Thatcher was No Feminist, The Guardian 10 April 2013

296 Albright, K Madeleine K, Women in the World Summit, March 8 2012, http//www.thedailybeast.com/articles/2012/03/09/women-in-the-world-highlights-angelina-jolie-madeleine-albright-more-video.html cited in Sandberg, Sheryl, Lean In, Penguin Random House 2015 pp. 164-165

297 Jeffers, Susan, Feel The Fear And Do It Anyway, Arrow Books Ltd, 1987, pp. 178-179

298 Passant, John, How the Poor Are Shunted Into Deeper Poverty Just for Political Capital, Sydney Morning Herald, 4 January 2013

299 Henriques-Gomes, Luke, Right Intention: Kelly O'Dwyer Rules Out Changes to ParentsNext Before Next Election, The Guardian, 1 March 2019 and Hermant, Norman, ParentsNext Program Comes Under Fire From Single Mothers Who Say 'It Makes Life Harder', ABC 1 February 2019

300 Henriques-Gomes, Luke, ParentsNext: Coalition Makes Changes to Welfare Program After Scathing Report, 12 April 2019

301 Hutchins, Gareth, Julie Bishop Calls out Appalling Behaviour in Politics saying 'Enough is Enough', The Guardian, 6 September 2018

302 Davey, Melissa, Why Australia's Royal Commission into Child Sexual Abuse Had to Happen—Explainer, The Guardian, 11 December 2017

303 Murphy, Damien and Coorey, Phillip, Insults and Chaff Bags Leave Jones in Bad Odour, Sydney Morning Herald, 2 October 2012

304 Beard, Mary, Women And Power, p. 79

305 'Slut Shaming Senator's Absurd Apology Demands,' The Queensland Times, 3 July 2018 and 'Stop Being a Pussy: Leyonhjelm attacks Prime Minister, by Seniors News, 4 July 2018

306 Beard, Mary, Women and Power, pp. 95-96

Chapter Twelve: What Makes Good Leadership?

[307] Goleman, Daniel et. al, The New Leaders, pp. 276-277

[308] Ibid p. 328

[309] Watson, Don, Death Sentence: The Decay of Public Language, Vintage 2004

[310] Maxwell, John, Good Leaders Learn How to Trust Intuition, Not Just Logic, Pittsburgh Business Times, 5 May 2003

[311] Goleman, Daniel et. al, The New Leaders, pp. 52-53

[312] Bamber, David, Gut Feelings Help Solve Crimes, The Telegraph, 10 June 2001

[313] Goleman, Daniel et. al, The New Leaders, pp. 3, 5, 327-332

[314] Hanh, Thich Nhat, The Art of Power, HarperOne 2007 pp. 208-210

[315] Parker, Jean, Lessons To Be Learnt From The Pink Batts Disaster, ABC The Drum, 21 May, 2014

[316] Jung CG, The Earth Has A Soul: C.G Jung on Nature, Technology and Modern Life, p. 149

[317] Gare, Shelley, The Great Creativity Turn-Off, The Age, The Good Weekend, The Cultural Issue. October 6, 2018, pp. 33-36 See also, Cadzow, Jane, Culture Clash, same issue. pp. 18-20

[318] Walter, Ekaterina, Reaping the Benefits of Diversity for Modern Business Innovation, Forbes, 14 Jan 2014

[319] Groysberg, Boris, and Conolly, Katherine, Great Leaders Who Make the Mix Work, Harvard Business Review, September 2013 Issue.

[320] Comey, James, A Higher Loyalty, p. 242

[321] Ibid, p. 104

[322] Ibid p. x

[323] See for further information Cohn, Carol, Sex and Death in the Rational World of Defence Intellectuals, Signs 12, 4: 687-718

[324] Roddick, Anita, Corporate Social Responsibility? Global Issues Video, Published March 11, 2009

[325] Rolland, Romain, The Life of Vivekananda and the Universal

Gospel, Published by Swami Tattwavidananda, 31ˢᵗ reprint 2016, pp. 137-161

[326] Aurelius, Marcus, Meditations, p. 81

[327] Ibid pp. 4-6

[328] Ibid pp. xix, 6, 7, 27

[329] Ibid p. 24

Chapter Thirteen: True Power

[330] Jung CG, The Undiscovered Self, Mentor, 1958, pp. 117-118

[331] Harvey, Andrew, The Hope, A Guide to Sacred Activism, Hay House, 2009, p. 188

[332] Johnson Robert, Owning Your Own Shadow, HarperCollins, 1991, p. 112

[333] See Hayman, Ronald, A Life of Jung, Bloomsbury, 1999, for an exploration of Jung's shadow side including his own sexist views such as believing if a woman took up a masculine profession she was injuring her femininity, and also his extra-marital affairs.

[334] Staff Writer AP, Aung San Suu Kyi Stripped of Amnesty's Highest Honour Over 'Shameful Betrayal', news.com.au 13 November 2018

[335] Source of quote: Jung, Carl, Psychological Reflections, Princeton University Press, 1953 p. 82

[336] Johnson, Robert, Owning Your Own Shadow, HarperCollins 1991 p. 46

[337] Ibid p. 32

[338] Ibid p. 10

[339] Xenophon, Memorabilia, 4.8.3 cited in Hughes, Bettany, The Hemlock Cup

[340] Panayi, Stephanie, Above the Battleground—The Courageous Path to Emotional Autonomy and Inner Peace, Published by Stephanie Panayi 2019, pp. 3-28, 58

[341] Aurelius, Marcus, Meditations, p. 25

[342] Ibid p. 114

[343] Epictetus, The Enchiridion of Epictetus, SMK Books, Wilder Publications, 2012, p. 6
[344] Aurelius, Marcus, Meditations, p. 33
[345] Han Thich Nhat, The Art of Power, p. 156
[346] McLeod, Anne, The Summit of Her Ambition—The spirited life of Marie Byles, Published by Anne McLeod, 2016, p. 4
[347] Ibid pp. 21-24
[348] Ibid p. 15
[349] Ibid p. 21
[350] Ibid p. 23
[351] Ibid p. 26
[352] Ibid p. 97
[353] Ibid p. 46
[354] Ibid, pp. 85-87
[355] Ibid p. 87
[356] Ibid p. 89
[357] Ibid p. 99
[358] Ibid p. 104
[359] Ibid p. 125
[360] Ibid p. 126
[361] Ibid p. 122
[362] Ibid p. 145
[363] Byles, Marie, Paths to Inner Calm, George Allen & Unwin, London 1965, as cited by McLeod, Anne, The Summit of Her Ambition, p. 146
[364] Byles, Marie, Paths to Inner Calm, p207, as cited by Anne McLeod, The Summit of Her Ambition, p. 157
[365] McLeod, Anne, The Summit of Her Ambition, p. 149
[366] Ibid p. 156
[367] Ibid p. 168
[368] Ibid p. 174
[369] Ibid p. 175
[370] Ibid p. 176
[371] Ibid p. 181
[372] Ibid p. 187

Made in the USA
Columbia, SC
06 April 2021